Teach®
Yourself

Essential Italian Grammar

Anna Proudfoot

For UK order enquiries: please contact Bookpoint Ltd, 130 Milton Park, Abingdon, Oxon OX14 4SB. *Telephone:* +44 (0) 1235 827720. *Fax:* +44 (0) 1235 400454. Lines are open 09.00–18.00, Monday to Saturday, with a 24-hour message answering service. Details about our titles and how to order are available at www.teachyourself.co.uk

For USA order enquiries: please contact McGraw-Hill Customer Services, PO Box 545, Blacklick, OH 43004-0545, USA. *Telephone:* 1-800-722-4726. *Fax:* 1-614-755-5645.

For Canada order enquiries: please contact McGraw-Hill Ryerson Ltd, 300 Water St, Whitby, Ontario L1N 9B6, Canada. *Telephone:* 905 430 5000. *Fax:* 905 430 5020.

Long renowned as the authoritative source for self-guided learning – with more than 40 million copies sold worldwide – the *Teach Yourself* series includes over 300 titles in the fields of languages, crafts, hobbies, business, computing and education.

British Library Cataloguing in Publication Data: a catalogue record for this title is available from the British Library.

Library of Congress Catalog Card Number: on file.

First published in UK 2000 as Teach Yourself Italian Grammar by Hodder Education, 338 Euston Road, London, NW1 3BH.

First published in US 2000 as Teach Yourself Italian Grammar by Contemporary Books, a Division of the McGraw-Hill Companies, 1 Prudential Plaza, 130 East Randolph Street, Chicago, IL 60601 USA.

This edition published 2010.

The *Teach Yourself* name is a registered trade mark of Hodder Headline.

Copyright © 2000, 2003, 2010 Anna Proudfoot

In UK: All rights reserved. Apart from any permitted use under UK copyright law, no part of this publication may be reproduced or transmitted in any form or by any means, electronic or mechanical, including photocopy, recording, or any information, storage and retrieval system, without permission in writing from the publisher or under licence from the Copyright Licensing Agency Limited. Further details of such licences (for reprographic reproduction) may be obtained from the Copyright Licensing Agency Limited, of 90 Tottenham Court Road, London W1T 4LP.

In US: All rights reserved. Except as permitted under the United States Copyright Act of 1976, no part of this publication may be reproduced or distributed in any form or by any means, or stored in a database or retrieval system, without the prior written permission of Contemporary Books.

Typeset by Transet Limited, Coventry, England.

Printed in Great Britain for Hodder Education, a division of Hodder Headline, 338 Euston Road, London NW1 3BH.

The publisher has used its best endeavours to ensure that the URLs for external websites referred to in this book are correct and active at the time of going to press. However, the publisher and the author have no responsibility for the websites and can make no guarantee that a site will remain live or that the content will remain relevant, decent or appropriate.

Hodder Headline's policy is to use papers that are natural, renewable and recyclable products and made from wood grown in sustainable forests. The logging and manufacturing processes are expected to conform to the environmental regulations of the country of origin.

Impression number 10 9 8 7 6 5 4 3 2
Year   2014 2013 2012 2011 2010

Contents

Meet the author

Ciao! I'm Anna Proudfoot, the author of **Essential Italian grammar**.

I've been teaching Italian to adult students for quite a long time, writing and using my own materials, and I hope that you'll enjoy using my book to teach yourself Italian grammar.

I was brought up in Scotland, where there was a large Italian community, and spent summers in Italy. I loved speaking Italian and I always wanted to help other people learn to speak it, too!

After graduating in Italian from the University of London, I started to teach the language. My first posts were in London, Cambridge and Pasadena (California). Then I came to live in Oxford, where I was Head of Italian at Oxford Brookes University for several years.

In 2006, I moved to the Open University to design and launch Andante, the beginners' Italian course. We have around 500 adult students learning Italian each year all over the UK, with face-to-face and online tutorial support. We are currently designing and planning the intermediate Italian course, Vivace, which will run in 2011 for the first time.

Apart from **Essential Italian grammar**, I've written several other Italian grammar books and textbooks aimed at adults, and in 2007, I was honoured to receive from the Italian Government the award of **Cavaliere della Stella della Solidarietà Italiana** (Knight of the Star of Italian Solidarity) for my services to Italy and the Italian language.

So if you are learning Italian and you want a firm basis of grammar to build on, then **Essential Italian grammar** is written for you.

Only got a minute?

Italian comes from Latin, the language spoken by the ancient Romans. Like French and Spanish, Italian is one of the family of 'romance languages'. It's an easy language to learn, since the pronunciation is straightforward, but it helps to have a good foundation of grammar to build on.

Present-day Italian is a relatively new language; Italy became a nation only in 1867, and even as recently as 50 years ago, many Italians only spoke their own regional language or dialect. Now almost everyone speaks standard Italian.

Apart from in Italy itself, Italian speakers can be found in the Italian-speaking cantons of Switzerland, and in a few areas of Slovenia and Croatia. Of course, you will also find Italian speakers in all the countries to which Italians have emigrated: Great Britain, countries of mainland Europe (particularly France and Germany), the USA, Canada, Australia and South America, particularly Argentina.

Why learn Italian?

Unlike English, which has several different ways of pronouncing the same combinations of letters (just think of *laugh*, *tough*, *cough*, etc.), Italian pronunciation is easy. Once you know the rules, you can't really go wrong. And Italians love people who try and speak Italian; they really appreciate them making the effort.

The other good point is that – unlike German or Latin – there are no 'cases'; a noun has the same form regardless of its function in the sentence.

Why buy this book?

Of course, there are some challenges in learning Italian. As in other European languages, Italian does have some grammar rules to learn. Nouns, for example, have genders. They can be masculine or feminine, singular or plural, and the adjectives and articles have to match. And Italian verbs change form a lot more than English verbs. But this book will show you how to do it.

5 Only got five minutes?

Italian comes from Latin, the language spoken by the ancient Romans. Like French and Spanish, Italian is one of the family of 'romance languages'. It is an easy language to learn, since the pronunciation is straightforward, but it helps to have a good foundation of grammar to build on.

Present-day Italian is a relatively new language; Italy became a nation only in 1867, and even as recently as fifty years ago, many Italians only spoke their own regional language or dialect. Even now, Italy is still divided into regions. There are twenty regions, each with several provinces; in all, there are over a hundred provinces.

Each region has its own traditions, cuisine and language variations. In some regions, there is even a second national language (for example German in the Trentino-Alto Adige region and French in Valle d'Aosta). Like the cuisine, regional languages are heavily influenced by history. In Sicily, long dominated by the Arabs, there are Arabic elements in both language and cooking, for example **zaffarana** (*saffron*, from **za'farān**, *yellow*) and **cassata** (a dessert made with ricotta cheese, from **qa'sat**, *a deep bowl*). In Naples, ruled by the Angevins and later the Bourbons, there are both French and Spanish elements in the region's language and cooking; for example, a favourite Neapolitan dish, made with potatoes, eggs and cheese, is known as a **gattò di patate** (from French **gâteau**).

Nowadays, everyone in Italy is able to speak standard Italian. They may still choose to speak dialect as well, with friends or family, but they are able to speak and write the form of Italian accepted as standard. This is due to several factors. Firstly, the unification of Italy in 1867 meant that a standard language had to be adopted. However, it was World War I which really saw Italians from different regions coming together on a wide scale and having to communicate with speakers of other regional dialects. Another factor was the process of urbanization, whereby Italians left the poorer rural areas (particularly in the south) and moved to the cities. As they couldn't understand each others' dialects, each group had to communicate in standard Italian. Another major factor was the raising of the school-leaving age to fourteen, which extended compulsory education, helping to reduce illiteracy and encouraging the spread of standard Italian. Finally, the advent of radio then television brought standard Italian into homes where previously only dialect or regional languages were spoken.

Standard Italian itself was originally a regional language. Its origins lie in the Florentine dialect of the fourteenth and fifteenth centuries. One of the main reasons why this dialect came to be the 'gold standard' can be found in three of the greatest names in Italian literature: Dante, Petrarch and Boccaccio. The other reason was the importance of Florence in the commercial and diplomatic world, which gave its dialect a standing above that of others.

Apart from in Italy itself, Italian speakers can be found in the Italian-speaking cantons of Switzerland, and in a few areas of Slovenia and Croatia. Of course, you will also find Italian speakers in all the countries to which Italians have emigrated: Great Britain, countries of mainland Europe (particularly France and Germany), the USA, Canada, Australia and South America, particularly Argentina. Many Italians who emigrated in the late nineteenth century were from poor backgrounds and were illiterate; not only were they unable to write, in many cases they were unable to speak standard Italian. In the new country where they settled, they often met other dialect speakers from the same region with whom they could communicate.

The descendants of those early migrants grew up knowing only dialect and the language of their new country. Many later wanted to return to their roots or explore their heritage and found they needed to speak standard Italian to communicate in an Italy which was very different from the one their grandparents had left.

In many countries with large Italian communities, the Italian consular school service organizes classes of Italian language and culture for the children of Italian families. In other localities, consular teachers are integrated into local schools.

You yourself may be descended from an Italian family and want to learn more about your language; or you may just have a love of Italy and want to be able to communicate in Italian.

Italian is an easy language to learn. Here are just a few reasons why you should learn Italian!

Unlike English, which has several different ways of pronouncing the same combinations of letters (just think of *laugh*, *tough*, *cough*, etc.), Italian pronunciation is easy. Once you know the rules, you can't really go wrong. And Italians love people who try and speak Italian; they really appreciate them making the effort.

Another good point is that – unlike German or Latin – there are no 'cases'; a noun has the same form regardless of its function in the sentence.

Italian is a musical language. Because most Italian words end in vowels, it flows in a soft and rhythmic way.

Of course, there are some challenges in learning Italian. As in other European languages, Italian *does* have some grammar rules to learn. Nouns, for example, have genders. They can be masculine or feminine, singular or plural, and the adjectives and articles have to match. In other words, you have to make nouns, articles and adjectives 'agree'. Verbs also have rules. Unlike English, which relies mainly on pronouns to indicate who is carrying out the action (*I eat*, *you eat*, etc.), Italian changes the verb endings (**mangio, mangi**). There are three main groups of verbs, and each of them has a different set of patterns. Like English, there are different tenses to learn: future tense, past tenses and so on.

But this book will show you how to do all that and more!

Introduction

This fully revised edition is designed as a reference guide for all those studying Italian on their own or in a class, and particularly for those using textbooks written along communicative lines, who feel they need some grammar back-up. You do not need a specialized knowledge of grammar terms in order to use this book, because everything is explained in a non-technical way. There is also a short **Glossary of grammatical terms**.

The book is suitable for all levels, from complete beginners to A-level and even beyond. It is designed for the independent user, but can also be used as back-up in a class situation. It is particularly helpful in that it explains grammar points in English, since many students find it hard to follow explanations in textbooks written entirely in Italian.

The book is divided into units, each one covering a basic communicative function, such as 'Asking for and giving personal information', 'Talking about location', 'Describing the past'. In each unit, you will find the constructions you need to carry out the particular language function covered, along with the essential vocabulary and important grammar points. You will also find language exercises which allow you to practise the points learned.

For each unit, the contents pages list both the language functions and the grammar points covered, so that you can see at a glance what is included. If, on the other hand, you want to check specific grammar points, look up the Index at the back of the book.

How to use this book

Each of the units in this book is free-standing, so if you want to learn or revise all your Italian grammar, you can work through the units in any order you like. If there is a particular language function that you need to use, you can check the **Contents** pages to find out which unit deals with the function that interests you. Unit 16, for example, teaches you how to express your likes and dislikes; Unit 7 shows you how to talk about your daily routine.

Start by looking at the first page of each unit, where you will find listed the language functions to be studied and, under **Language points**, the grammar constructions you are going to need in order to carry out those functions. The **Introduction** gives a few examples (with English translation) of these constructions, along with a very brief explanation. When you have looked at these examples, you are ready to study the **Focus on grammar**, in which all the grammar points are dealt with one by one. Detailed explanations are illustrated by examples.

Once you feel confident about using the language points you have just learned, you can expand your knowledge by reading the section **Language plus**.

The **Insight** boxes give additional information about points covered in the unit which, in my experience, students find particularly tricky.

The **Language in action** section at the end of each unit shows you how these language functions are used in the context of everyday life and gives you practical exercises to do on each point, with examples taken from both spoken language and written language.

The **Test yourself** section at the end of each unit will allow you to measure your progress and check whether you are ready to go on to the next unit.

The **Index** lists specific grammar points, as well as key words in alphabetical order.

1

Asking for and giving personal information

In this unit, you will learn how to:
- *say who you are / what your name is*
- *say where you are from / what nationality you are*
- *say what region or city you are from*
- *say what your occupation and marital status is*
- *ask other people for similar information*
- *give similar information about other people*

Language points
- io, tu, lui, *etc. (subject pronouns)*
- essere *(present tense)*
- chiamarsi *(present tense)*
- *adjectives of nationality, region, city of origin*
- *plurals of adjectives*
- *profession, marital status, titles*

Introduction

To give or ask for personal information, you need to know the subject pronouns io, tu, Lei, etc. (*I, you*, etc.), the verb **chiamarsi** (*to be called*), and the verb **essere** (*to be*). Look at these examples before going on:

Mi chiamo Anna.   *My name's Anna.*
Sono inglese.   *I'm English.*

Sono di Oxford.	*I'm from Oxford.*
Lei è italiana?	*Are you Italian?*
È di Roma?	*Are you from Rome?*
Lui si chiama George.	*He's called George.*
È inglese.	*He's English.*
E lei?	*And (what about) her?*
Lei si chiama Georgina.	*She's called Georgina.*
È inglese.	*She's English.*

Focus on grammar

1 Io, tu, lui, lei, Lei, noi, voi, loro

The subject pronouns **io, tu, lui, lei, Lei,** etc. (English *I, you,* etc.)
are not normally needed in Italian, because the ending of the verb
indicates the person carrying out the action. They can, however,
be used:

a when you want to distinguish between *he* and *she*, which have
the same verb form.

Lui è inglese.	*He is English.*
Lei è italiana.	*She is Italian.*

b when you want to emphasize a difference or contrast.

Io sono italiano. **Lui** è inglese.	*I am Italian. He is English.*
Noi siamo inglesi ma **loro** sono scozzesi.	*We are English, but they are Scottish.*

c after **anche** (*also, too*).

Noi siamo italiani, di Roma. Anche **voi** siete di Roma?	*We are Italian, from Rome. Are you from Rome, too?*

d to make a question sound less abrupt, particularly when using the polite form.

Lei è italiana? *Are you Italian?*

Here are all the subject pronouns:

Singular		Plural	
io	*I*	**noi**	*we*
tu	*you (informal)*	**voi**	*you*
lui	*he*	**loro**	*they*
lei	*she*		
Lei	*you (formal)*	**Loro**	*you (formal)*

Insight

It's hard for English speakers to get out of the habit of using subject pronouns all the time (**io vado, tu mangi** ...). But it will sound much more natural if you just use the verb on its own (**vado, mangi**) and use the subject pronouns only for emphasis or contrast or after **anche**.

2 Tu *or* Lei?

Italian has two forms of address meaning *you* in the singular: **tu** (the informal form) used with friends, family, children and animals; and **Lei** (the formal form, normally written with upper case 'L'), which is used in business situations, such as in a shop or a bank, with new acquaintances (until invited to use **tu**) and with people older than you or considered worthy of respect. **Lei** uses the same form of the verb as **lui** (*he*) or **lei** (*she*).

Lui è inglese? *(he)*
Lei è inglese? *(she)*

Lei è inglese? *(you)*

There is also a formal form of address for more than one person (**Loro**) which a waiter or hotel receptionist may use when addressing more than one client. It uses the same form of verb as **loro** (*they*).

Signore, (**Loro**) sono inglesi?

But it is probably more common to use the more informal **voi** form:

Signore, siete inglesi?

Insight

It's tricky knowing whether to use **tu** or **Lei** with Italian friends and acquaintances. But if in doubt, use **Lei** unless invited to use **tu**. It's also age related – young people tend to use **tu** with each other as soon as they meet.

3 Essere

The verb **essere** (*to be*) is used to give information about yourself, such as where you are from or what nationality you are.

Italian verbs come into three main groups, with their infinitive forms ending -**are**, -**ere**, or -**ire**. Usually they follow a set pattern according to the group they 'belong' to, but **essere** (*to be*) does not follow such a pattern. Here are all the forms of the verb **essere** with the subject pronouns.

	Singular			*Plural*	
(io)	**sono**	*I am*	(noi)	**siamo**	*we are*
(tu)	**sei**	*you are*	(voi)	**siete**	*you are*
(lui)	**è**	*he is*	(loro)	**sono**	*they are*
(lei)	**è**	*she is*			
(Lei)	**è**	*you are (formal)*	(Loro)*	**sono**	*you are (formal)*

*The **Loro** form (formal *you*) is shown here and in the **chiamarsi** table below. It is always the same as the **loro** (*they*) form, so is not shown separately in later units.

> **Insight**
>
> **Irregular verbs** Languages evolve and change over the centuries, and the verbs which are used most change most. **Essere**, for example, is a common verb which has an irregular pattern. And it's a verb you'll need to use a lot!

4 Chiamarsi

The Italian for *My name is ...* is **Mi chiamo ...** (lit.: *I call myself*). To say this, you need the reflexive verb **chiamarsi** (*to call oneself*), whose forms are shown below. (See Unit 7 for a fuller explanation of reflexive verbs.)

Singular		
(io)	**mi** chiamo	*I am called*
(tu)	**ti** chiami	*you are called*
(lui)	**si** chiama	*he is called*
(lei)	**si** chiama	*she is called*
(Lei)	**si** chiama	*you are called (formal)*

Plural		
(noi)	**ci** chiam**iamo**	*we are called*
(voi)	**vi** chiam**ate**	*you are called*
(loro)	**si** chiam**ano**	*they are called*
(Loro)	**si** chiam**ano**	*you are called (formal form)*

Come ti chiami?   **Come si chiama?**

Italians don't say *What are you called?* but *How are you called?*

For more verbs that end in -are (**mangiare, parlare** etc.), see Units 5 and 6. For more reflexive verbs (actions you do to or for yourself and which require reflexive pronouns), see Unit 7.

> ## Insight
> When introducing yourself, you use a reflexive verb **chiamarsi** (*to call oneself*). It's just a normal verb (**chiamare**) with a reflexive pronoun added (**mi, ti, si**). To use a reflexive verb correctly, you have to find both the correct verb form and the correct reflexive pronoun.

5 Nationality and other adjectives

An adjective tells you about someone or something. Use one with the verb essere to say what nationality someone is:

Sara è italiana.   *Sara is Italian.*

In Italian, the adjective has to agree with the person (or object) it describes, i.e. it must have a masculine or feminine, singular or plural ending to match the person (people) or thing (things) it is describing. In Italian, objects – like people – are either masculine or feminine, singular or plural. For further notes on agreement, see Unit 2.

There are two main types of adjective in Italian:

a Those ending in -e (same for masculine or feminine) whose plural ends in -i:

Henry è ingles**e**.   *Henry is English.*
Henrietta è ingles**e**.   *Henrietta is English.*
Henry e Henrietta sono ingles**i**.   *Henry and Henrietta are English.*

b Those ending in **-o** (masculine) or **-a** (feminine) whose plural is **-i** (masculine) or **-e** (feminine):

Mario è italian**o**.	*Mario is Italian.*
Maria è italian**a**.	*Maria is Italian.*
Mario e Piero sono italian**i**.	*Mario and Piero are Italian (men).*
Maria e Teresa sono italian**e**.	*Maria and Teresa are Italian (women).*
Mario e Maria sono italian**i**.	*Mario and Maria are Italian (one man, one woman).*

The last example shows how, when there is one male and one female subject, the adjective becomes masculine for both of them.

Insight

The adjective has to match the noun in gender and number. So if the noun (person or object) is masculine, the adjective is too; if the noun is feminine, the adjective must be feminine. The same applies to number: a singular noun needs a singular adjective, a plural noun needs a plural adjective.

6 Town or region

Just as important as nationality is the region of Italy a person comes from. Italians are very loyal to their region, town, city or village. So the following questions and answers might be heard:

Di dove sei?	*Where are you from?*
Sono di Bari. E tu?	*I'm from Bari. And you?*
Io sono milanese (di Milano).	*I'm from Milan.*
Mia madre è pugliese però.	*My mother is from Puglia, however.*

7 Greetings

With close friends and amongst younger people, **ciao** is used for both *hello* and *goodbye*. With acquaintances and in more formal situations, there is a range of greetings, depending on the time of day: **buongiorno** (*good morning, good day*), **buonasera** (*good afternoon/good evening*) and **buona notte** (*goodnight*, when going to bed).

Insight

Greetings in Italy have to fit within the cultural context. **Buongiorno** (*good morning*) is appropriate up until 1 p.m. After that comes lunch and sometimes – at least in the hot summer of the south – a siesta, so it is only after that (around 5 p.m.) that you can safely say **buonasera**.

8 Titles

Titles are important in Italy as an acknowledgement of someone's professional status. Specific titles are used for an engineer (**ingegnere**), lawyer (**avvocato**), accountant (**ragioniere**), lecturer or secondary school teacher (**professore, professoressa**), doctor or even just graduate (**dottore, dottoressa**). You can also use just **signore** or **signora** (**signorina** is used only for young girls), but it is very common, particularly in the south, for all men of any status to be addressed as **dottore**. Before a surname, a final **e** is dropped from titles:

Buongiorno, Avvocato.
Buongiorno, Avvocato Bruni!
Buona notte, Dottore.
Buona notte, Dottor Esposito!
Buongiorno, Dottoressa.
Buongiorno, Dottoressa Tondello!
Buonasera, Ingegnere.
Buonasera, Ingegner Bianchi!

Language plus

1 Profession or occupation

You can extend a conversation by asking someone his or her profession or occupation:

Lei è professore?	*Are you a teacher?*
No. Sono medico. E Lei?	*No. I'm a doctor. What about you?*
Io sono avvocato.	*I'm a lawyer.*

a The indefinite article **un, uno, un', una** is usually omitted when saying what you do or asking someone about their occupation. (See Unit 2 for more on the indefinite article.)

b The names of some professions have distinct forms for men and for women:

Masculine	Feminine	
maestro	maestra	*teacher*
professore	professoressa	*lecturer, teacher*
sarto	sarta	*tailor, dressmaker*
dottore	dottoressa	*doctor, graduate*
cuoco	cuoca	*cook*
infermiere	infermiera	*nurse*
studente	studentessa	*student*
cameriere	cameriera	*waiter, waitress*
attore	attrice	*actor, actress*
ragioniere	ragioniera	*accountant*
scrittore	scrittrice	*writer*
direttore	direttrice	*manager*

c The names of some professions and occupations have the same forms for both male and female:

··

-e			
cantante	*singer*		
insegnante	*teacher*		
-ista			
dentista	*dentist*	turista	*tourist*
artista	*artist*	pianista	*pianist*
autista	*driver*	ciclista	*cyclist*
giornalista	*journalist*		

··

d For some professions, the masculine form is used for both male or female:

Carlo è medico. Carla è medico. Giulia è avvocato.

Use of the corresponding female forms – e.g. **avvocatessa** – is considered condescending.

For more information on nouns and indefinite articles **un, una** etc., see Unit 2.

2 Marital status

The verb **essere** is used also to give information about marital status:

Giovanni **è** sposato.	*Giovanni is married.*
Maria **è** sposata.	*Maria is married.*
Giovanni e Maria **sono** sposati.	*Giovanni and Maria are married.*
Sono separata.	*I am separated.*
Alfredo **è** divorziato.	*Alfredo is divorced.*
Gabriella **è** fidanzata.	*Gabriella is engaged.*

Although the terms **celibe** (*bachelor*) and **nubile** (*spinster*) exist, and are used on official documents, it's more common to say:

| **Non è sposato.** | *He isn't married.* |
| **Non è sposata.** | *She isn't married.* |

You can even use the English single:

| **Carlo è single.** | *Carlo is single.* |

3 Asking questions

A statement can be turned into a question in two different ways:

a Change the order, putting the subject (**tu**, **Lei**) at the end.

| **Lei è inglese.** | *(statement)* |
| **È inglese Lei?** | *(question)* |

b Raise the intonation of the voice at the end of the sentence.

Lei è inglese?

4 Negative sentences

Negative sentences (statements or questions) are formed simply by adding **non** immediately before the verb:

Sono inglese.	*I'm English.*
Non sono inglese.	*I'm not English.*
Siamo studenti.	*We are students.*
Non siamo studenti.	*We are not students.*
Sei studente?	*Are you a student?*
Non sei studente?	*Aren't you a student?*
Lei è italiana?	*Are you Italian?*
Lei **non** è italiana?	*Aren't you Italian?*

Language in action

Exercise 1

Note and learn how people introduce themselves in the first three scenes, then try to complete the conversation in Scene 4.

1 Al lavoro

In this scene, where Simon is being introduced to his new colleagues at the **Città d'Acqua** offices in Venice, the **Lei** form is used, because people are meeting for the first time. Otherwise in a work situation, colleagues may use **tu**. **Questo** is used to indicate the person being introduced (see Unit 2).

Bruna, questo è Simon, lo studente inglese.	*Bruna, this is Simon, the English student.*
Simon, questa è Bruna, la mia collega.	*Simon, this is Bruna, my colleague.*
Piacere, Bruna.	*Pleased to meet you, Bruna.*
Anche Lei è di Venezia?	*Are you from Venice, too?*
No. Sono francese, di Nizza.	*No. I'm French, from Nice.*
E tu?	*And you?*
Io sono di Londra.	*I'm from London.*

2 Ad un ricevimento

At a drinks party, you might introduce yourself to someone, again using the **Lei** form to ask their name.

Io sono Marco Baralle, della ditta Baralle e Carpaldi.	*I'm Marco Baralle, of Baralle and Carpaldi.*
Lei come si chiama?	*What's your name?*
Mi chiamo Cristina Caria. Sono una collega di Gianni Prestini.	*My name's Cristina Caria. I'm a colleague of Gianni Prestini.*

3 Ad una festa di studenti

Children or younger people starting up a conversation will probably address each other informally, using the **tu** form, right from the start.

Ciao, come ti chiami?
Io sono Marina. E tu?
Mi chiamo Filippo. E questa è mia sorella, Chiara.
Ciao, Chiara.
Ciao.

4 Al bar

Now complete the conversation in this scene. Choose from among the options **la mia amica inglese / uno studente inglese / un turista tedesco**.

Ciao, Valentina. Questa è Mary, (a) _LA MIA AMICA INGLESE_
Ciao, Mary. Io sono Daniela, questo è Hans.
Piacere. Io sono Hans, sono (b) _UN TURISTA TEDESCO_ di Monaco di Baviera.

Scusa, Valentina, il tuo ragazzo come si chiama?
Io sono James, (c) _UN STUDANTE INGLESE_

Exercise 2

Choose to be one of the characters described below and imagine you are introducing yourself. Using the information given, tell someone your name, nationality and occupation.

1
Tracy Jones
Milton Keynes
Student, English

2
Massimiliano Lusardi
Genova
Student, Italian

3
Dr Joe Barnes
Oxford
Lecturer, Welsh

4
Camilla Pennino
Roma
Doctor, Italian

Exercise 3

Say what nationality everyone is by completing the sentences below with the correct form of the adjectives in the box.

americano   austriaco   gallese   inglese   irlandese
italiano   scozzese   tedesco

Di che nazionalità sono?
Esempio: Pierre-Philippe è di Bayeux. È *francese*.

1 Heinz è di Mainz. È _Tedesco_
2 Blodwen è di Llangollen. È _IRLANDese_
3 Callum e Malcolm sono di Aberdeen. Sono _scozzese_
4 Padraig è di Laoghaire. È _gallese_
5 Maria Teresa e Aldo sono di Genova. Sono _italiane_
6 Oswald e Mathilde sono di Vienna. Sono _AUSTRIACO_
7 Jim e Mary-Jo sono di New Orleans. Sono _Americano_
8 Charlotte e Sophie sono di Chobham, Surrey. Sono _INglese_

Test yourself

Check your progress! Do you know how to do the following in Italian?

1 Say who you are.
SONO Anna.
2 Ask someone's name informally and formally.
   a ____ chiami?   _Como si chiama_
   b ____ chiama?   _Como ti chiama._
3 Say where you are from.
____ Milano.
4 Say what nationality you are.
Sono _BRASiliano_

5 Ask someone else what nationality he/she is, informally and formally.

a E tu, ____ sei? *DA DOVE Sei?*

b E Lei, ____ ? *DA DOVE è?*

6 Ask where someone is from, both informally and formally.

a Di *Dov*sei?

b Di *Dove è?*

7 Say whether you are married, single, etc.

10 . Mio marito si chiama Giorgio.

8 Ask your friend whether someone else is married.

Marco *e* ? *SPOSATO?*

9 Ask someone what work he/she does, informally and formally.

a E tu, *CO*? *SA FA?*

b E Lei, *Do*? *Che cosa se oCuLPA?*

10 Remember some of the titles you give to someone in Italian.

Esempio: Doctor Dottore/Dottoressa

a Teacher *PROFFeSoR*

b Lawyer *AVOCCIATo*

c Engineer *ENGeNKeiRi*

2

Identifying people and things

In this unit, you will learn how to:
- *ask for something*
- *ask or say what something is*
- *ask or say who someone is*
- *indicate or point out something or someone*

Language points
- *nouns (an object, a person, or an animal)*
- *indefinite articles* un, uno, una, un'
- *plurals of nouns*
- Chi è?
- Cos'è? (Cosa è?)
- questo, questa, questi, queste

Introduction

Study these examples of things you might want to ask for in Italy:

Un cappuccino, per favore.	*A cappuccino, please.*
Una cioccolata, per piacere	*A hot chocolate, please*
... e una spremuta.	*... and a fresh fruit juice.*
Due paste e due cappuccini.	*Two cakes and two cappuccinos.*

You might want to know what something is:

Che cos'è?	*What is it?*
È un telefonino.	*It's a mobile phone.*

Or what several things are:

Che cosa sono questi?	*What are these?*
Sono biscotti per Carnevale.	*They're biscuits for Carnival.*

Or who somebody is:

Chi è?	*Who is he?*
È un collega americano.	*He's an American colleague.*
Chi sono?	*Who are they?*
Sono amici inglesi.	*They're English friends.*

Focus on grammar

1 *Nouns and indefinite articles* **un**, **una**, *etc.*

A noun is a person, animal, object or abstract thing. In Italian, objects, as well as people, are either masculine or feminine. There are several different ways of saying *a* or *an* (**un, uno, una, un'**); the forms depend on whether the noun is masculine or feminine, and whether it starts with a vowel or a consonant.

Insight

Not only do people have a gender (masculine or feminine) in Italian, but objects do as well. Knowing the gender of nouns is important, since it determines the form of any article (**il** or **la, un** or **una**) and adjective (**bello** or **bella**) used with them.

It can be helpful to look at the ending of the word.

a *Nouns that end in* **-o**
Nouns that end in -o are usually masculine. The most common definite article for masculine nouns is **un**, but before a word starting with **s** and another consonant, **gn, ps, z, pn** or **x**, **uno** is used instead. **Uno** is also used before **y** and **i** followed by another vowel.

un cappuccino	*a cappuccino*
un espresso	*an espresso*
uno spuntino	*a snack*
uno gnomo	*a gnome*
uno psicologo	*a psychologist*
uno zoo	*a zoo*
uno pneumatico	*a tyre*
uno xilofono	*a xylophone*
uno ionizzatore	*an ioniser*
uno yogurt	*a yogurt*

Exceptions: a few nouns end in -o but are feminine and take **una**, for example:

una mano	*a hand*
una radio	*a radio*

Insight

Un or **uno**? The indefinite article **un, una, uno**, etc. (English *a, an*) has different forms depending on the gender (masculine or feminine) and number (singular or plural) of the word it refers to. For masculine nouns, the indefinite article is either **un** or **uno**; the choice depends on which letter the following word starts with.

b *Nouns that end in* **-a**
Nouns that end in **-a** are usually feminine. These take the indefinite article **una**, or **un'** if they start with a vowel (**a, e, i, o, u**).

una pasta	a cake
una spremuta	a fresh fruit juice
un'aranciata	an orangeade

Exceptions: a few nouns end in **-a** but are masculine and take **un**, **uno**, for example:

un programma	a programme
un tema	an essay
uno stratagemma	a stratagem

> ## Insight
>
> **Una** or **un'**? The choice of indefinite article (**una** or **un'**) for feminine nouns depends on the letter that the following word starts with. Before consonants, use **una**. Before a vowel, particularly **a**, the elided form **un'** is often used: **un'aranciata, un'esperienza, un'isola, un'ora.**

In Unit 1, you saw some words denoting professions that end in **-ista** for both sexes. Referring to men, these nouns use the masculine indefinite articles **un** or **uno**; referring to women, the feminine indefinite articles **una** or **un'** are used.

un dentista / una dentista	a dentist
un artista / un'artista	an artist
uno specialista / una specialista	a specialist

c *Nouns that end in -e*
Some nouns that end in **-e** are masculine (these take **un** or **uno**) and some are feminine (these take **una** or **un'**). You have to learn which are which.

| un giornale | a newspaper | una lezione | a lesson |
| uno studente | a student (male) | un'automobile | a car |

d Foreign words

Words borrowed from other languages, particularly those without a final vowel, are usually masculine and take **un** or **uno**.

un bar	*a café, bar*	**un** toast	*a toasted sandwich*
un sandwich	*a sandwich*	**un** weekend	*a weekend*
un club	*a club*	**un** whisky	*a whisky*

A few foreign words are feminine and take **una**.

una brioche   *a brioche, cake*

Summary

Here are examples of the various types of nouns set out in table form, with the indefinite articles **un**, **una**, etc.

Masculine	Singular nouns
un cappuccino	Before word starting with consonant or vowel (but see below)
un buon cappuccino	
un aperitivo	
un Amaretto di Saronno	
un giornale	
un bar	
uno spuntino	Before word starting with s and consonant, **gn**, **pn**, **ps**, **x**, **z**, or **y** or **i** combined with a vowel
uno splendido pranzo	

Feminine	Singular nouns
una pizza	Before word starting with a consonant
una buona pizza	
una chiave	
un'aranciata	Before word starting with a vowel.
un'unica occasione	
un'automobile	

e Male and female

You may be surprised to learn that – grammatically speaking – Italian does not always have a male and a female of each animal species.

Una giraffa (*giraffe*) is always female.

Un ippopotamo (*hippopotamus*) is always male.

In order to provide the other half of the species, you have to say:

una giraffa maschio	*a male giraffe*
un ippopotamo femmina	*a female hippopotamus*

Some animals – as in English – have a different name for the male and the female of the species:

un cane	*dog*	**una cagna**	*bitch*
un gallo	*cock*	**una gallina**	*hen*

2 Nouns (plural forms)

a *Masculine nouns ending in* **-o**
Masculine nouns ending in **-o** have plural ending in **–i**.

un cappuccino	*a cappuccino*	**due cappuccini**	*two cappuccinos*
uno spuntino	*a snack*	**due spuntini**	*two snacks*

b *Feminine nouns ending in* **-a**
Feminine nouns ending in **-a** have plural ending in **-e**.

una cioccolata	*a hot chocolate*	**due cioccolate**	*two hot chocolates*
una spremuta	*a fresh fruit juice*	**due spremute**	*two fresh fruit juices*

c *Nouns ending in* **-e**
Both masculine and feminine nouns ending in **-e** have plural in **-i**.

un giornale	*a newspaper*	**due giornali**	*two newspapers*
uno studente	*a student*	**due studenti**	*two students*
una lezione	*a lesson*	**due lezioni**	*two lessons*
un'automobile	*a car*	**due automobili**	*two cars*

d Other noun patterns
• The following nouns have an irregular pattern.

un **uomo**	*a man*	due **uomini**	*two men*
una man**o**	*a hand*	due man**i**	*two hands*

• Nouns which are foreign in origin have the same form for singular and plural.

un bar	*a bar*	due bar	*two bars*
una brioche	*a brioche*	due brioche	*two brioches*

• Words ending in an accented syllable have the same form for singular and plural.

un caff**è**	*a coffee*	due caff**è**	*two coffees*
un t**è**	*a tea*	due t**è**	*two teas*
una citt**à**	*a city*	due citt**à**	*two cities*

• Some nouns ending in -a can be either masculine or feminine and have different plural forms according to their gender.

un pianista	*a pianist* (m.)	due pianisti	*two pianists* (m.)
una pianista	*a pianist* (f.)	due pianiste	*two pianists* (f.)
un artista	*an artist* (m.)	due artisti	*two artists* (m.)
un'artista	*an artist* (f.)	due artiste	*two artists* (f.)
uno stilista	*a designer* (m.)	due stilisti	*two designers* (m.)
una stilista	*a designer* (f.)	due stiliste	*two designers* (f.)

For further examples of nouns that do not fit the main patterns, please refer to the **Grammar Appendix §1**.

Summary
Here are examples of the various types of regular nouns and their plural forms set out in table form:

un cappuccin**o**	due cappuccin**i**	una past**a**	due past**e**
uno spuntin**o**	due spuntin**i**	una spremut**a**	due spremut**e**
un amar**o**	due amar**i**	un'aranciat**a**	due aranciat**e**
un giornal**e**	due giornal**i**	una chiav**e**	due chiav**i**

Insight
In English, the plural form of nouns is usually easy to learn (*cat*, *cats*; *box*, *boxes*), with a few exceptions (*sheep*, *sheep*). In Italian, there are three main singular–plural patterns, depending on the type of noun and its gender. Adjectives also have a singular–plural pattern, depending on their ending, as you will see in the next section.

3 Adding an adjective

In Unit 1, you met adjectives of nationality with two different patterns: adjectives ending in -o/-a (**italiano/italiana**) and adjectives ending in -e (**inglese**). An adjective has to 'agree' with the person or object it refers to, both in gender (masculine/feminine) and number (singular/plural).

The adjective may not have the same pattern of singular/plural endings as the noun, so the endings will not necessarily look the same.

un ragazzo italiano	*an Italian boy*
due ragazzi italiani	*two Italian boys*
una ragazza italiana	*an Italian girl*
due ragazze italiane	*two Italian girls*
un ragazzo inglese	*an English boy*
due ragazzi inglesi	*two English boys*
una ragazza inglese	*an English girl*
due ragazze inglesi	*two English girls*
uno studente italiano	*an Italian student* (m.)
due studenti italiani	*two Italian students* (m.)
una studentessa italiana	*an Italian student* (f.)
due studentesse italiane	*two Italian students* (f.)
uno studente inglese	*an English student* (m.)
due studenti inglesi	*two English students* (m.)
una studentessa inglese	*an English student* (f.)
due studentesse inglesi	*two English students* (f.)
un pianista famoso	*a famous pianist* (m.)
due pianisti famosi	*two famous pianists* (m.)
una pianista famosa	*a famous pianist* (f.)
due pianiste famose	*two famous pianists* (f.)
un violinista giapponese	*a Japanese violinist* (m.)
due violinisti giapponesi	*two Japanese violinists* (m.)
una violinista giapponese	*a Japanese violinist* (f.)
due violiniste giapponesi	*two Japanese violinists* (f.)

4 Order of nouns and adjectives

In English, the order 'article–adjective–noun' is inflexible.

a bad hotel the famous artist an Italian friend

In Italian, word order is more flexible. The most common arrangement is 'article–noun–adjective'.

un aperitivo sardo una bibita fresca un caffè freddo

Adjectives of nationality, shape or colour always come after the noun.

uno studente **spagnolo** una tavola **rotonda** una casa **bianca**

Many common adjectives (**nuovo, bello, buono, giovane, vecchio, piccolo, grande**) can come either before or after the noun, with a slightly different meaning, depending on position: when they come after, there is more emphasis on that particular quality or characteristic.

Abito in **una piccola casa**.	*I live in a small house.* (description of house)
Abito in **una casa piccola**.	*I live in a small house* (emphasising its small size).
Giorgio ha **una nuova macchina**.	*Giorgio has a new car.* (a new car, not his old one)
Giorgio ha **una macchina nuova**.	*Giorgio has a new car.* (a new car, not a second-hand one)

Insight

In English, word order is fairly inflexible: for noun groups, it is always 'article–adjective–noun', so *a black cat*, never *a cat black*. In Italian, word order is more flexible: **una bella ragazza** or **una ragazza bella**.

5 Chi è?

To ask who someone is, **chi** (*who*) and **è** (*he/she/it is*) are used.

Chi è?	*Who is it?*
È Giorgio.	*It's Giorgio.*

And for more than one person, **Chi sono?**

Chi sono?	*Who are they?*
Sono Paolo e Giulia.	*They're Paolo and Giulia.*

6 Che cos'è?

To ask what something is, you use **che** (*what*), **cosa** (*thing*) and **è**. You can also just use **cosa** and **è**. Before **è**, **cosa** is usually abbreviated.

Che cos'è? / Cos'è?	*What is it?* (lit.: What thing is it?)
È un elenco telefonico.	*It's a telephone directory.*

For more than one thing, you say:

Che cosa sono? / Cosa sono?	*What are they?*
Sono biscotti per Carnevale.	*They're biscuits for Carnival.*

Language plus

Questo

To make it quite clear who or what you are referring to, you can point and/or add **questo** to your question or your reply. **Questo** (this, this one, this object, this person) indicates something or someone near you. The forms of **questo** vary according to the gender (masculine/feminine) and number (singular/plural) of the object/person it is referring to, but if you don't know what something is called in Italian, far less its gender, just point and use the masculine form **questo** (or **questi** if plural).

a Pointing out an object
Masculine singular:

Cos'è questo?	*What's this?*
(**Questo**) è un aperitivo sardo.	*(This) is an aperitif from Sardinia.*

Feminine singular:

Cos'è **questa**?	*What is this?*
È una bibita analcolica.	*It's a non-alcoholic drink.*

Masculine plural:

Cosa sono **questi**?	*What are these?*
Sono gnocchi di patate.	*They're potato gnocchi.*

Feminine plural:

Cosa sono **queste**?	*What are these?*
Sono paste di mandorla.	*They're almond cakes.*

Insight
• **Gnocchi** are very small dumplings made out of semolina or potato (**gnocchi di patate**), served with a sauce and usually eaten for the first course as a change from pasta.
• While pasta means pasta (**spaghetti, tagliatelle**, etc.), **una pasta** can also mean a cake, as in **una pasta di mandorla**. To avoid confusion, you can also call it **un pasticcino** (*a little cake*). The place where cakes are sold is called **una pasticceria**.
• All pasta is plural in Italian. You wouldn't eat just **uno spaghetto**. So always use the plural form, e.g. **cannelloni, lasagne, spaghetti, tortellini, penne, fusilli**.

b Indicating or introducing a person

Chi è **questo**?	*Who is this?*
È Luigi.	*It's Luigi.*
Chi è **questa**?	*Who is this (woman)?*
Questa è una collega americana.	*This is an American colleague.*
Chi sono **questi**?	*Who are these (people)?*
Sono Henry e Henrietta.	*They're Henry and Henrietta.*
Chi sono **queste**?	*Who are these (women)?*
Queste sono amiche italiane.	*These are Italian friends.*

c Questo *or* questa?

With people, you know whether their gender is masculine or feminine, so it's obvious when to use **questo** and **questa**, but with objects it's not so easy. It's safest to assume the object is masculine and use **questo** (**questi** for the plural).

Chi è **questo**?	*Who is this (man)?*
È un professore.	*He's a teacher.*
Chi è **questa**?	*Who is this (woman)?*
È un'amica.	*She's a friend.*
Cos'è **questo**?	*What's this?*
È una spremuta d'arancia.	*It's a fresh orange juice.*

For **questo** as adjective (*this*), see Unit 5.

Language in action

Exercise 1

Fill in the gaps with the correct form of indefinite article (**un, una, uno, un'**). If you have not met the word before, this is a chance to look it up in your dictionary and find out what gender it is.

a _UN_ cornetto   **f** _UN_ caffè   **j** _UNA_ spremuta

b _UNA_ birra   **g** _UNO_ cappuccino   **k** _UN'_ aperitivo

c _UN_ brioche   **h** _UN'_ aranciata   **l** _UNO_ digestivo

d _UN_ toast   **i** _UNA_ limonata

e _UNA_ bicchiere di acqua minerale

Exercise 2

Now you decide you want two of everything you have just ordered in Exercise 1.

e.g. Un cornetto? No, due cornetti.

Exercise 3

You are in a bar, ready to order some items for your friends! Order the items you see in the pictures below, using the words in Exercise 1. Here are some more words to help you.

per favore, per piacere	*please*
un cornetto	*Italian version of a croissant; can be plain or filled with jam or pastry cream and is generally eaten in the morning; also called una brioche or even un croissant in the north of Italy*
un cono	*ice-cream cone*
un aperitivo	*aperitif (for before the meal)*
un digestivo	*digestif (for after the meal)*

1 UNO CA UN CB

2 UN VINO UNI APERdiIVO UN TOST

3 UN CAFE UNI'ESPREMUTA

4 VNA bIRRA VNA SPREMUTA

5 VNA acqua Hue CAFE

6 due galati

Test yourself

Check your progress! Do you know how to do the following in Italian?

1 Ask for two cakes and two coffees. *Due torte e due caffè*
2 Ask what something is/what some things are. *che cosa è?*
3 Say that it is:
  a a mobile phone. *Un telefonino*
  b a non-alcoholic drink. *Una bolsi dia non-alcolica*
  c almond cakes. *Torta de almondega*
  d cheese rolls.
4 Ask who someone is/who some people are. *Chi è? chi sono?*
5 Say that he is/they are: *Lui è? Loro sono?*
  a an English student. *Un estudante inglese*
  b an Italian designer. *Un designer italiese.*
  c English tourists. *Turista inglese mal*
  d Italian friends. *Amico italiano*
6 Write the correct indefinite article **un, una**, etc.
  a ___Un___ spuntino
  b ___un___ caffè
  c ___Una___ spremuta di arancia
  d ___Uni___ aranciata
  e ___Un___ studente
  f ___Un___ automobile
7 Work out the correct plural form of these nouns.
  a un aperitivo
  b una pasta
  c un giornale
  d una lezione
  e un programma
  f un'artista
  g un bar
  h un caffè
8 Point to these people using **questo**.
  a ____ sono Carlos e Gianni.
  b ____ sono Maura e Teresa.
  c ____ è mia madre.
  d ____ è mio marito.

9 Write out the correct form of the adjective shown in brackets.

   a una ragazza _a_ (inglese)

   b un aperitivo _e_ (analcolico)

   c una birra _a_ (fresco)

   d paste di mandorla ____ (sardo)

   e gnocchi ____ (buono)

   f panini ____ (grande)

10 Put these phrases in the correct order.

   a studente   italiano   uno

   b tavola   rotonda   una

   c automobile una   italiana

   d signora   una   anziana

   e casa   una   piccola

3

Asking about availability

In this unit, you will learn how to:
* *ask and say if something or someone exists*
* *ask and say if something or someone is available*
* *say how much there is of something (or how many)*
*

Language points
* c'è, ci sono
* ne
* del, della, dei, delle, etc.
* alcuni, alcune
* qualche
* un po' di

Introduction

First, look at these examples:

C'è un telefono qui vicino?	*Is there a telephone near here?*
Sì, ce n'è uno al Bar Roma.	*Yes, there's one at the Roma bar.*
Ci sono tortellini oggi?	*Are there tortellini today?*
Sì. Ce ne sono.	*Yes. There are (some).*
Ci sono turisti a Lecce?	*Are there any tourists at Lecce?*
Sì, ce ne sono alcuni.	*Yes, there are a few.*
Ci sono anche degli stranieri?	*Are there foreigners too?*
Ci sono dei tedeschi e qualche inglese.	*There are Germans and a few English.*

Focus on grammar

1 C'è, ci sono

In Unit 1, you learned **essere** (*to be*). Together with **ci** (*there*), it forms **c'è** (*there is*), short for **ci è**, and plural **ci sono** (*there are*).

C'è una cabina telefonica all'angolo.	*There is a telephone box on the corner.*
Ci sono molti studenti italiani a Oxford.	*There are lots of Italian students in Oxford.*

Make it sound like a question by raising your voice at the end, as you learned in Unit 1.

C'è ...? *Is there ...?*	**Ci sono ...?** *Are there ...?*
C'è una toilette?	*Is there a toilet?*
Sì, c'è una toilette.	*Yes, there's a toilet.*
C'è un medico?	*Is there a doctor?*
Sì, c'è un medico.	*Yes, there's a doctor.*
Ci sono pesche oggi?	*Are there peaches today?*
Sì, oggi ci sono pesche.	*Yes, today there are peaches.*

Insight

This is a very useful phrase for learners of Italian, since you can use it to ask about things (**C'è un bagno?**) or people (**C'è un medico?**). At the shops, you can ask about English newspapers (**Ci sono giornali inglesi?**) or anything else you want.

2 Ne

When answering a question such as **C'è un telefono?**, instead of repeating the object (**Sì, c'è un telefono**) you can use **ne** (*of it, of them*) and either **uno/una** or another number, quantity or weight. Ci and **ne** combine to form **ce ne** as in **ce n'è** (**ce ne è**), meaning *there is* (*one, some*), and **ce ne sono** meaning *there are* (*some*).

C'è un telefono?	*Is there a telephone?*
Sì, **ce n'è** uno al pianterreno.	*Yes, there is one (of them) on the ground floor.*
Ci sono delle guide?	*Are there any guides?*
Sì, **ce ne sono** due.	*Yes, there are two (of them).*
Ci sono dei fichi freschi oggi?	*Are there any fresh figs today?*
Sì, **ce ne sono** tanti.	*Yes, there are lots (of them).*
Ci sono delle carote?	*Are there any carrots?*
Sì, **ce ne sono** due chili.	*Yes, there are two kilos (of them).*

One will be either **uno** or **una**, depending on whether the object or person is masculine or feminine.

C'è un medico?	*Is there a doctor?*
Sì, ce n'è **uno**.	*Yes, there is one (of them).*
C'è una toilette?	*Is there a toilet?*
Sì, ce n'è **una** al primo piano.	*Yes, there is one on the first floor.*

To say that there aren't any:

C'è un telefono?	*Is there a telephone?*
No. **Non c'è.**	*No. There isn't one.*
Ci sono studenti qui?	*Are there any students here?*
No. Non **ce ne sono.**	*No. There aren't any.*

Generally, in the singular, **ne** is used only when there is a number or other indication of quantity.

C'è un bicchiere pulito?	*Is there a clean glass?*
Sì, **c'è.**	*Yes, there is.*
Sì, ce **n'è uno** in cucina.	*Yes, there is one in the kitchen.*
C'è dell'olio d'oliva?	*Is there any olive oil?*
Sì, **c'è.**	*Yes, there is.*
Sì, **ce n'è** un litro.	*Yes, there is a litre (of it).*

> **Insight**
> Ci or ce? The particle **ci** (there) is shortened to **c'** before **è** (*there is*). It also changes to **ce** before another pronoun, such as **ne**. Compare these examples: **c'è** (*there is*), **ci sono** (*there are*), **Ce n'è** un **chilo** (*There is a kilo (of it)*), **Ce ne sono due chili** (*There are two kilos (of them)*).

3 Expressing *some*

There are several ways of saying *some/a little/several* in Italian, as shown in Sections 4–7 below. Some can only be used when there is more than one thing or person involved, others can be used both for singular and plural. Some can only be used after a negative, translating the English *any*.

4 Del, della, dei, delle, *etc.*

The forms of **del, della, dei, delle**, etc. (*some, any*) vary according to the gender and number of the noun they refer to.

Vorrei **del** vino.	*I'd like some wine.*
Metti **dello** zucchero?	*Do you put sugar in?*
C'è **della** marmellata?	*Is there any jam?*
Vorrei **dell'**aranciata.	*I'd like some orangeade.*
Vuole **dell'**Amaretto di Saronno?	*Would you like some Amaretto di Saronno?*
Ci sono **dei** biscotti al cioccolato.	*There are some chocolate biscuits.*
Ci sono **delle** paste di mandorla.	*There are some almond cakes.*
Ci sono **degli** zucchini al burro.	*There are courgettes cooked in butter.*
Ci sono **degli** alberghi economici in centro.	*There are some cheap hotels in the centre.*

Here is the pattern in table form:

Masculine singular noun	Context
del vino **del** buon Amaretto	Before a word starting with a consonant (except the consonant groups below)
dello zucchero **dello** strutto **dello** yogurt	Before a word starting with: **s** and consonant; **gn**, **pn**, **ps**, **x** or **z**; **y** or **i** + vowel
dell'Amaretto di Saronno	Before a word starting with a vowel

Feminine singular noun	Context
della marmellata	Before a word starting with a consonant
dell'aranciata	Before a word starting with a vowel.

Masculine plural noun	Context
dei biscotti	Before a word starting with a consonant (except the consonant groups below)
degli spaghetti	Before a word starting with: **s** and consonant; **gn**, **pn**, **ps**, **x**, **z**; **y** or **i** + vowel
degli alberghi	Before a word starting with a vowel

Feminine plural noun	Context
delle melanzane	Before a word starting with any vowel or consonant

5 Alcuni, alcune

Another way of expressing *some* (plural nouns only) is to use
alcuni (for masculine nouns) or **alcune** (for feminine nouns). **Alcun**
(singular) is used only with a negative meaning (see **Grammar
Appendix** §5.1). **Alcuni** can be used as an adjective (describing a
noun) or as a pronoun (on its own) meaning *some/a few things*,
some/a few people.

Ci sono **alcuni** problemi.	*There are some/a few problems.*
Ci sono **alcune** cose da fare prima di partire.	*There are some/a few things to do before leaving.*
Molti passeggeri sono ancora in aeroporto.	*There are lots of passengers still in the airport.*
Alcuni dormono, altri telefonano a parenti ed amici.	*Some are sleeping, others are phoning relatives and friends.*

Ne can also be used with **alcuni** (see §2, **ne**, above).

Ci sono dei giornali italiani?	*Are there any Italian newspapers?*
Ce ne sono **alcuni**.	*There are a few (of them).*

6 Qualche

Qualche – like **alcuni** – means *a few*, *some*. But, although the
meaning is plural, it is always used with a singular noun. It can
only be used with 'countable' nouns, not with 'uncountable' nouns
such as *sugar*, *butter*.

C'è **qualche programma** interessante alla TV stasera?	*Are there any interesting programmes on TV tonight?*
C'è **qualche amica** di Camilla a casa.	*There are a few friends of Camilla's at home.*

Compare the use of **alcuni** with the use of **qualche**.

alcuni programmi – qualche programma
alcune amiche – qualche amica

Insight

Countable/uncountable nouns The distinction between 'countable' and 'uncountable' nouns is only important if you want to use **qualche**. **Qualche** is singular, but refers to plural nouns, so you can only use it for items you can 'count', e.g. biscuits, bottles, not for things like sugar or coffee.

7 Un po' di

The phrase **un po' di** (short for <u>un poco di</u>, *a little*, *a few*) can be used both for singular 'uncountable' nouns (such as *sugar*, *wine*, *bread*) and plural 'countable' nouns (such as *cakes*).

un po' di vino	*a little wine*
un po' di grissini	*a few breadsticks*
un po' di caffè	*a little coffee*
un po' di paste	*a few cakes*

Insight

The ways of saying some or a few in Italian include **del**, **alcuni**, **qualche**, **un po' di**. **Un po' di** is easiest of all and can be used for both singular and plural, but it tends to imply few rather than some: **un po' di zucchero**, **un po' di caffè**.

Language plus

1 Non ... nessun(o)

To emphasize that there isn't or there aren't any, use **non** and the negative form **nessuno** (no, not any), which varies in the same way as **un, uno, una, un'**. **Nessuno** can only be used with the singular form.

Non c'è **nessuna** guida.	*There is no guide.*
Non c'è **nessun'**automobile disponibile.	*There are no cars available. (lit.: There is no car).*
Non c'è **nessun** posto libero.	*There is no seat free.*
Non c'è **nessuno** scrittore italiano qui.	*There is no Italian writer here.*

It is also possible to omit **nessuno** in common phrases.

Non c'è posto.	*There is no room.*

With a plural noun, just use **non** without **nessuno**.

Non ci sono ospiti.	*There are no guests.*
Non ci sono concerti durante l'inverno.	*There are no concerts in winter.*

In Unit 19, you will find out what happens when you 'qualify' statements such as the above with an additional specification.

Non c'è **nessuno** scrittore moderno **che mi piaccia**.	*There is no modern writer that I like.*

Insight

To form a negative statement or question, Italian normally uses **non** and another negative element, for example **non (viene) nessuno, non (mangio) niente, non (è) ancora (arrivato)**. When the other negative element is at the beginning of the sentence, the **non** is omitted, e.g. **Nessuno viene**.

---

2 Qualcosa, qualcuno, nessuno, niente

While **qualche** and **nessun** are adjectives and are used with a noun, **qualcosa** (*something*, *anything*), **qualcuno** (*someone*, *anyone*) and **nessuno** (*nobody*) are pronouns and can be used on their own, as can **niente**.

C'è **qualcosa** da mangiare?	*Is there anything to eat?*
C'è **qualcuno**?	*Is anyone there?*

Non c'è **nessuno**.	*There's no one there.*
È venuto **qualcuno**.	*Someone came.*
Non c'è **niente** da mangiare.	*There is nothing to eat.*

Language in action

Exercise 1

Silvia's party

What is there to eat and drink at Silvia's party? Below is a list of items. Add the appropriate form of **del**, **alcuni**, **qualche** or **un po' di** to each item. There may be more than one correct answer. Practise using as many *some/a* few words as possible.

Esempio: panini

dalle

dei panini / alcuni panini / qualche panino / un po' di panini

a salatini	**e** patatine	**i** pasticcini	**m** stuzzicchini	**q** grissini
b pizzette	**f** spuntini	**j** bibite	**n** aperitivi	**r** coca cola
c aranciata	**g** vino	**k** birra	**o** bevande alcoliche	**s** bevande analcoliche
d acqua frizzante	**h** liquori	**l** gelato	**p** dolci	**t** uova sode

Insight

• The prefix **an-** means without; **analcolico** means without alcohol. So **una bevanda analcolica** (or **un analcolico**) is a non-alcoholic drink. **Un bitter analcolico** is a type of alcohol-free aperitif, red in colour and often sold in small, triangular-shaped bottles.

• **L'uovo**, *egg*, has an irregular plural (feminine, but ending in **-a**): **le uova**. Any adjective used with it also has to agree in gender. So while one hard-boiled egg is **un uovo sodo**, two hard-boiled eggs are **due uova sode**.

Exercise 2

Use the pictures to say how much there is of each item:

1 *DIECE UOVA*

2

3

4

5

e.g. Quanto parmigiano c'è? **Ce n'è un chilo.**

CI SONO

1 Quante uova ci sono? *DiECi UOVA*
2 Quanto latte c'è? *Cé UN LATTE*
3 Quante bottiglie di vino ci sono? *CI SONO 5éi bottiglie di Vino*
4 Quanta farina c'è? *Ce UN cHiLO di FARiNA*
5 Quante bustine di lievito ci sono?
Ce NE SONO due bustiNe di LievTo.

For more on **quanto,** see Unit 5.

Test yourself

Check your progress! Do you know how to do the following in Italian?

1 Ask if there is …
  a a toilet. *C'e un bagno?*
  b a telephone. *C'è il telefono ?*
2 Reply that there is one …
  a on the first floor. *Si, ce né una al primo piano.*
  b in the bar. *Si, ce n'é uno al bar.*
3 Ask if there are any …
  a peaches. *Ci sono le pesche?*
  b rolls/sandwiches. *Ci sono dei panini?*
4 Reply that there are …
  a two kilos of them. *Si, ce n'é due. chilo*
  b rolls with cheese or ham. *Ce*
5 Express *some* in four different ways:
  _____ panini
  _____ panini
  _____ panini
  _____ panino
6 Say that there is no …
  a train for Milan.
  b bottle of wine in the house.
7 Ask if there are any …
  a English students in the hotel.
  b Italian newspapers.
8 Say that there are no …
  a friends at the party.
  b interesting programmes on TV.
9 Ask if there is …
  a anything to eat.
  b anybody there.
10 Say that there is …
  a nothing to eat.
  b nobody there.

4

Talking about location

In this unit, you will learn how to:
- *ask where something or someone is*
- *say where something or someone is*
-

Language points
- *il, la, lo, etc. (definite article)*
- *plurals of definite articles*
- *Dov'è? Dove sono?*
- *in, a, da, su and combined forms* nel, al, dal, sul
- *phrases indicating location:* in centro, in primo piano, *etc.*
- ecco *and* mi, ti, lo, la *(direct object pronouns)*

Introduction

Study these examples of questions and answers about location.

Dov'è il Bar Roma?	*Where is Bar Roma?*
È in Via dei Sette Santi.	*It's in Via dei Sette Santi.*
Dove sono gli scavi?	*Where are the excavations?*
Sono in fondo a questa strada.	*They're at the bottom of this road.*
Dov'è il telefono?	*Where is the phone?*
È nell'angolo.	*It's in the corner.*
Dove sono gli elenchi telefonici?	*Where are the telephone directories?*
Sono dietro il banco.	*They're behind the counter.*

Peter e Mara abitano a Londra,   *Peter and Mara live in London,*
  in Inghilterra.   *England.*

Focus on grammar

1 Il, lo, la, *etc.*

A noun is a person, animal, object or abstract thing. In Unit 2, you
saw that, in Italian, objects, as well as people, are either masculine
or feminine. You also saw how the indefinite article **un** (English *a,
an*) varies, depending on the gender of the noun (person or object)
it refers to and also depending on the first letter of the word that
follows it. The same rule applies to **il, lo, la, l'** (the definite article,
English *the*) and its plural forms. It is usually helpful to look at the
ending of the noun which often indicates whether it is masculine or
feminine.

Look at these examples:

Singular	
Dov'è **il** bar?	*Where is the café?*
Dov'è **la** banca?	*Where is the bank?*
Dov'è **la** stazione?	*Where is the station?*
Dov'è **l'**automobile?	*Where is the car?*
Dov'è **lo** stadio?	*Where is the stadium?*
Dov'è **l'**albergo?	*Where is the hotel?*

Plural	
Dove sono **i** bambini?	*Where are the children?*
Dove sono **le** ragazze?	*Where are the girls?*
Dove sono **gli** studenti?	*Where are the students?*
Dove sono **gli** alberghi?	*Where are the hotels?*

Insight

Noun group: agreement of noun, adjective and article A noun group (e.g. **il gatto nero**) consists of a noun (**gatto**), an adjective (**nero**) and a definite or indefinite article (**il** or **un**). Both the article and the adjective have to match the noun in gender (masculine or feminine) and number (singular or plural). So if the noun is masculine plural (e.g. **gatti**), the definite article and the adjective have to match: **i gatti neri**.

a *Masculine nouns ending in* **-o** *or* **-e**

Masculine nouns ending in -o or -e take the definite article **il**; **lo** is used if the following word starts with s and a consonant; **gn**, **pn**, **ps**, **x** or **z**; **y** or **i** followed by a vowel. **L'** is used if the following word starts with a vowel.

In the plural, masculine nouns take the definite article **i**; but **gli** is used if the following word starts with s and consonant; **gn**, **pn**, **ps**, **x** or **z**; **y** or **i** followed by a vowel.

Singular		Plural	
il ragazzo	*the boy*	**i** ragazzi	*the boys*
lo stupido ragazzo	*the stupid boy*	**gli** stupidi ragazzi	*the stupid boys*
il giornale	*the newspaper*	**i** giornali	*the newspapers*
lo stadio	*the stadium*	**gli** stadi	*the stadiums*
il grande stadio	*the big stadium*	**i** grandi stadi	*the big stadiums*
lo studente	*the student*	**gli** studenti	*the students*
l'albergo	*the hotel*	**gli** alberghi	*the hotels*
il grande albergo	*the big hotel*	**i** grandi alberghi	*the big hotels*
lo yogurt	*the yogurt*	**gli** yogurt	*the yogurts*
il nuovo yogurt	*the new yogurt*	**i** nuovi yogurt	*the new yogurts*

> **Insight**
>
> The choice of the definite article for masculine nouns (**il**, **lo**, **l'**) depends on the initial letter of the word it precedes, whether noun or adjective: **il ragazzo, l'unico ragazzo; l'albergo, il bell'albergo; lo specchio, il grande specchio; lo studente, il bravo studente.**

b *Feminine nouns ending in* **-a** *or* **-e**

Feminine nouns ending in **-a** or **-e** take the definite article **la**; this is usually elided (shortened) to **l'** if the word it precedes starts with a vowel. The feminine plural definite article is **le** which is NOT elided before a vowel.

Singular		Plural	
la ragazza	*the girl*	**le** ragazze	*the girls*
la lezione	*the lesson*	**le** lezioni	*the lessons*
la student-essa	*the student (f.)*	**le** student-esse	*the students (f.)*
l'aranciata	*the orange-ade*	**le** aranciate	*the orange-ades*
l'automobile	*the car*	**le** automobili	*the cars*
l'unica ragazza della mia vita	*the only girl in my life*		

> **Insight**
>
> For singular feminine nouns, the choice of **la** or **l'** as definite article depends on the initial letter of the word following it, whether noun or adjective: **la ragazza, l'unica ragazza; l'automobile, la nuova automobile; l'aranciata, la buona aranciata (buon'aranciata); la studentessa.**

c Nouns that do not follow either of these patterns

• Feminine nouns ending in -o

A few feminine nouns end in -o and take definite article **la**. The plural is also irregular:

Singular		Plural	
la man**o**	*the hand*	**le** man**i**	*the hands*
la rad**io**	*the radio*	**le** rad**io**	*the radios*

• Masculine words ending in -a

Some nouns of Greek origin end in –a, but are masculine with definite article **il** or **lo**. The plural is regular, taking definite article **i** or **gli**.

Singular		Plural	
il programm**a**	*the pro-gramme*	**i** programm**i**	*the pro-grammes*
il tem**a**	*the essay*	**i** tem**i**	*the essays*

• Masculine/feminine words ending in -ista

There are several words ending in **-ista** which denote professions or occupations (see Unit 2) and which can be either masculine (with definite article **il, lo, l'**) or feminine (with definite article **la, l'**).

In the plural, the masculine nouns end in **-i**, and take definite article **i** or **gli**, while the feminine nouns end in **-e** and take definite article **le**.

Singular		Plural	
il pianista	*the pianist (m.)*	**i** pianisti	*the pianists (m.)*
la pianista	*the pianist (f.)*	**le** pianiste	*the pianists (f.)*
lo specialista	*the specialist (m.)*	**gli** specialisti	*the specialists (m.)*
la specialista	*the specialist (f.)*	**le** specialiste	*the specialists (f.)*
l'artista	*the artist (m./f.)*	**gli** artisti (m.)	*the artists (m.)*
		le artiste (f.)	*the artists (f.)*

Summary of articles

Masculine singular nouns	Context
il vino **il** buon vino **il** giornale	Before a word starting with a consonant (but see below)
lo zucchero **lo** stupido ragazzo **lo** studente	Before a word starting with: **s** and consonant; **gn**, **pn**, **ps**, **x** or **z**; **y** or **i** followed by a vowel
l'Amaretto di Saronno **l'**artista **l'**unico problema	Before a word starting with a vowel

Feminine singular nouns	Context
la marmellata	Before a word starting with a
la bella ragazza	consonant
la lezione	
l'aranciata	Before a word starting with a vowel
l'unica ragazza	
l'automobile	

Masculine plural nouns	Context
i biscotti	Before a word starting with a
i buoni biscotti inglesi	consonant (but see below)
i giornali	
gli alberghi	Before a word starting with a vowel
gli unici stranieri	
gli spaghetti	Before a word starting with: **s** and
gli stupidi bambini	consonant; **gn**, **pn**, **ps**, **x** or **z**
gli studenti	

Feminine plural nouns	Context
le melanzane	Before a word starting with any
le belle ragazze	consonant or vowel
le automobili	
le lezioni	

2 Order of noun group (noun, article, adjective)

In Italian, word order is flexible. The most common arrangement
of the noun group is article–noun–adjective.

l'aperitivo sardo
la bibita fresca
il caffè freddo

Common adjectives such as **bello, grande, piccolo** can also come before the noun.

la **bella** ragazza
la **buona** pizza napoletana
il **grande** caos

Adjectives of nationality, shape and colour always come after the noun.

lo studente spagnolo
la tavola rotonda
la casa Bianca

See Unit 2 for more information on the position of the adjective.

3 Dov'è ...?, Dove sono ...?

The word **dove** means *where*: combine it with è to ask where something is, or with **sono** to ask where several things are.

Dov'è il cameriere?	*Where is the waiter?*
Dove sono i biscotti?	*Where are the biscuits?*
Dove sono gli studenti?	*Where are the students?*
Dov'è l'Ufficio Cambio?	*Where is the Bureau de Change?*

4 *Location:* **a**, **in**, **da**, *etc.*

To say where something is, or where you are going, you use a preposition (such as **a, in**).

in centro	*in the centre*
a Roma	*in Rome*
in Italia	*in Italy*

Whether staying *in* or going *to* a place, the same prepositions are used in Italian: **a** with a town, city or small island, and **in** with a region, country or large island.

a Londra	in/to London
a Capri	in/to Capri
in Toscana	in/to Tuscany
in Inghilterra	in/to England
in Sicilia	in/to Sicily

Insight

English speakers learning Italian sometimes think it would be logical to use **a** to talk about going to a place, and **in** to talk about staying in a place. Italian, however, makes no such distinction: **in** and **a** are used both for going to a place (**Vado a Palermo, Vado in Sicilia**) and living or staying in a place (**Vivo a Londra, Vivo in Inghilterra**).

Da means *at/to the house* of or *at/to the shop of.*

| **Andiamo da Marco.** | *Let's go to Marco's house.* |
| **Compro il formaggio dal salumiere.** | *I buy cheese at the delicatessen.* |

It is often used in the name of a restaurant.

| **Da Lorenzo** | *Lorenzo's* |

Depending on the verb used with it and the context, it can also mean *from*.

| **Torno dal lavoro alle 18.00.** | *I get back from work at 6 p.m.* |
| **Arriva da Londra alle 19.00.** | *He gets here from London at 7 p.m.* |

Insight

Da can be used to express many things including location. It has no exact equivalent in English. It can mean *to, at, by* or *from*. It can be combined with the definite article **il, la,** etc. to form **dal, dalla,** etc.

5 *Prepositions combined with definite article:* **al, dal, del, nel, sul**

The prepositions **a, da, di, in, su** can combine with the definite article (**il, la, lo, l'**, etc.) to produce forms which vary according to number (singular/plural) and gender (masculine/ feminine): e.g. **al, da, del, nel, sul**. They translate into English as *at the, to/from the, of the, in the, on the* and so on.

al cinema	*at the cinema*
alla televisione	*on the television*
allo specchio	*in the mirror*
all'albergo	*at the hotel*

This list shows the forms of combined preposition and definite article and their approximate translation in English.

al ristorante	*at/to the restaurant*
allo specchio	*in the mirror*
all'albergo	*at/to the hotel*
all'accademia	*at/to the academy*
alla spiaggia	*at/to the beach*
ai laghi	*at/to the lakes*
agli alberghi	*at/to the hotels*
agli sportelli	*at/to the ticket windows*
alle Isole Eolie	*in/to the Aeolian islands*
nel ristorante	*in the restaurant*
nell'ufficio	*in the office*
nello stadio	*in the stadium*
nell'acqua	*in the water*
nella camera	*in the bedroom*
nei giardini	*in the gardens*
negli alberi	*in the trees*
negli scavi	*in the excavations*
nelle camere	*in the bedrooms*
dal medico	*at the doctor's*
dallo psichiatra	*at the psychiatrist's*
dall'amico	*at the (male) friend's (house)*
dall'amica	*at the (female) friend's (house)*

dalla zia	*at the aunt's house*
dai ragazzi	*at the boys' house*
dagli americani	*at the Americans' house*
dagli studenti	*at the students' house*
dalle ragazze	*at the girls' house*
sul banco	*on the counter*
sullo sgabello	*on the stool*
sull'albero	*on the tree*
sull'isola	*on the island*
sulla sabbia	*on the sand*
sui gradini	*on the steps*
sugli alberi	*on the trees*
sugli scalini	*on the steps*
sulle scale	*on the stairs*

Insight

• Italian and English don't always use the same or equivalent preposition, for example, **alla televisione** (*on the television*), **allo specchio** (*in the mirror*), **sul giornale** (*in the newspaper*), **in autobus** (*on the bus*).

The choice of simple preposition or combined form depends on the context.

Ho lasciato la valigia all'albergo.   *I left my suitcase at the hotel.*

(Where actual location is important)

Stiamo in albergo.   *We are staying in a hotel.*

(Where reference is to accommodation, i.e. hotel rather than apartment)

In common and frequently used phrases, the simple form – **in, a,** etc. – is generally used.

in centro	*in the centre*
in giardino	*in the garden*
a casa	*at home*
in casa	*in the house/at home*
a scuola	*at school*
in città	*in town*
in montagna	*in the mountains*
in campagna	*in the country*

The simple form is also used for means of transport.

in treno	*by train*
in macchina	*by car*
in aereo	*by plane*
in autobus	*by bus*
in bicicletta	*by bike*
a piedi	*on foot*
a cavallo	*on horseback*

Insight

Where there is a specific reference (a particular theatre, a certain house) or where location is important, you will probably use the combined preposition and article **al, del,** etc. But some common everyday expressions use the simple preposition: **a teatro** (*at the theatre*), **a casa** (*at home*).

6 Phrases expressing location

Adverbs and prepositions
The following words and phrases can be used both as adverbs and prepositions. Used as preposition, they are normally (but not always) combined with another simple preposition such as **a, di, da,** shown in brackets below.

accanto (a)	accanto a noi
davanti (a)	davanti a casa mia
dentro (di)	dentro l'armadio, dentro di me

dietro (a, di)	dietro il banco, dietro al banco, dietro di lui
di fronte (a)	di fronte alla stazione
dopo (di)	dopo la banca, dopo di noi
fuori (di)	fuori di casa
lontano (da)	lontano dal centro
prima (di)	prima del semaforo
sopra (di)*	a 600 m sopra il livello del mare, sopra di noi
sotto (di)	sotto di noi
vicino (a)	vicino a casa mia

* **Sopra** can also be followed by **a**, e.g. **la montagna sopra a casa mia.**

In each of the pairs of examples below, the first shows the adverbial use, while the second shows the prepositional use.

Vado davanti?	*Shall I go in front?*
Puoi lasciare la macchina davanti a casa mia.	*You can leave the car in front of my house.*
Vai sopra e prendi l'agendino.	*Go upstairs and get the diary.*
L'agenda è sopra la scrivania.	*The diary is on the desk.*
Abito qui vicino.	*I live near here.*
Abito vicino alla scuola.	*I live near the school.*
Non lasciare fuori la bicicletta.	*Don't leave your bike outside.*
Abito fuori del centro.	*I live outside the centre.*

Some prepositions need a preposition only when used with a personal pronoun.

dentro l'armadio	*but*	dentro **di** me
verso la stazione	*but*	verso **di** noi
dietro il castello	*but*	dietro **di** lui
sopra la scrivania	*but*	sopra **di** me

Sometimes the use of a second preposition is optional.

dietro il banco	*but* also	dietro **al** banco

Other phrases indicating location
Those followed by a preposition in brackets (e.g. **di**) can also be used as prepositions.

qui	*here*
lì, là	*there*
in alto	*high up, up there*
in basso	*down there, at the bottom*
giù	*down (below)*
su	*above, on*
in mezzo (a)	*in the middle*
a sinistra (di)	*on the left*
a destra (di)	*on the right*
fra/tra	*between*
in cima (a)	*at the top of*
in fondo (a)	*in the background, at the bottom of*
in primo piano	*in the foreground*
in vetrina	*in the shop window*
verso (di)	*toward*

Language plus

1 Ecco!

An easy way to reply to *where* questions is to use the word **ecco** which means *Here is, Here are* or *There is, There are*.

Dov'è il telefono?	*Where is the telephone?*
Ecco il telefono!	*There's the telephone!*
Dove sono gli elenchi telefonici?	*Where are the telephone directories?*
Ecco gli elenchi!	*Here are the directories!*

Ecco can also stand on its own, and can be used when someone hands you something (*There you are!*) or has just completed something, in which case **ecco** is often combined with the word **fatto** (*done*).

Ecco fatto!   *That's that!*

2 Ecco *and* mi, ti, lo, la, *etc.*

Ecco can also be combined with **mi, ti, lo, la,** etc. to form a phrase meaning *Here I am* or *Here it is*. **Mi, ti, lo, la,** etc. are pronouns; they are used in place of a noun, whether person or inanimate object. They are usually found linked directly to a verb as the object of that verb (see Unit 14), which is why they are known as direct object pronouns. Their form will depend on whether the person or object they are replacing is masculine or feminine, singular or plural. Here are some examples:

Dove sei, Susy?	*Where are you, Susy?*
Ecco**mi**!	*Here I am!*
Dov'è il barista?	*Where is the barman?*
Ecco**lo**!	*Here he is!/There he is!*
Dov'è la stazione?	*Where is the station?*
Ecco**la**!	*There it is!*
Dove sono i bambini?	*Where are the children?*
Ecco**ci**!	*Here we are!*
Dove sono le pile?	*Where are the batteries?*
Ecco**le**!	*Here they are!*

Finally, here is a table of all the direct object pronouns.

Singular		Plural	
mi	*me*	ci	*us*
ti	*you (informal)*	vi	*you (plural)*
lo	*it, him*	li	*them*
la	*it, her*	le	*them*
La	*you (formal)*		

Language in action

Exercise 1

Your friend is coming to stay in your house while you are away.
Tell her where everything is. You will need to fill in the gaps either
with the plain preposition **in** or a combination of the definite article
and appropriate preposition **a, in, su** (**al, nel, sul,** etc.).

1 Il latte è ____ frigorifero.
2 Le tazzine sono ____ armadietto ____ cucina.
3 L'impianto stereo è ____ soggiorno.
4 Il gatto è ____ giardino.
5 La lavatrice è ____ bagno.
6 Le lenzuola sono ____ cassettone.
7 Il telecomando è vicino ____ poltrona.
8 I libri italiani sono ____ camera degli ospiti.
9 I dizionari sono ____ scaffale ____ studio.
10 Le chiavi sono ____ cassetto della credenza.

Exercise 2

Dialogo
Using the map of Pisa for information, tell a tourist where he can
find certain places.

Esempio: Scusi, dov'è l'albergo Rondinella?

L'albergo Rondinella? È in Piazza Treviso, vicino alla stazione.

1 Dove sono i grandi magazzini?
  Sono in ____ vicino a ____ .
2 Dov'è l'Ente Provinciale di Turismo?
  È in ____ vicino a ____ .
3 Dove sono le cabine telefoniche?
  Sono in ____ vicino a ____ .

4 Dov'è la biblioteca?
 È in _____ vicino a _____ .
5 Dov'è la Pensione Ginestra?
 È in _____ vicino a _____ .
6 Dov'è il parcheggio?
 È in _____ vicino a _____ .

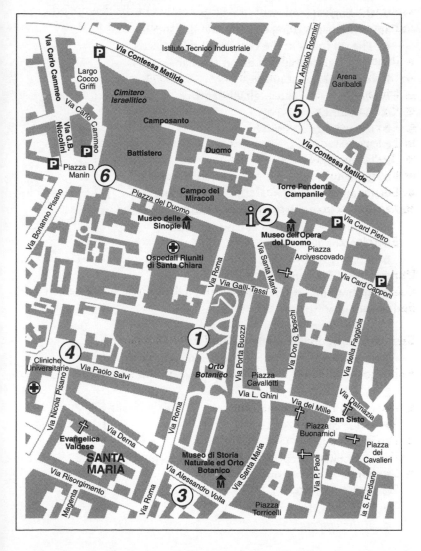

Test yourself

Check your progress! Do you know how to do the following in Italian?

1 Ask where these things/people are.
   a the station
   b the English students
2 Say where something or someone is.
   a The station is at the bottom of this street.
   b The English students are at the bar.
3 Form the plural of nouns.
   Esempio: lo studente – gli studenti
   a la pianista
   b il cameriere
   c la chiave
   d lo spuntino
   e l'albergo
   f l'aranciata
4 Make the noun, definite article and adjective agree.
   Esempio: casa (bianco) la casa bianca
   a automobile (rosso)
   b bibita (fresco)
   c alberghi (costoso)
   d programma (interessante)
   e specialisti (bravo)
   f scarpe (nuovo)
5 Use phrases indicating location.
   Esempio: *in the mountains* in montagna
   a *in town*
   b *in the garden*
   c *at school*
   d *in the country*
   e *at home*
6 Use combined preposition and article forms.
   Esempio: *at the seaside* al mare
   a *at the doctor's*
   b *at the ticket window*
   c *at the cinema*

d *in the stadium*
e *in the restaurant*
f *in the trees*

7 List five more adverbs or adverbial phrases expressing location.
davanti, ...

8 Translate these prepositions and prepositional phrases.
  a *in front of*
  b *opposite*
  c *on the left of*
  d *at the bottom of*
  e *near (to)*

9 Translate these phrases using ecco with a pronoun.
  a *Here I am!*
  b *Here she is!*
  c *Here it is!* (it = elenco telefonico)
  d *Here they are!*
  e *Here you are!* (to a friend)

10 Translation these sentences using **da**.
  a We're eating dinner at Maura's.
  b I buy rolls at the delicatessen.
  c My husband comes back from work at 8 p.m.
  d He comes from Naples.

5

Stating choice and preference

In this unit, you will learn how to:
- **ask the cost of a thing or things**
- **express a preference**
- **specify which item you want**
- **use numbers**
- **ask how much or how many**

Language points
- **questo/quello**
- **quanto?**
- *verbs ending in -are, e.g.* **costare**
- *verbs ending in -ere, e.g.* **prendere**
- *numbers*
- **quale?**

Introduction

Look at these examples:

Quanto costa questo?	*How much does this cost?*
Quanto costano questi sandali?	*How much do these sandals cost?*
Questi costano settantasei euro.	*These cost 76 euros.*
Prendiamo queste due cartoline.	*We'll take these two postcards.*
Quanto costa quello?	*How much does that cost?*
Quanto costano quelle scarpe?	*How much do those shoes cost?*
Prendo quel borsellino in vetrina.	*I'll take that purse in the window.*
Prendo quelli.	*I'll take those ones.*

Focus on grammar

1 Questo *or* quello

Demonstrative adjectives and pronouns (English *this*, *that*) are used to indicate or 'demonstrate' the object or person referred to. The most frequently used demonstratives in Italian are **questo** (*this*) and **quello** (*that*).

2 Questo

Questo (*this*) is used to indicate something or someone near the speaker. It can be an adjective, used with a noun, or a pronoun, standing on its own. In Unit 2, you saw **questo** used as a pronoun meaning *this (one)*, *these (ones)*.

Questi sono i miei amici Gina e Paolo.	*These are my friends Gina and Paolo.*
Quale* gonna vuole misurare? **Questa?**	*Which skirt do you want to try on? This one?*

*See Language plus.

When **questo** is used as an adjective, describing a person or object, it changes its ending according to whether the person or object referred to is singular or plural, masculine or feminine. There are four possible forms:

Masculine singular	*Feminine singular*
Questo museo è chiuso. *This museum is shut.*	**Questa** casa è sporca. *This house is dirty.*
Masculine plural	*Feminine plural*
Questi biglietti sono cari. *These tickets are dear.*	**Queste** camere sono piccole. *These rooms are small.*

> ## Insight
>
> **Questo** is both an adjective (*this*, *these*) and a pronoun (*this one*, *these ones*). In both cases, its forms have to agree in gender (masculine/feminine) and number (singular/plural) with the person or object it refers to.

3 Quello

Use **quello** (*that*, *those*) to indicate something or someone not near the speaker. Its endings follow the definite article **il**, varying according to whether the noun is masculine, feminine, singular or plural and according to the initial letter of the word it precedes. Here are the forms of **quello** when used as an adjective:

Singular	
Quel ristorante è sporco.	*That restaurant is dirty.*
Quell'albergo è costoso.	*That hotel is expensive.*
Quello scontrino è sbagliato.	*That receipt is wrong.*
Quella pensione costa poco.	*That pension is cheap.*
Quell'agenzia è chiusa.	*That agency is closed.*

Plural	
Quei sandali sono di plastica.	*Those sandals are plastic.*
Quegli stivali sono brutti.	*Those boots are ugly.*
Quegli alberghi sono economici.	*Those hotels are cheap.*
Quelle scarpe sono di pelle.	*Those shoes are made of leather.*

Like **questo**, **quello** can also be used as a pronoun, standing on its own. It has four possible forms, depending on gender (masculine/feminine) and number (singular/plural). If you are uncertain of the gender, use the masculine form:

Quello è incredibile.	*That (person or thing) is unbelievable.*
Quelli sono antipatici.	*Those (people) are unpleasant.*
Quella è carina.	*That (girl) is pretty.*
Quelle sono simpatiche.	*Those (girls) are nice.*

Insight

Quello is both an adjective (*that*, *those*) and a pronoun (*that one*, *those ones*). As an adjective, its forms follow the endings of the definite article **il**, **la**, **lo**, etc. As a pronoun, it has only four possible endings. Referring to people only as **quelli** can sound quite dismissive, so is best avoided.

4 Quanto

Quanto can be used as an adjective, referring to a person/object, meaning *how much* or *how many*. **Quanto** varies according to whether the noun is masculine, feminine, singular, or plural.

Quanto zucchero prendi?	*How much sugar do you take?*
Quanta pasta mangi?	*How much pasta do you eat?*
Quanti panini prendi?	*How many sandwiches are you having?*
Quante sigarette fumi al giorno?	*How many cigarettes do you smoke a day?*

Quanto can also be used on its own, meaning *how much* (*time, money*, etc.), in which case the form doesn't change.

Quanto costa?	*How much does it cost?*
Quant'è?	*How much is it? (How much does it cost?)*
Quanto ti fermi?	*How long are you staying?* (fermarsi = *to stop*)

> **Insight**
> **Quanto** is both an adjective, in which case its endings change
> to agree with the noun (**quanto zucchero? quanta birra?**),
> and a pronoun, in which case it doesn't change form (**quanto
> costa?**).

5 **-are** *and* **-ere** *verbs*

The subject pronouns io, **tu**, **lui**, etc. (see Unit 1) are not needed
with the verb because in Italian verbs, the endings show who or
what is doing the action – in other words, who or what is the
subject of the sentence. They can, however, be used for emphasis,
as shown below in brackets.

> **Insight**
> English grammar is simpler than Italian, and English verb
> forms don't vary much: *I go, you go, we go.* (The pronoun
> indicates who is carrying out the action.) So English learners
> sometimes find it complicated having to choose the correct
> verb ending ... but once you get into the habit, it's not too
> difficult!

Most Italian verbs follow one of three main patterns, depending on
whether they end in **-are**, **-ere** or **-ire**. Verbs are usually listed in a
dictionary in a form known as the infinitive, but each group has a
whole set of endings depending on the subject, i.e. the person
carrying out the action. The patterns for **-are** and **-ere** verbs are
shown below.

a *Verbs ending in* **-are**

parlare (to speak)

(io)	parl**o**	*I speak*	(noi)	parl**iamo**	*we speak*
(tu)	parl**i**	*you speak*	(voi)	parl**ate**	*you speak*
(lui)	parl**a**	*he speaks*	(loro)	parl**ano**	*they speak*
(lei)	parl**a**	*she speaks*			
(Lei)	parl**a**	*you speak* (formal)			

b *Verbs ending in* **-ere**

prendere (to take, to have e.g. something to eat or drink)

(io)	prend**o**	*I take*	(noi)	prend**iamo**	*we take*
(tu)	prend**i**	*you take*	(voi)	prend**ete**	*you take*
(lui)	prend**e**	*he takes*	(loro)	prend**ono**	*they take*
(lei)	prend**e**	*she takes*			
(Lei)	prend**e**	*you take* (formal)			

c *Verbs ending in* **-ire**

There is a third group of verbs ending in **-ire** (see Unit 6). The endings do not vary much from those of **-ere** verbs. Examples include **partire, finire, capire**.

d Irregular verbs

Unfortunately, some verbs don't follow a pattern; these are called 'irregular'. There is a list of the most common irregular verbs at the end of the book.

Insight

Italian verbs come in three main groups ('conjugations') distinguished by their ending: **-are** (**parlare**), **-ere** (**vedere**) or **-ire** (**capire, partire**). Each group has its own distinct pattern of endings. Occasionally, verbs follow a different pattern, and these are known as irregular verbs. Unfortunately, these tend to be some of the most commonly used ones, so you just have to learn them!

6 Numbers

1 to 20

0 zero	6 sei	12 dodici	18 diciotto
1 uno	7 sette	13 tredici	19 diciannove
2 due	8 otto	14 quattordici	20 venti
3 tre	9 nove	15 quindici	
4 quattro	10 dieci	16 sedici	
5 cinque	11 undici	17 diciassette	

21 to 30

21 ventuno	26 ventisei
22 ventidue	27 ventisette
23 ventitré	28 ventotto
24 ventiquattro	29 ventinove
25 venticinque	30 trenta

31 to 40 and up ...

31 trentuno	60 sessanta
32 trentadue	70 settanta
33 trentatré	80 ottanta
38 trentotto	90 novanta
40 quaranta	100 cento
50 cinquanta	

hundreds ...

101 centouno, centuno
102 centodue
140 centoquaranta
142 centoquarantadue
200 duecento
etc.

thousands ...

1.000 mille
1.001 mille (e) uno
1.500 millecinquecento
1.550 millecinquecentocinquanta
1.555 millecinquecentocinquantacinque
2.000 duemila
10.000 diecimila

millions ...

1.000.000 un milione
2.000.000 due milioni
1.500.255 un milionecinquecentomiladuecentocinquantacinque

billions ...

1.000.000.000 un miliardo

Notes

- The middle consonants are doubled in **diciassette** and **diciannove**.

- In **ventuno** and **ventotto**, the **i** is dropped from **venti**.

- In **trentuno** and **trentotto**, the **a** is dropped from **trenta**; the same applies to all similar numbers from 30 upwards (**quarantuno, quarantotto, cinquantuno, cinquantotto**, etc.).

- There is no accent on the final vowel of **tre**, but there is one on all the compound numbers which include **tre** from **ventitré** upwards.

- **Cento** can lose its final **o**, as in **centottanta** (**cento ottanta**), **centotto** (**cento otto**). but this is optional.

- The plural of **mille** is **mila**, as in **duemila, tremila**.

- **Cento abitanti, mille abitanti** BUT **un milione di abitanti**

- Several-digit numbers are generally written as one word.

142	centoquarantadue
1.145	millecentoquarantacinque
2.360	duemilatrecentosessanta

- Decimal points are expressed with a comma (**virgola**).

  10,2 dieci virgola due
  1,5 uno virgola cinque

- Long numbers after a thousand are broken up by a point not a comma.

  600.000 seicentomila
  100.000 centomila

Insight

Never translate directly from English into Italian, as language structures are not always used in the same way. Even small points can catch you out, for example *a million tourists* is **un milione di turisti**. Learn as many long numbers by memory as you can – when you ask the price of something, it will help you understand the reply!

The euro and prices

Italy has been part of the eurozone for several years now, though occasionally you may still find reference to the old Italian lire. Euro has no plural form: **un euro, due euro**. The fractions of the euro are **centesimi** ('hundredth parts'). In spoken Italian, when asking a price, you might hear **quattro cinquanta**. Depending on the context, this could be either **quattrocentocinquanta euro** (450 euro) or it could be **quattro euro cinquanta centesimi** (4,50 euro). If in doubt, ask again!

Approximate numbers

Certain numbers also have an 'approximate' version.

dieci (*ten*)	una decina (*about ten*), e.g. una decina di amici (*about ten friends*)
dodici (*twelve*)	una dozzina (*a dozen*), e.g. una dozzina di uova (*a dozen eggs*)
quindici (*fifteen*)	una quindicina (*about fifteen*)
venti (*twenty*)	una ventina (*about twenty*)
trenta (*thirty*)	una trentina (*about thirty*)
cento (*a hundred*)	un centinaio (*about a hundred*), delle centinaia (*hundreds*)
mille (*a thousand*)	un migliaio (*about a thousand*), delle migliaia (*thousands*)

Ordinal numbers and fractions

In Italian, ordinal numbers (English *first, third*) end in **-esimo**, e.g. **quindicesimo, ventesimo, centesimo**. The exceptions are the first ten ordinal numbers: **primo, secondo, terzo, quarto, quinto, sesto, settimo, ottavo, nono, decimo**. These can be abbreviated to **1°**, **2°**, etc.

Ordinal numbers are used in Italian to express fractions: **una decima parte** (*a tenth share*); **un quarto** (*a quarter*); **due terzi** (*two-thirds*).

Dates

Dates in Italian are normally expressed with cardinal numbers (not ordinal).

il 24 settembre (il **ventiquattro** settembre)	*the 24th of September*
il 15 agosto (il **quindici** agosto)	*the 15th of August*

An exception to this is the first day of every month, which is expressed with the ordinal number.

il 1° maggio (il **primo** maggio)	*the 1st of May*

The days of the week and the months of the year are listed in Unit 11.

Time

Time is normally expressed in the plural, since it refers to **le ore** (*hours*).

Sono le due.	*It's two o'clock.*
Sono le otto di sera.	*It's 8.00 p.m.*
Sono le otto di mattina.	*It's 8.00 a.m.*

The exceptions are midnight, midday and one o'clock.

È' mezzanotte.	*It's midnight.*
È' mezzogiorno.	*It's midday.*
È' l'una.	*It's one o'clock.*

The minutes or fractions of an hour can be expressed in different ways.

Sono le otto **e un quarto**.	*It's quarter past eight.*
Sono le otto **e mezzo**.	*It's half past eight.*
Sono le otto **e trenta**.	*It's eight thirty.*
Sono le nove **meno un quarto**.	*It's quarter to nine.*
Sono le otto **e quarantacinque**.	*It's eight forty-five.*

In official or formal contexts, e.g. radio announcements and timetables, the 24-hour clock is used with minutes rather than fractions of an hour.

Sono le **ore venti**.	*It's 20.00.*
Sono le **ore ventidue e trenta**.	*It's 22.30.*

In Unit 6, you will see how to express time at which actions take place, for example **alle due, a mezzanotte, a mezzogiorno**.

Language plus

Quale

Quale (plural **quali**) is an adjective (*which*) and a pronoun (*which one*).

Quale gelato vuoi?	*Which ice-cream do you want?*
Quale pizza preferisci?	*Which pizza do you prefer?*
Quali biscotti prendiamo?	*Which biscuits shall we get?*
Quali scarpe metti?	*Which shoes are you putting on?*

As a pronoun, **quale** can also be used to translate English *what* (see Unit 10).

Quale has the same form for both masculine and feminine nouns: **quale pasta, quale panino.** Similarly, the plural **quali** is used for both masculine and feminine: **quali sandali, quali scarpe.**

Language in action

Exercise 1

Quale preferisci?
You have a choice of items. Choose one of the two words or phrases supplied, making the adjective agree where necessary. (See Unit 14 for more on **preferire**.)

Esempio: Quale tavolo preferisci? (*antico, moderno*)
Preferisco quello moderno.

1 Quale casa preferisci? (*in campagna, in città*)
2 Quale giacca prendi? (*economico, caro*)
3 Quali sandali metti? (*sportivo, elegante*)
4 Quali scarpe compri? (*con tacco alto, senza tacco*)
5 Quali studenti inviti? (*italiani, inglesi*)
6 Quale panino prendi? (*con prosciutto, con formaggio*)
7 Quali biscotti mangi? (*alle nocciole, al cioccolato*)
8 Quale vino bevi? (*rosso, bianco*)
9 Quale giornale leggi? (*inglese, italiano*)
10 Quali film vedi? (*comico, romantico*)

Exercise 2

Opposites
Everything has an opposite. Fill in the gaps with the appropriate form of **quello** and a suitable adjective.

Esempio: Queste scarpe sono comode. **Quelle** scarpe sono **strette**.

1 Quest'aranciata è fresca. ____ aranciata è ____ .
2 Questo palazzo è vicino. ____ palazzo è ____ .
3 Questi studenti sono intelligenti. ____ studenti sono ____ .
4 Questo albergo è di lusso. ____ albergo è ____ .
5 Questi giornalisti sono onesti. ____ giornalisti sono ____ .
6 Questa bottiglia è piena. ____ bottiglia è ____ .
7 Questo film è interessante. ____ film è ____ .
8 Questo museo è chiuso. ____ museo è ____ .
9 Questo straniero è simpatico. ____ straniero è ____ .
10 Questo specialista è anziano ____ specialista è ____ .

_____

Test yourself

Check your progress! Do you know how to do the following in Italian?

1 Write the correct form of **questo**.

   a _____ biglietto   c _____ gonna
   b _____ scarpe   d _____ sandali

2 Write the correct form of **quello**.

   a _____ scontrino   e _____ scarpe
   b _____ agendino   f _____ stuzzicchini
   c _____ pensione   g _____ sandali
   d _____ ristorante   h _____ alberghi

3 Say *how much* or *how many* of these things.

   a _____ panini   d _____ lasagne
   b _____ sigarette   e _____ zucchero
   c _____ pasta

4 Form the present tense of verbs ending in -**are**. **abitare**:

   a (io)   _____   c (noi)   _____
   b (tu)   _____   d (loro)   _____

5 Form the present tense of verbs ending in -**ere**. **prendere**:

   a (io)   _____   c (voi)   _____
   b (lui)   _____   d (loro)   _____

6 Say the numbers from 10 to 20.

10 _____   16 _____
11 _____   17 _____
12 _____   18 _____
13 _____   19 _____
14 _____   20 _____
15 _____

7 Say these numbers.

  a 25 _____   **d** 1.450 _____
  b 38 _____ **e**   10,5 _____
  c 128 _____

8 Say these prices.

  a 10€   **c** 2.000€
  b 100€   **d** 1.000.000€

9 Say these dates in full.

  a 31 August   **c** 1 March
  b 8 January

10 Say these times.

  a It's 9.15 (p.m.).   **d** It's midnight.
  b It's half past five in the   **e** It's 4.45 p.m.
    morning.
  c It's 1 p.m.

6

··

Talking about the present

In this unit, you will learn how to:
- *ask or talk about the present*
- *ask or talk about where someone lives or works*
- *ask or talk about the time when someone does something*
-

Language points
- *introduction to verbs ending in* -ire
- *practice of regular verbs ending in* -are, -ere
- *question words* dove?, a che ora?, come?
- *stare and gerund* -ando, -endo *(immediate present)*
- *expressions of time*

Introduction

Study these examples of how to ask and answer questions about one's life and work.

Dove abita, dottoressa Pellegrini?	*Where do you live, Dr Pellegrini?*
Abito in centro.	*I live in the centre.*
Lavori in città, Marco?	*Do you work in town, Marco?*
Sì, io lavoro in centro, mia moglie invece lavora qui vicino.	*Yes, I work in the centre; my wife, on the other hand, works near here.*
A che ora cominciate a lavorare?	*What time do you start work?*
Io comincio alle otto; mia moglie comincia alle otto e mezzo.	*I start work at eight o'clock; my wife starts at half past eight.*

A che ora finite?	*What time do you finish?*
Io finisco alle sette; mia moglie finisce alle sette e mezzo.	*I finish at seven o'clock; my wife finishes at half past seven.*
Come arrivi al lavoro?	*How do you get to work?*
Prendo l'autobus.	*I take the bus.*
Com'è il tuo lavoro?	*What is your work like?*
È interessante ma faticoso.	*It's interesting but tiring.*

And how to talk about what you are doing right now ...

Sto mangiando!	*I'm eating!*
Sto leggendo un libro.	*I'm reading a book.*

Focus on grammar

1 -ire *verbs*

In Unit 5, you saw verbs ending in **-are** and **-ere**. Here we meet another group of verbs, this time ending in **-ire**.

finire *to finish*

(io)	fini**sco**	*I finish*	(noi)	fin**iamo**	*we finish*
(tu)	fini**sci**	*you finish*	(voi)	fin**ite**	*you finish*
(lui)	fini**sce**	*he finishes*	(loro)	fin**iscono**	*they finish*
(lei)	fini**sce**	*she finishes*			
(Lei)	fini**sce**	*you finish* (formal)			

There are lots of verbs which follow this pattern; one very common one is **preferire** (*to prefer*).

There is also another group of verbs ending in -ire which follow a simpler pattern.

dormire *to sleep*

(io)	dorm**o**	*I sleep*	(noi)	dorm**iamo**	*we sleep*
(tu)	dorm**i**	*you sleep*	(voi)	dorm**ite**	*you sleep*

(lui)	dorm**e**	*he sleeps*	(loro)	dorm**ono**	*they sleep*
(lei)	dorm**e**	*she sleeps*			
(Lei)	dorm**e**	*you sleep* (formal)			

There are a lot of similarities between the endings of the three groups of verbs, especially for some forms.

(io) mangio / prendo / dormo / (finisco)
(noi) mangiamo / prendiamo / dormiamo / (finiamo)

2 Dove ...?

Dove means *where* (see Unit 4). You can use **dove** to ask where someone works or lives.

| **Dove** lavora Lei? | *Where do you work?* |
| **Dove** abitano i Rossi? | *Where do the Rossi family live?* |

Dove is elided before è (*(it) is*).

| **Dov'è** il bar? | *Where is the bar?* |
| Dove sono i bambini? | *Where are the children?* |

Although not strictly necessary, the pronoun **Lei** is often used when asking a question in the formal form, to make the question sound less abrupt.

| Dove abita **Lei**? | *Where do you live?* |

3 A che ora?

A che ora means literally *At what hour?*

A che ora comincia a lavorare?	*What time do you start work?*
	(using formal you)
A che ora chiude il negozio?	*What time does the shop close?*
A che ora parte il treno?	*What time does the train leave?*

Since the hours are generally plural, time is expressed using the plural form.

Comincio a lavorare **alle** otto e mezzo.	*I begin work at 8.30.*
Il negozio chiude **alle** sette e mezzo.	*The shop closes at 7.30.*
Il treno parte **alle** dieci e trenta.	*The train leaves at 10.30.*

The exceptions are midnight, midday and one o'clock, which are singular.

Torno a casa all'ora di pranzo, **all'una.**	*I go home at lunchtime, at one o'clock.*
Finisco di lavorare **a mezzanotte.**	*I finish working at midnight.*
Arrivo a casa **a mezzogiorno.**	*I get home at midday.*

For expressing time, see also Unit 5.

4 Come ...?

Come used in a question means *how*.

Come arrivi in centro?	*How do you get to the centre?*
Come comincia il film?	*How does the film begin?*
Come finisce la storia?	*How does the story end?*
Come va il lavoro?	*How's work going?*
Va abbastanza bene, grazie.	*It's going quite well, thanks.*
Come sta tua sorella?	*How is your sister?*
Sta meglio, grazie.	*She's better, thanks.*

It can also translate the English *What is it like?/What are they like?*

Com'è il tuo lavoro?	*What is your work like?*
È' noioso.	*It's boring.*
Come sono i fichi?	*What are the figs like?*
Sono buonissimi!	*They're really good!*

Come is generally elided before **è** to **com'è**. For other uses of **come**, see Grammar Appendix §§10 and 11, at the end of the book.

Insight

If you want to ask about someone's health (e.g. *How is your father?*), don't translate literally from English to Italian. If you use **essere** (**Com'è tuo padre?**), you are asking what someone's father is like (tall, short, fat, thin, etc.)! So, always use **stare** in this context (**Come sta tuo padre?**).

5 Stare *(to be) and gerund (-ing form)*

The construction of **stare** and gerund is used to either express something you are doing right now or talk about something ongoing. Here, we look at the verb **stare**, the gerund form and finally the combination of **stare** + gerund.

a stare

Stare means to be, but is not synonymous with **essere**; it is generally used only in the following contexts:

- with **come**, e.g. to ask how someone is: **Come sta?**
- with the gerund: **Sto mangiando, Sto leggendo,** etc.
- to express geographical location: **Dove sta la casa?**
- to express the idea of staying (in), rather than going out: '**Esci stasera?**' '**No, sto a casa.**'

However, it is sometimes used by southern Italian speakers in situations where northern and central Italian speakers would simply use essere:

Dove stai? (Dove sei?)   *Where are you?*

The verb **stare** is irregular. Here are the present tense forms:

(io)	**sto**	*I am*	(noi)	**stiamo**	*we are*
(tu)	**stai**	*you are*	(voi)	**state**	*you are*
(lui)	**sta**	*he is*	(loro)	**stanno**	*they are*

(lei)	**sta**	*she is*
(Lei)	**sta**	*you are* (formal)

Insight

Stare is not interchangeable with **essere**. It can only be used in certain contexts, as shown above. It can suggest permanent location (**Dove stai di casa?** *Where do you live?*), whereas **Dove sei?** can be used to ask where you are just now.

b Gerund

The gerund in Italian (**mangiando, leggendo, partendo**) is a near-equivalent of the English *-ing* (*eating, reading, leaving*). It is formed by taking the infinitive form of the verb (for example **parlare**), removing the ending **-are** and adding the gerund ending **-ando**. For **-ere** and **-ire** verbs, remove the endings **-ere** or **-ire** and add **-endo**.

parl**are**	*to speak*	parl**ando**	*speaking*
legg**ere**	*to read*	legg**endo**	*reading*
part**ire**	*to leave*	part**endo**	*leaving*
fin**ire**	*to finish*	fin**endo**	*finishing*

A few verbs (mainly those with a shortened infinitive) have irregular gerund forms, which derive from an older form of the verb.

bere	*to drink*	bev**endo**	*drinking*
d**ire**	*to say*	dic**endo**	*saying*
f**are**	*to do*	fac**endo**	*doing*
trad**urre**	*to translate*	traduc**endo**	*translating*

c stare *and the gerund*

Stare and the gerund are used to express something you or someone else are doing right now.

Cosa **stai facendo**?	*What are you doing (right now)?*
Sto mettendo in ordine.	*I'm tidying up.*
I ragazzi **stanno leggendo**.	*The boys are reading.*
Sto facendo i compiti.	*I'm doing my homework.*

Stare + gerund can also express an ongoing action or event, rather than an immediate one.

Sto facendo un corso di laurea.   *I'm doing a degree course.*
Stiamo rifacendo la casa in Italia. *We are doing up the house in Italy.*

The combination of **stare** and the gerund cannot be used to talk about an action or event in the future, even if it's the immediate future. For this, you must use the plain present or the future tense.

Cosa **fai** stasera?   *What are you doing tonight?*
Esco.   *I'm going out.*

Compare these three sentences:

Ogni settimana **preparo** la cena per gli amici.
(regular action expressed by present tense)

Stasera **preparo** la cena per gli amici.
(near future expressed by present tense)

Mi puoi chiamare dopo? **Sto preparando** la cena.
(ongoing current action expressed by stare and gerund).

Other uses of the gerund are described in the Grammar Appendix §12.1.

Insight

Stare + gerund is a more immediate way of expressing the present. It's the appropriate form to use when someone calls by or phones you and asks what you are doing at that very moment in time. It's also the correct form to express an ongoing action or event. Don't use it to express the future, even the immediate future, e.g. tonight.

Language plus

1 Expressions of time

oggi	*today*
ieri	*yesterday*
domani	*tomorrow*
Oggi mangio il gelato.	*Today, I'm eating ice cream.*
Domani comincio la dieta.	*Tomorrow, I'll start my diet.*
oggi pomeriggio	*this afternoon*
stasera	*this evening*
stamattina	*this morning*
stanotte	*this night (last night)*
questa settimana	*this week*
ieri sera	*yesterday evening*
ieri pomeriggio	*yesterday afternoon*
ieri notte	*last night*
l'altro ieri (l'altrieri)	*the day before yesterday*
la settimana scorsa	*last week*
domani mattina	*tomorrow morning*
domani pomeriggio	*tomorrow afternoon*
domani sera	*tomorrow evening*
dopodomani	*the day after tomorrow*
la settimana prossima	*next week*

Insight

Expressions of time are frequently used in everyday conversation, as well as in letters and emails to friends. Italian often uses the present tense to talk about the future, so adding an expression of future time such as **domani, dopodomani, la settimana prossima** helps to indicate the period in question.

2 Expressions of frequency

tutti i giorni	*every day*
ogni giorno	*every/each day*
tutte le settimane	*every week*

ogni settimana	every/each week

See Unit 7 for more examples of expressions of time and frequency.

3 Pairs of adjectives

Italian uses pairs of adjectives to emphasize a quality. These are colloquial expressions whose use is limited to informal conversation or emails.

stanco morto	*dead tired*
ubriaco fradicio	*dead drunk (lit.: soaking drunk)*
bagnato fradicio	*soaking wet*
pieno zeppo	*packed out*

Sometimes the adjective or adverb is doubled to produce the same effect:

piano piano	*softly, softly (slowly, slowly)*

Alternatively, you can just use molto or tanto for emphasis.

Sono molto stanca.	*I am very tired.*
Il treno è tanto pieno.	*The train is so full.*

Insight

The use of pairs of adjectives is limited to certain combinations – you can't just make them up. If you want to emphasize a particular quality, you can just use **molto** or **tanto**. But of course, if you do know these colloquial expressions, feel free to use them, for variety and authenticity.

Language in action

Exercise 1

Interview with a commuter

– Dove abita, signor Ruzzini? Abita a Firenze?
– No, abito a Pisa, ma lavoro a Firenze.
– E viaggia ogni giorno?
– Sì. Prendo il treno tutti i giorni. Parto alle sette e arrivo alle otto. Comincio a lavorare alle 8.15.

Now write up the information supplied as a brief account of Signor Ruzzini's day:

Il signor Ruzzini comincia a lavorare alle otto e quindici ...

Exercise 2

Interview with a working mother
– Signora Giannini, a che ora comincia a lavorare?
– Comincio alle otto e trenta. Lavoro in centro.
– A che ora finisce?
– Finisco alle sette. Torno a casa stanca morta.
– E suo marito?
– Mio marito non lavora. Resta a casa con la bambina.
– E la sera?
– La sera guardiamo la TV.

Now write up this information in the form of a brief account:

La signora Giannini lavora in centro ...

Exercise 3

Dialogue between friends

CARLA	Vieni al cinema, Marco?
MARCO	Sì, vengo volentieri.
CARLA	Sbrigati, allora, stiamo uscendo proprio adesso.
MARCO	Sto venendo. Mi sto mettendo le scarpe.
CARLA	Sei sempre l'ultimo.
MARCO	Stai scherzando! Tu sei la più lenta di tutti.

Highlight all the examples of **stare** + gerund. Now replace them by a normal present tense.

Esempio: sto mangiando → mangio

Exercise 4

Although Nick is married to an Italian teacher and has spent a lot of time in Italy, he has never studied the language and has problems with the verbs. Sometimes he uses the infinitive form (**-are**, etc.) and sometimes he just misses the verbs out altogether. Can you help him out by adding the appropriate verbs in his part of the conversation with his friend Gloria and making any other necessary changes?

GLORIA	Allora, Nick, dove andate in vacanza quest'anno?
NICK	(1) Noi Argentina. Voi Sardegna come sempre?
GLORIA	Sì, partiamo domani. E voi invece, quando partite?
NICK	(2) Noi partire Oxford il 19 agosto di sera. Arrivare Buenos Aires il 20. E tornare Oxford il 5 settembre.
GLORIA	Come stanno i ragazzi?
NICK	(3) Bene. Malcolm lavorare come medico, Alex lavorare a Londra. Molta musica, molti amici, cinema la sera.

GLORIA	Ah, ho capito. Francesca studia ancora, va tutti i giorni a Milano. E Anna?
NICK	(4) Anna sempre al lavoro. A casa solo per la cena. Molto stressata. Scrivere sempre libri. Finire libro di grammatica prima delle vacanze, spero!

Exercise 5

Use **stare** and an appropriate gerund to say what you or someone else is doing. If you are already familiar with the object pronouns (see Units 4 and 14), use these too, where appropriate:

Esempio: Gianna, cosa fai con quella maglietta? (*lavare*)
Sto lavando la maglietta per stasera.
La sto lavando. (Sto lavandola.)

1 Loredana, cosa fai con la teiera? (*preparare, fare un tè*)
2 Gabriele, cosa fai con la patente? (*andare a noleggiare la macchina*)
3 Sabrina e Max, dove andate con il cane? (*portare a spasso*)
4 Giulio, cosa fai con la radio? (*riparare*)
5 Tania, cosa fai con tutta quella carta? (*scrivere un romanzo*)
6 Paolo, cosa fai con le forbici? (*tagliare le unghie*)
7 Nino, cosa fai con la valigia? (*partire*)
8 Camilla, cosa fai con la tazzina? (*bere un caffè*)
9 Eliana, cosa fai con la macchina fotografica? (*fare una foto della nuova casa*)
10 Alessandro, cosa fai al computer? (*tradurre una lettera*)

Test yourself

Check your progress! Do you know how to do the following in Italian?
1 Use the present tense of verbs like **finire**.
   Esempio: (io) finisco

a (tu) _____
b (lui) _____
c (noi) _____
d (loro) _____

2 Use the present tense of verbs like **dormire**.

   a (io) _____
   b (lei) _____
   c (voi) _____
   d (loro) _____

3 Use **dove** to ask these questions.

   a *Where do you live?* (using **tu**)
   b *Where do you work?* (using **Lei**)
   c *Where do you study?* (using **voi**)

4 Use **come** to ask these questions.

   a *How do you get to school?*
   b *How is your mother?*
   c *How is your work going?*
   d *What is London like?*
   e *What is the lasagne like?*

5 Ask what time things happen.

   a *What time does the film start?*
   b *What time does the supermarket close?*
   c *What time do you finish work?*

6 Use **stare** and the gerund.

   Esempio: i ragazzi (leggere) I ragazzi stanno leggendo.

   a mia madre (cucinare)
   b mio marito (lavorare)
   c noi (cenare)
   d voi cosa (fare)?

7 Say these expressions of present time.

   a *this afternoon*
   b *this morning*
   c *this evening/tonight*
   d *today*

8 Say these expressions of past time.

   a *yesterday morning*
   b *the day before yesterday*

  c *last week*
  d *yesterday evening*

9 Say these expressions of future time.
  a *tomorrow*
  b *the day after tomorrow*
  c *next week*
  d *tomorrow evening*

10 Complete these colloquial expressions (pairs of words).
  Esempio: stanco morto
  a ubriaco _____
  b bagnato _____
  c pieno _____ (= *packed out*)
  d piano _____ (= *softly, softly*)

7

Talking about routine and habits

In this unit, you will learn how to:
- *talk or ask about regular actions and daily routine*
- *talk about something one does for oneself*
- *talk about how one does things*
- *say how frequently one does something*

Language points
- *reflexive verb forms (alzarsi, sedersi, vestirsi)*
- *phrases and adverbs of time (prima, più tardi)*
- *phrases and adverbs of frequency*
- *forming adverbs*

Introduction

Study these short conversations about morning routine.

A che ora ti alzi, Gianna?	*What time do you get up, Gianna?*
Di solito mi alzo alle sei.	*I usually get up at 6 a.m.*
Signora, a che ora si alza la mattina?	*What time do you get up in the morning, signora?*
Io mi alzo tardi, in genere verso le 8.00, e mi preparo un caffè.	*I get up late, usually around 8 a.m., and make myself a coffee.*

Focus on grammar

1 Reflexive verbs

Verbs expressing actions that one does to oneself are known as reflexive verbs (verbs that refer back to the subject or person carrying out the action). In Italian, reflexive verbs are often used to talk about everyday actions such as getting dressed or putting one's make-up on. The reflexive verb is formed by taking the basic verb form and adding a reflexive pronoun e.g. **mi alzo, ti alzi, si alza**. The infinitive form of reflexive verbs is the basic infinitive form (**alzare**) with the final -**e** dropped and the reflexive pronoun -**si** attached to the end. If you want to look up the verb in the dictionary, search for it under its infinitive form (e.g. **alzarsi, sedersi, vestirsi**) or else under the infinitive form of the basic verb (e.g. **alzare, sedere, vestire**).

alzare (*to get someone up*) + **si** = **alzarsi** (*to get oneself up*)
sedere (*to sit*) + **si** = **sedersi** (*to sit down*)
vestire (*to dress someone*) + **si** = **vestirsi** (*to dress oneself*)

a Reflexive verb forms

alzarsi *to get up*			
Singular		Plural	
mi alzo	*I get up*	**ci** alziamo	*we get up*
ti alzi	*you get up*	**vi** alzate	*you get up*
si alza	*he/she gets up*	**si** alzano	*they get up*
si alza	*you get up* (formal 'you')		

Many of the verbs expressing this type of action are -**are** verbs, but there are -**ere** or -**ire** verbs as well, including some irregular verbs.

sedersi *to sit down*
Singular   *Plural*

mi siedo	*I sit down*	**ci** sediamo	*we sit down*
ti siedi	*you sit down*	**vi** sedete	*you sit down*
si siede	*he/she sits down*	**si** siedono	*they sit down*
si siede	*you sit down* (formal 'you')		

vestirsi *to get dressed*
Singular   *Plural*

mi vesto	*I get dressed*	**ci** vestiamo	*we get dressed*
ti vesti	*you get dressed*	**vi** vestite	*you get dressed*
si veste	*he/she gets dressed*	**si** vestono	*they get dressed*
si veste	*you get dressed* (formal 'you')		

b Other uses of the reflexive construction

The reflexive construction – used with any suitable verb – can also describe an action one carries out for oneself. In this case, using the reflexive pronoun implies more involvement on the part of the person carrying out the action. Compare these examples:

Preparo un caffè.   *I'll make a coffee.*
Mi preparo un bel caffè.   *I'll make myself a nice coffee (and sit down and drink it!).*

Frequently, Italian uses the reflexive pronoun (**mi**, **ti**, etc.) as a way of expressing belonging, particularly when talking about articles of clothing or parts of the body. Where English uses the possessive adjective, e.g. *I put my jacket on*, Italian says *I put the jacket on myself*.

Mi metto la giacca per uscire.	*I put my jacket on to go out.*
Mia figlia **si** lava i capelli tutti i giorni.	*My daughter washes her hair every day.*

See Unit 10 for further examples of the reflexive pronoun replacing the possessive adjective.

In the cases above, the reflexive pronoun is not the direct object of the action as in **mi lavo** (*I wash myself*) but the indirect object: **mi lavo i capelli** (*I wash the hair for/to myself*).

c Reflexive infinitives: changing the pronoun
When using the infinitive form of a reflexive verb (e.g. **truccarsi**) after another verb, remember that the reflexive pronoun is not always si, but will change according to the person carrying out the action.

truccarsi (*to put on one's make-up*)

Devo[1] truccarmi per andare alla festa.	*I must do my make-up to go to the party.*

vestirsi (*to get dressed*)

Bambini, preferite vestirvi da soli?	*Kids, do you prefer to get dressed by yourselves?*

prepararsi (*to get ready*)

Perché ci metti[2] tanto a prepararti?	*Why do you take so long to get ready?*

Notes

1 The forms of the verb **dovere** are shown in Unit 18.
2 The combination **mettere + ci** means *to take time*.

Insight

A reflexive verb is just a normal verb with a reflexive pronoun attached to it. With a true reflexive verb, one carries out the action on oneself, but reflexive pronouns can also be used with a range of verbs to convey a sense of involvement.

2 Phrases of time

prima	*first*
prima di me	*before me*
dopo	*after*
dopo di noi	*after us*
più tardi	*later*
poi	*then*
alle tre	*at three o'clock*
verso le tre	*about three o'clock*
dalle nove in poi	*from nine o'clock on*
dalle nove all'una	*from nine till one (o'clock)*
fino all'una	*until one o'clock.*
lunedì	*on Monday (this Monday)*

See also Unit 5 for more ways of expressing time and Unit 6 for more expressions of time.

Insight

Expressions of time can mark a chronological progression: **prima, poi, dopo, più tardi**. They can also refer to events happening *at* a specific time (**alle tre**), *from* a specific time (**dalle nove in poi**), *up until* a specific time (**fino alle due**) or *over* a duration of time (**dalle nove a mezzogiorno**).

3 Phrases expressing frequency

Expressions of frequency can specify how regularly events occur.

il lunedì	*every Monday*
ogni lunedì	*every Monday*

tutti i lunedì	every Monday
sempre	always
di solito	usually
normalmente	normally
generalmente	generally
ogni tanto	every so often
qualche volta	sometimes
(non) ... mai	never
spesso	often
raramente	rarely
una volta al mese	once a month
due volte al mese	twice a month
una volta al giorno	once a day
una volta all'anno	once a year
una volta alla settimana	once a week

Insight

Days of the week Unlike English, Italian doesn't need to use a preposition with the day of the week. **Lunedì** means *on Monday* or *this Monday*. To say *every Monday*, use **ogni lunedì, tutti i lunedì** or just **il lunedì**.

Language plus

1 Position of reflexive pronouns

Normally, the reflexive pronoun comes before the verb, but in certain cases it follows and is joined to it.

a with imperative forms

With the **tu, noi, voi** forms of the imperative, used for giving orders (see Unit 9), the reflexive pronoun is joined to the end of the verb.

Ti metti il vestito nuovo?	*Are you putting your new dress on?*
Metti**ti** il vestito nuovo.	*Put your new dress on!*
Ci prepariamo.	*We're getting ready.*

Prepariamo**ci**.	*Let's get ready.*
Vi mettete le scarpe?	*Are you putting your shoes on?*
Mettete**vi** le scarpe.	*Put your shoes on!*

b with the gerund

With the gerund form, the reflexive pronoun is normally joined on the end, as in the first example below. But when **stare** is used, the pronoun can go either at the end of the gerund -**ando**, -**endo** or (more commonly) before **stare**.

Alzandomi alle sette, ho piu tempo per studiare.	*Getting up at seven, I have more time to study.*
Luisa **si sta truccando**.	*Luisa's doing her make-up.*
Luisa **sta truccandosi**.	*Luisa's doing her make-up.*

c with the infinitive

| Vado a lavarmi. | *I'm going to wash.* |
| Cominciano a prepararsi. | *They start to get ready.* |

Insight

The reflexive pronoun normally comes before the verb (**mi alzo**), except in the case of the infinitive (**alzarsi**) or some imperative forms (**alzati**, **alzatevi**) or the gerund (**alzandosi**).

2 Adverbs

An adverb is similar in purpose to an adjective, but instead of describing a person or a thing, it describes the way someone does something, in other words it qualifies the verb.

| Gli italiani guidano **velocemente**. | *Italians drive fast.* |
| I miei amici prendono **regolarmente** l'aereo. | *My friends take the plane regularly.* |

An adverb can also qualify an adjective.

L'albergo è **particolarmente** adatto agli ospiti anziani.	*The hotel is particularly suitable for elderly guests.*
Questo programma è **facilmente** adattabile alle vostre esigenze.	*This programme is easily adaptable to your needs.*

There are two common ways in which adverbs are formed in Italian, and a few exceptions.

• Adjectives that end in -o, such as **rapido, educato,** change to the feminine form (**rapida**) and add **-mente** to become **rapidamente, educatamente.**
• Adjectives that end in -e, such as **veloce,** add **-mente** to form adverbs such as **velocemente.** In the case of adjectives ending in **-le** or **-re,** such as **facile** and **regolare,** the e is dropped first: **facilmente, regolarmente.**

Some common adjectives and their comparative forms have their own distinct adverb forms.

Adjective	Adverb
buono (*good*)	bene (*well*)
cattivo (*bad*)	male (*badly*)
migliore (*better*)	meglio (*better*)
peggiore (*worse*)	peggio (*worse*)

(See Grammar Appendix §§3.3 and 3.4.)

Insight

Bene and male are two of the most commonly used adverbs in Italian, for example in phrases such as **Sto bene, Sto male, Va bene, Non va bene.** Their comparative forms (**meglio** and **peggio**) are also frequently used: **Va meglio, Va peggio.**

Adverbial phrases, often formed with **con, senza** or **in modo/ maniera,** can take the place of adverbs.

con attenzione	*with care, carefully*
in modo educato	*in a polite way, politely*

| **senza** cura | *without care, carelessly* |
| **in maniera** sgarbata | *in an impolite way, rudely* |

Many adjectives have a dual role as adverbs, for example **certo, chiaro, duro, lontano, vicino, piano, forte**.

| Chi va **piano** va **sano** e va **lontano**. | *He who goes slowly goes safely and goes far.* |
| Mangiate **sano**! | *Eat healthily!* |

Adjectives expressing quantity such as **molto, poco, quanto, tanto, troppo, tutto** (see Grammar Appendix §6 for their use as adjectives) can also be used as adverbs and are often found qualifying an adjective or even another adverb.

Questo treno è **molto veloce**.	*This train is very fast.*
I bambini sono **poco entusiasti**.	*The children are not very enthusiastic.*
Sei **tanto brava**!	*You are so clever!*
Guidi **troppo velocemente**.	*You drive too fast.*
Sono **tutto agitata**!	*I'm all agitated!*

Insight

As adjectives, **molto, poco, tanto, troppo** and **tutto** change ending to agree with the noun (e.g. **molto zucchero, poca pasta, tanti errori, troppe ragazze**). As adverbs, they use the masculine singular form and do not change (**Bevo molto, Mangio poco, Dormo tanto, Studio troppo, Sono tutto rilassata**).

Simple adverbs which are not derived from adjectives are covered elsewhere in the book, for example adverbs of time and frequency, such as those shown in section 2 above, and adverbs of place (see Unit 4).

Language in action

Exercise 1

Getting ready
In this 'dialogue', highlight or underline the verbs used reflexively.

Piero e Maddalena, perché non andate a farvi la doccia? Su,* cercate di sbrigarvi! Poi mettetevi i vestiti puliti e pettinatevi un pochino. (Bevete il latte ...)

Now continue giving the children orders, along these lines, using a range of different verbs (see Exercise 2 below for ideas). Alternatively, for a change, try giving orders to an imaginary partner, in the **tu** form.

* Come on! Get a move on!

Exercise 2

Say what you do first in the morning, using **preferire** and the infinitive form of the reflexive.

Esempio: Ti fai prima la doccia o prendi il caffè? **Preferisco farmi** prima la doccia.

1 Ti fai prima la doccia o ti vesti?
2 Ti metti prima i vestiti o prendi il caffè?
3 Ti metti prima le scarpe o i calzini?
4 Ti trucchi prima o ti pettini?
5 Ti lavi i capelli prima o ti vesti?
6 Ti lavi prima i denti o fai colazione?

Exercise 3

Use the example below as a basis to write an account of what you (and your friends or family) do every morning. Practise asking your partner (imaginary if you prefer) what he or she does in the morning. Use expressions of time such as **prima, dopo, poi** to say what order you do things in and use the verbs illustrated.

Esempio:

A casa
La mattina mio marito si alza prima di me e mi prepara il caffè. Io mi alzo dopo, mi faccio la doccia, mi lavo i capelli, mi vesto e poi mi preparo ad uscire.

Now it's your turn.

alzarsi   fare la doccia   farsi la barba.

preparare il caffè   fare colazione   lavarsi i capelli

lavarsi i denti   mettersi le scarpe   pettinarsi

svegliarsi   truccarsi   vestirsi

Test yourself

Check your progress! Do you know how to do the following in Italian?

1 Say four things about your daily routine.
   Esempio: Mi alzo alle sette.
2 Say four things about your children's daily routine.
   Esempio: I bambini si alzano alle otto.
3 Talk about what clothes everyone is putting on.
   Esempio: Sandra (*puts her shoes on*) Sandra si mette le scarpe.
   a Davide (*puts his jacket on*)
   b Carlo and Maura (*put their coat on*)
   c I bambini (*put their gloves on*)
   d Io (*put my trousers on*)
   e Tu (*put your sweater on*)
4 Write the correct reflexive pronoun.
   Esempio: Devo prepararmi.
   a Luisa deve truccar__.
   b Devi preparar__?
   c Preferiamo vestir__ prima di cena.
   d Preferite metter__ il cappotto pesante?
   e Gli studenti preferiscono preparar__ dopo.
5 Say these frequency expressions.
   a *once a day*
   b *twice a week*
   c *once a month*
   d *once a year*
   e *often*
   f *rarely*
   g *sometimes*
   h *every so often*
6 Say these time expressions.
   a *before you*
   b *after him*
   c *from ten to two*
   d *then*
   e *later*

7 Form adverbs from adjectives.

Esempio: veloce velocemente

a rapido

b buono

c facile

d migliore

8 Make up adverbial phrases based on adjectives.

Esempio: attento con attenzione

a educato

b sgarbato

c brusco

d entusiasta

9 Turn these sentences into orders.

Esempio: Ti metti il vestito? Mettiti il vestito!

a Vi mettete le scarpe?

b Ci mettiamo la giacca?

c Ti lavi i capelli?

d Ti trucchi per la festa?

e Vi preparate adesso?

10 Complete this proverb.

Chi va ____ va ____ e va ____ .

8

Talking about possibility and asking permission

In this unit, you will learn how to:
- **ask permission to do something**
- **ask someone if he/she is able to do something for you**
- **say you can or can't do something**
- **ask if something is allowed/possible**

Language points
- **potere**
- *impersonal* **si può?**
- **È possibile?**
- **sapere**

Introduction

Study these ways of asking permission and asking if someone can do something.

Può indicarmi la strada per Pisa?	*Can you show me the road to Pisa?*
Posso telefonare da qui?	*Can I telephone from here?*
Si può parcheggiare?	*Can one park?*
È possibile telefonare?	*Is it possible to phone?*
Sa dirmi quanto costa?	*Can you tell me how much it costs?*

Focus on grammar

1 Potere

Potere means *to be able to* (*I can*). It is an irregular verb, i.e. it does not follow the pattern of any of the main verb groups. Here are the forms of the present tense.

posso	*I can*	possiamo	*we can*
puoi	*you can*	potete	*you can*
può	*he/she can* (formal)	possono	*they can you can*

Use **potere** say what *one is able*, or *not able*, *to do*; *to ask permission*; or *to ask other people if they can do something*.

Possiamo prendere l'autobus?	*Can we get the bus?*
Non **posso** mangiare le fragole, perché sono allergica.	*I can't eat strawberries because I'm allergic (to them).*
Posso telefonare in Inghilterra?	*Can I phone England?*
Può cambiare questo biglietto da 50 euro?	*Can you change this 50-euro note?*
Potete indicarmi la strada per Roma?	*Can you show me the road for Rome?*

In the last question above, the pronoun can also be placed before **potete**:

Mi potete **indicare** la strada per Roma?

2 Si può?

This is a general way of asking if one can do something where no specific person is mentioned.

Si può parcheggiare qui?	*Can one park here?*
Si può entrare?	*Can one come in?*
Si può telefonare in Inghilterra?	*Can one phone England?*

....

Insight

The expression **si può** is general and makes no mention of a specific person. It can be translated into English as *One can .../Can one ...?* (or, more informally *You can .../Can you ...?*) and is used with the infinitive of the verb: **Si può lasciare la macchina qui?** (*Can you/one leave the car here?*). You can also ask permission to enter, simply by putting your head round the door and asking **Si può?** (*May I?*).

....

3 È possibile?

You can also use **È possibile** in the same way.

È possibile parlare con il direttore?	*Is it possible to speak to the manager?*
È possibile andare in macchina?	*Is it possible to go by car?*

Language plus

sapere

When *I can* means *I know how to*, use **sapere**.

So nuotare bene.	*I can swim well. (= I know how to swim well.)*
Sai cucinare?	*Can you cook? (= Do you know how to cook?)*

Sapere also means to know a piece of information.

Sai a che ora parte l'autobus?	*Do you know what time the bus leaves?*
Sa dirmi a che ora parte il treno?	*Can you tell me what time the train leaves?*
Sai che ore sono?	*Do you know what time it is?*

Compare these examples:

So parlare italiano.	*I can speak Italian. (= I know how to)*
Posso parlare italiano con la mia collega.	*I can speak Italian with my colleague. (i.e. because circumstances permit)*

Insight

English *I can* can be either **posso** or **so**. While **sapere** means *to know a piece of information, a fact or a skill* (**So suonare il pianoforte** *I can play the piano*), **potere** means you can do something because you are allowed, because circumstances permit it or because you have the time/money/opportunity.

4 Omitting **potere**

When any of the five senses are involved, e.g. *to see, hear, feel, taste* or *smell* (in Italian **vedere, sentire**), the verb **potere** is often omitted. The same applies to verbs of similar meaning such as **toccare** (*to touch*).

Mi senti?	*Can you hear me?*
Non sento niente.	*I can't hear/feel/taste/smell anything.*
Non vediamo nessuno.	*We can't see anyone.*
Non tocco! L'acqua è troppo alta.	*I can't touch (the bottom). The water is too deep.*

Insight

Sentire in Italian can mean *to hear, to feel, to taste* or *to smell*. Usually, the precise meaning will be obvious from the context. **Vedere** means *to see*. With both of these, the verb **potere** is generally left out. The particle **ci** is often added, as in **Ci vedi?** (*Can you see?*).

5 *Other tenses and moods of* **potere**

All of these tenses are covered in more detail later in the book, as indicated in brackets below, so you might prefer to read this section later, when you have learned those tenses.

• **Potere** when used in the conditional mood (see Unit 20) means *could*.

Potresti farmi un favore?	*Could you do me a favour?*
Potrei passare domani.	*I could pass by tomorrow.*

• **Potere** in the past conditional (see Unit 21) means *could have*:

Avresti potuto avvertirmi.	*You could have warned me.*
Avrei potuto farne a meno.	*I could have done without it.*

....

Insight
   The conditional mood is a verb form which expresses actions
   or events in a less certain way than the indicative (normal)
   verb form. While **posso** means *I can*, **potrei** means *I could*. It
   has a present tense (e.g. **potrei**) and a past tense (e.g. **avrei
   potuto**).
....

• **Potere** can be used in the perfect tense (see Unit 11) or the imperfect tense (see Unit 12). If the sentence refers to one action or event, use the perfect. If it is a continuing situation or incomplete action where you would normally use the imperfect, then use the imperfect of **potere**.

Non **ho potuto** telefonargli.	*I couldn't ring him.*
Non **potevo** aspettare. Avevo troppe cose da fare.	*I couldn't wait. I had too much to do.*

• **Potere** normally takes **avere** in the perfect tense, but when followed by a verb taking **essere**, it can use **essere**. In spoken Italian, either is acceptable. When used with essere, the past participle (**potuto**) has to agree with the subject in number and gender.

Non **ho potuto** venire./Non **sono** **potuto** venire.	I couldn't come.
Non **abbiamo potuto** andare./ Non **siamo potuti** andare.	We couldn't go.
Luisa non **ha potuto** venire./ Luisa non **è potuta** venire.	Luisa couldn't come.

6 Other ways of saying 'to be able to'

a essere in grado di
Essere in grado (di) means *to be able to, to be up to*.

| Non **è in grado di** fare questo lavoro. | He is not up to this work. |
| **Sei in grado di** darmi una risposta? | Are you able to give me a reply? |

b farcela
Farcela is an idiomatic expression composed of **fare**, **ci** and **la**, meaning *to be able to, to manage to, to cope*. It can be followed by the preposition **a**. Ce la does not change, while the **fare** part of the expression changes according to who is carrying out the action.

| Non **ce la faccio** più. | I can't cope. |
| **Ce la fai** a spostare quel divano? | Can you manage to move that sofa? |

7 Non ne posso più

Non ne posso più is an expression meaning *I can't bear it, I can't stand it any longer*.

| Non ne possono più. | They can't stand it any more. |

It can be followed by **di**.

| Non ne posso più **di** questa storia. | I can't bear this nonsense any longer. |

Insight

Italian has a range of colloquial expressions which cannot be translated literally into English. Many of these use pronouns or the particle **ci**, for example **metterci**, **farcela**, **non ne posso più**.

Language in action

Exercise 1

Complete this exercise with the appropriate form of **potere** in the present tense.

1 (Io) non _____ finire i compiti, perché ho ospiti in casa.
2 I nostri amici non _____ andare in vacanza perché la bambina è malata.
3 (Tu) non _____ andare al cinema perché hai una lezione di pianoforte alle cinque.
4 (Noi) non _____ ospitare i nostri amici perché stiamo facendo i lavori in casa.
5 (Voi) non _____ vedere il film perché il cinema è chiuso.
6 Mio figlio non _____ uscire stasera perché è senza soldi.

Exercise 2

Suggest things you or your friend(s) might do, to solve your problems. Your answer must include an appropriate form of the verb **potere**.

Esempio: Come arrivo in centro? Non ho la macchina. (*prendere l'autobus*)
Puoi prendere l'autobus.

1 Gloria non ha niente da mettere. (*comprare un vestito nuovo*)
2 Andrea non viene alla festa, deve fare i compiti. (*venire dopo*)
3 I ragazzi si annoiano a casa. (*andare al cinema*)

4 Non abbiamo soldi per andare in vacanza. (*fare lo scambio di casa*)

5 Voglio andare al mare ma in agosto lavoro. (*andare a luglio*)

6 Al ristorante non c'è una tavola per sei persone. Che facciamo? (*andare domani*)

7 Ho paura di guidare da sola. (*accompagnarti se vuoi*)

8 Domani c'è la festa di Barbara ma siamo senza macchina. (*venire con noi, se volete*)

Exercise 3

Planning a holiday in Italy

Amanda and Tony are going to Tuscany for a short holiday. Their friend Maura helpfully tells them all the things they can see in five days! Fill in the gaps with the correct form of **potere** or **sapere** (present tense).

AMANDA	Abbiamo cinque giorni per visitare Firenze, Pisa, Siena e Lucca. Non **(1)** _____ (sapere) come organizzarci. Tony vuole vedere il Palio di Siena, mentre io preferisco visitare le gallerie d'arte e i musei. I nostri amici non **(2)** _____ (sapere) consigliarci. Tu **(3)** _____ (sapere) darci qualche indicazione, Maura?
MAURA	Eh ... sono troppe cose da vedere in poco tempo. Arrivate a Pisa e ripartite da Pisa, vero? **(4)** _____ (potere) prendere un volo da Firenze per risparmiare tempo. **(5)** _____ (sapere) l'orario dei voli da Londra? Oppure **(6)** _____ (potere) cominciare la vostra vacanza a Pisa, andando a vedere la Torre ... Io non **(7)** _____ (sapere) a che ora chiude, ma posso chiedere al mio amico, che forse lo **(8)** _____ (sapere). Dopo **(9)** _____ (potere) prendere il pullman da Pisa a Lucca e fare una passeggiata lungo le mura antiche. Poi da Lucca si **(10)** _____ (potere) prendere il pullman per Firenze ... è più veloce del treno. Il centro di Firenze

non è molto grande e si **(11)** _____ (potere) girare anche a piedi. In una giornata **(12)** _____ (potere) vedere i principali monumenti: il Duomo, Palazzo Pitti, il Ponte Vecchio. Se veramente volete andare anche a Siena, **(13)** _____ (potere) prendere il pullman da Firenze a Siena. Tu, Amanda, **(14)** _____ (potere) visitare i musei e le gallerie d'arte, mentre tu, Tony, **(15)** _____ (potere) andare a vedere il Palio. Tony, **(16)** _____ (sapere) dove si fa il Palio, vero?

Test yourself

Check your progress! Do you know how to do the following in Italian?

1 Write the present tense of **potere**. **Esempio:** (io) posso
  a (tu) _____   **d** (voi) _____
  b (lui) _____   **e** (loro) _____
  c (noi) _____

2 Ask permission to do things. **Esempio:** You want to phone England. Posso telefonare in Inghilterra?
  a *You want to go to the bathroom.*
  b *You want to see the photos.*
  c *You want to speak to the director.*

3 Ask someone to do something for you.
  a Scusi, mi _____ cambiare cinquanta euro?
  b Signora, _____ indicarmi la strada per il centro?
  c Ragazzi, _____ indicarmi la fermata dell'autobus?
  d Maura, _____ prestarmi il tuo telefonino?

4 Ask if it is possible to do something (using **si può** or **è possibile**).
  a _____ parcheggiare qui?   **c** _____ parlare con il direttore?
  b _____ visitare il Duomo? **d** _____ comprare un giornale italiano?

5 Write the present tense of **sapere**. **Esempio:** (io) so

a (tu) _____

b (lui, lei, Lei) _____

c (noi) _____

d (voi) _____

e (loro) _____

6 Choose between **potere** and **sapere**. **Esempio:** Io so parlare italiano.

   a Gli studenti _____ nuotare alla piscina dell'Università.

   b Io non _____ venire alla festa, sono senza macchina.

   c Marco, _____ a che ora parte il pullman?

   d Mio marito _____ cucinare molti piatti italiani ma non _____ cucinare stasera perché è in Italia per lavoro.

7 Decide which is the correct option (the one with **potere** or not).

   a **i** Puoi sentire la musica?

      ii Senti la musica?

   b **i** Ragazzi, potete vedere le stelle?

      ii Ragazzi, vedete le stelle?

   c **i** Senti che buon odore?

      ii Puoi sentire che buon odore?

   d **i** Non sento niente.

      ii Non posso sentire niente.

8 Say these sentences using the present conditional of **potere**.

   a _Could you do me a favour?_ (farmi un piacere)

   b _Could you pass the salt?_ (passare il sale)

   c _Could you close the window?_ (chiudere la finestra)

9 Say these sentences using the present conditional of **potere**.

   a _I could come by tomorrow._ (passare domani)

   b _I could call later._ (telefonare più tardi)

   c _I could give you a hand._ (darti una mano)

10 Complete these sentences with the most suitable colloquial expression out of **essere in grado (di)**, **farcela (a)**, **non ne posso piu (di)**.

   a (Marco) non _____ di finire questo progetto.

   b (Io) non _____ a mangiare tutta questa pasta.

   c Sei veramente antipatica – (io) non _____ di sentire le tue critiche.

   d Sono già le 17.00. (Noi) _____ a finire per le 18.00?

9

Giving orders and instructions

In this unit, you will learn how to:
- **request, order or give instructions**
- **read written instructions**
- **tell someone not to do something**

Language points
- **imperative (command) form: tu, lei, noi, voi, loro**
- **written instructions using the infinitive**
- **negative forms of the imperative**

Introduction

A command or order is expressed in Italian by the imperative verb form. These examples show how the imperative form is used to give orders or instructions:

Prendi un dolce, Marco!	*Have a cake, Marco.*
Mangia un panino!	*Eat a sandwich!*
Non fare complimenti!	*Don't stand on ceremony!*
Senta! Scusi! Come arrivo alla stazione?	*Listen. Excuse me. How do I get to the station?*
Prenda Via Manzoni.	*Take Via Manzoni.*
Al primo semaforo giri a sinistra.	*At the first traffic lights, turn left.*
Non giri a destra!	*Don't turn right.*
Andiamo al cinema! C'è un film di Troisi.	*Let's go to the cinema! There's a Troisi film.*

Non facciamo tardi.	*Let's not be late.*
Bambini, andate a giocare in giardino!	*Children, go and play in the garden!*
Non andate fuori scalzi, mettetevi le scarpe!	*Don't go out with bare feet, put your shoes on!*
Signorine, si accomodino!	*Ladies, please be seated! (Please make yourselves comfortable!)*
Non si preoccupino!	*Don't worry!*
Aprire con cautela.	*Open with care. (Instructions on a packet)*

Focus on grammar

1 Imperative (**tu** form)

When giving an instruction to someone you are on friendly terms with, use the **tu** (informal you) form. The ending is -**a** for -**are** verbs or -**i** for -**ere** and -**ire** verbs (the same as the **tu** form of the present tense).

....

parlare	**Parla** chiaro!	*Speak clearly!*
prendere	**Prendi** qualcosa da mangiare!	*Have something to eat!*
sentire	**Senti** questo!	*Listen to this!*
pulire	**Pulisci** la bocca!	*Wipe your mouth!*

....

2 Imperative (**Lei** form)

When giving an order to someone you are on formal terms with, use the **Lei** (formal *you*) form. For -**are** verbs, the imperative ends in -i; for -**ere** and -**ire** verbs, it ends in –a.

portare	**Mi porti** il menù!	*Bring me the menu!*
prendere	**Prenda** un biscotto!	*Take a biscuit!*
sentire	**Senta!**	*Listen!*
finire	**Finisca** pure!	*Do finish!*

3 *Imperative (**noi** form)*

The **noi** form is not exactly a command; it is a way of exhorting one's friends to do something when the speaker himself/herself is part of the group. The form of the imperative is the same as the **noi** form of the present tense.

portare	**Parliamo** italiano!	*Let's talk Italian!*
prendere	**Prendiamo** un gelato!	*Let's have an ice-cream!*
sentire	**Sentiamo** cosa vuole.	*Let's hear what he wants!*
finire	**Finiamo** domani!	*Let's finish tomorrow!*

4 *Imperative (**voi** form)*

This is the form of imperative or order normally used when addressing more than one person (see section 5 for the polite **loro** form). The form is exactly the same as the **voi** form of the present tense.

cercare	**Cercate** di finire il progetto oggi!	*Try and finish the project today!*
mettere	**Mettete** i guanti, fa freddo.	*Put your gloves on, it's cold.*
dormire	**Dormite** bene!	*Sleep well!*
finire	**Finite** di mangiare!	*Finish eating!*

5 *Imperative (**Loro** form)*

Loro (the formal plural *you* form) is not common. It is sometimes used by shop assistants, waiters, hotel employees, etc. when addressing more than one customer.

accomodarsi	**Si accomodino!**	*Please make yourselves comfortable! (Please sit down, come in.)*
sedersi	**Si siedano!**	*Please sit down!*
dormire	**Dormano** bene!	*Sleep well!*
finire	**Finiscano** pure di mangiare, signori! Non c'è fretta.	*Do finish eating, there's no hurry.*

Insight

The imperative is the verb form used for orders, whether it is telling a friend to close the window or asking the waiter to bring the bill. Sometimes you may prefer just to use the normal verb form, but you should at least be able to recognise and use the more common imperative forms.

6 Giving instructions using the infinitive

Recipes, instruction manuals and other written instructions often use the infinitive (the *to* form of the verb).

Tagliare la cipolla e **mettere** in un tegame.
Chop the onion and place in a frying pan.

Moderare la velocità!
Reduce your speed!

For example, here is part of an instruction manual for a mobile phone:

Accensione del cellulare

1 Per accendere il cellulare, **tenere** premuto il tasto di accensione e spegnimento.
2 Se il cellulare richiede un codice PIN o un codice di protezione, **immettere** il codice e **selezionare** OK.
3 Per spegnere il cellulare, **tenere** premuto il tasto di accensione e spegnimento.

Insight

Written instructions such as instruction manuals and recipes either use the **voi** form of imperative (**Prendete**) or the infinitive form (**Prendere**), which is seen as more impersonal. Recipes are usually quite easy to understand, while instruction manuals may have more technical vocabulary.

7 Telling someone not to do something

For the **Lei**, **noi**, **voi** and **loro** forms, add **non** before the relevant imperative form of the verb.

Non esca, signora!	*Don't go out, signora!*
Non andiamo da Maria!	*Let's not go to Maria's!*
Non girate a sinistra!	*Don't turn left!*
Non si preoccupino!	*Don't worry!*

For the **tu** form, use **non** and the infinitive form (the -are, -ere, -ire form).

Non mangiare troppo!	*Don't eat too much!*
Non prendere tutto!	*Don't take all of it!*
Non dormire fino a tardi!	*Don't sleep in!*

Non is also added to instructions given in the infinitive.

Non parlare con il conducente!	*Don't speak to the driver!*

Insight

Making the **Lei**, **noi** and **voi** imperatives negative is easy: you simply add **non** (**Non vada veloce! Non andiamo fuori! Non andate via!**). For the **tu** imperative, the verb form changes (**Mangia! Non mangiare!**).

Language plus

1 Irregular imperatives

Many verbs have an imperative form which does not follow the form shown above. Some of the most common irregular imperative forms are:

Infinitive		tu	Lei	voi	Loro
andare	(to go)	va'	vada	andate	vadano
fare	(to do)	fa'	faccia	fate	facciano
stare	(to be)	sta'	stia	state	stiano
dare	(to give)	da'	dia	date	diano
dire	(to say)	di'	dica	dite	dicano
essere	(to be)	sii	sia	siate	siano
avere	(to have)	abbi	abbia	abbiate	abbiano
sapere	(to know)	sappi	sappia	sapete	sappiano
venire	(to come)	vieni	venga	venite	vengano

The **Lei** form of the imperative is the same as the 3rd person form (*he, she, you*) of the present subjunctive (see Unit 17). (See Grammar Appendix §13.3 for the subjunctive forms of irregular verbs.)

The one-syllable imperatives shown above are also spelt: **va, fa, sta, dà, dì**. Perhaps because they sound so abrupt, there is a tendency for the first four to be replaced by the **tu** form of the present indicative: **vai, fai, stai, dai**.

Vai a prendere la mia sciarpa. (**Va'**   *Go and get my scarf.*
  a prendere la mia sciarpa).

Mi dai una mano? (**Dammi** una   *(Can you) give me a hand?*
  mano).

2 Pronouns – before or after?

Direct object pronouns were covered in Unit 4. Indirect object
pronouns and combined direct and indirect object pronouns
are covered later in the book (Unit 16 and Grammar Appendix
§4.1–§4.2 respectively), so you may wish to come back to this
section later.

With the **tu, noi, voi** imperative (order) forms, the object pronouns
(direct, indirect and combined) are joined to the end.

Chiamiamoli!	*Let's call them!*
Telefonagli!	*Ring him!*
Passatemelo!	*Pass it to me!*

When attached to the one-syllable **tu** imperative forms (**Da'! Fa'!
Di'! Sta'! Va'!**), the initial consonant of the pronoun doubles.

Dallo a tuo fratello!	*Give it to your brother!*
Dammelo!	*Give it to me!*
Dimmi cosa vuoi!	*Tell me what you want!*
Facci un piacere!	*Do us a favour!*

Except in the case of **gli**.

Digli di andare via!	*Tell him to go away!*

Insight

The use of one-syllable imperative forms and attached
object pronouns **mi, ti,** etc. gives rise to combinations such
as **dammi, dimmi** and **fammi,** which are very common in
children's speech (**Dammi la macchinina!**) and also in that of
adults (**Fammi un piacere!**).

With the negative imperative **tu, noi, voi** forms, the pronoun has two possible positions.

Non seguirmi!	*Don't follow me!*
or Non mi seguire!	
Non compriamolo!	*Let's not buy it!*
or Non lo compriamo!	
Non mangiateli!	*Don't eat them!*
or Non li mangiate!	

With the **Lei** imperative form (the polite form), the object pronouns always go before.

Lo prenda pure!	*Please take it!*
Non lo prenda!	*Don't take it!*

For other cases in which pronouns are joined to the end of the verb, see Grammar Appendix §4.3.

Insight

Unfortunately, there is no single rule that determines the position of the pronouns with the imperative form. Their position depends on whether it is the **tu, noi, voi** form (pronoun is attached to the end of the verb) or the **Lei** form (pronoun comes before the verb).

Language in action

Exercise 1

Cosa c'è da vedere a Napoli?

One of your friends is going to Naples soon, with his girlfriend. Tell him what to go and see and give him some advice on where and what to eat, where to stay, how to get around. Use the basic information supplied below. Try not to use **andare** all the time; here are some other suggestions: **assaggiare, bere, cercare, comprare, fare, mangiare, prendere, prenotare, provare, stare, visitare.**

Esempio: Va' a vedere i chiostri di Santa Chiara. Cerca di visitare anche la chiesa.

Da visitare
- Castel dell'Ovo

- Palazzo Reale
- Museo Nazionale

Da mangiare e bere
- Limoncello

- Sfogliatelle napoletane
- Pizza

Da comprare
- Figurine per il presepe (San Gregorio Armeno)
- Vestiti (Via Toledo o Vomero)
- Corallo

Alberghi
- Terminus (vicino alla stazione ferroviaria)
- Bella Napoli (Via Caracciolo)
- Majestic (Largo Vasto a Chiaia)

Da visitare fuori città
- Pompei (la Circumvesuviana)
- Capri (aliscafo o nave)
- Sorrento (la Circumvesuviana)

Exercise 2

Come si arriva a ...?

Read this dialogue in which a tourist is given directions by a local resident.

TOURIST	Senta, scusi! Come arrivo alla stazione?
RESIDENT	Dunque ... vada diritto per questa strada, al primo semaforo giri a sinistra, continui ancora un po', e in fondo a quella strada volti a destra ... attraversi la piazza e la stazione è proprio di fronte.
TOURIST	Ah, grazie. Lei è molto gentile.

Now make up your own dialogue in which you explain to a visiting Italian tourist how to get to the Bodleian Library (**Biblioteca Bodleiana**), Oxford, from the Museum of Oxford. Use the map below.

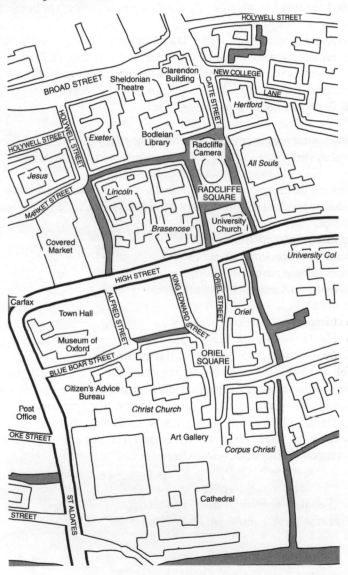

Test yourself

Check your progress! Do you know how to do the following
in Italian?

1 Give orders to someone using the **tu** form of the verb in brackets.
   a *Smell this!* (sentire)
   b *Speak slowly!* (parlare)
   c *Finish your homework!* (finire)
2 Give orders to someone using the **Lei** form of the verb in brackets.
   a *Have a cake!* (prendere)
   b *Bring me the bill!* (portare)
   c *Clean the table!* (pulire)
3 Encourage your friends to do something using the verb in brackets.
   a *Let's go out!* (uscire)
   b *Let's go to the pizzeria!* (andare)
   c *Let's put the sofa near the window!* (mettere)
4 Give orders to someone using the **voi** form of the verb
   in brackets.
   a *Put your gloves on!* (mettere)
   b *Finish your homework!* (finire)
   c *Study the verbs!* (studiare)
5 Give instructions in a recipe or manual using the verb
   in brackets.
   a *Chop the tomatoes.* (tagliare)
   b *Heat the olive oil.* (riscaldare)
   c *Boil the water for the pasta.* (far bollire)
6 Tell someone not to do something using the verb in brackets.
   a *Kids, don't eat all the chocolates.* (mangiare)
   b *Maura, don't forget your appointment.* (dimenticare)
   c *Dottor Di Giacomo, don't worry.* (preoccuparsi)
7 Give the imperative form of irregular verbs.
   Esempio: (Lei) andare – Vada!
   a (tu) fare
   b (voi) dare
   c (Lei) dire
   d (Lei) sapere
   e (tu) stare
   f (Lei) venire

8 Replace the noun with the appropriate object pronoun in the tu imperative.

Esempio: Non mangiare i cioccolatini! Non mangiarli!

a Mangia la pasta!

b Passa il sale!

c Non bere il vino!

9 Replace the noun with the appropriate object pronoun in the Lei imperative.

Esempio: Chiuda la finestra! La chiuda!

a Prenda il vino!

b Mangi i cannelloni!

c Non beva la birra!

10 Replace the noun with the appropriate object pronoun in the voi imperative.

Esempio: Lavate i piatti! Lavateli!

a Comprate il pane!

b Scrivete le cartoline!

c Pulite le vostre stanze!

10

Talking about possession

In this unit, you will learn how to:
- **ask to whom something belongs**
- **say to whom something belongs**
- **ask what other people have/own**

Language points
- **possessive adjectives** mio, tuo, suo, nostro, vostro, loro
- **possessive pronouns** il mio, *etc.*
- **possessive proprio**
- **di** *expressing ownership;*
- **Di chi è?**
- **avere**
- **Quale?**

Introduction

Look at these examples of possessives **mio, tuo,** etc:

La tua casa è grande.	*Your house is big.*
La mia è piccola.	*Mine is small.*
È tua questa giacca?	*Is this jacket yours?*
No, non è mia.	*No, it's not mine.*
Di chi è questa bicicletta?	*Whose is this bike?*
È di Franco.	*It's Franco's.*
Lei ha una macchina inglese?	*Do you have an English car?*
No, ho una macchina tedesca.	*No, I have a German car.*

Qual è la vostra macchina?	*Which is your car?*
Quella verde.	*That green one.*
Qual è il Suo indirizzo?	*What is your address?*

Focus on grammar

1 Mio, tuo, suo, etc.

To say to whom something belongs in Italian, use **mio, tuo, suo,** etc. (*my, your, his,* etc.); these are possessive adjectives. Like all adjectives, **mio, tuo, suo, nostro, vostro** change according to whether the person or thing they are describing is singular or plural, masculine or feminine.

Italian uses the definite article **il, la,** etc. with possessive adjectives (**il mio cane, la mia macchina**).

However, when talking about relatives, you don't need the definite article, except when there is more than one relative or the word is accompanied by an adjective or suffix: **mio padre, mia cugina, mia moglie** *but* **i miei fratelli, il mio fratello più grande, la mia sorellina.** A partner or fiancé is not considered a relative.

a mio *(my)*

il mio cane	*my dog*	**mia** madre	*my mother*
mio padre	*my father*	**i miei** jeans	*my jeans*
la mia bicicletta	*my bicycle*	**le mie** sorelle	*my sisters*

b tuo *(your)*

Use **tuo** when speaking informally to someone (**tu** form).

il tuo passaporto	*your passport*	**la tua** amica	*your friend*
i tuoi figli	*your children*	**le tue** scarpe	*your shoes*

c suo *(his, her)*
Suo means *his* or *her*.

il suo amico	*his/her friend*	**la sua** collega	*his/her colleague*
i suoi amici	*his/her friends*	**le sue** cose	*his/her things*

Suo can also mean *your* (when using the polite Lei form); with this meaning, it is sometimes written with capital S just as the Lei form is often written with a capital L.

È arrivato **Suo** marito?	*Has your husband arrived?*

d suo – di lui, di lei
Sometimes when **suo** is used, it is not clear whether it means *his* or *her*. Look at this sentence:

Ho visto Giorgio stasera. Era con Sandra. **Il suo** amico era appena tornato da Londra.	*I saw Giorgio tonight. He was with Sandra. His/Her friend had just got back from London.*

To avoid confusion between *his* and *her*, you can, if necessary, replace **suo** – or add to it – by the words **di lui** (*of him*) or **di lei** (*of her*).

Ho visto Giorgio oggi. Era con Sandra. L'amico **di lei** era appena tornato da Londra.	*I saw Giorgio today. He was with Sandra. Her friend had just got back from London.*

e nostro *(our)*

il nostro treno	*our train*	**la nostra** amica	*our friend*
i nostri mariti	*our husbands*	**le nostre** case	*our houses*

f vostro *(your)*
Use **vostro** when referring to more than one person.

il vostro errore	*your mistake*
la vostra macchina fotografica	*your camera*
i vostri biglietti	*your tickets*
le vostre valigie	*your suitcases*

g loro (their)

Loro is an exception to the rules above, because it never changes, whatever the gender or number of the object or person it describes, and it always takes the definite article (**il**, **la**, etc.).

il loro cane	*their dog*	**la loro** casa	*their house*
i loro amici	*their friends*	**le loro** cose	*their things*

Loro can also mean *your* when addressing people using the formal plural form **loro**, but this use is really limited to waiters, hotel staff, etc. addressing clients.

> ### Insight
> Italian uses the article **il**, **la** etc. with possessive adjectives (**il mio cane**, **la mia casa**). For relatives, in the singular only, the possessive article is omitted (**mio padre**, **mia madre**). The article is used, however, where there is an adjective (**la mia sorella maggiore**) or suffix (**la mia sorellina**). The article is always used with **loro**.

2 il mio, il tuo, il suo, *etc.*

To express ownership without naming the object, use the possessive pronouns **il mio**, **il tuo**, **il suo** (*mine, yours, his/hers*), etc. rather than the adjective **mio** (*my*). The article **il**, **lo**, **la**, etc. and the form of **mio**, **tuo**, **suo**, **nostro**, **vostro** still have to agree with the object or person owned, both in gender (masculine or feminine) and number (singular or plural).

Questa guida è **nostra. La vostra** dov'è?	*This guide is ours. Where's yours?*
La nostra è in macchina.	*Ours is in the car.*
Mio marito mi aiuta molto in cucina.	*My husband helps me a lot in the kitchen.*
Il mio non sa dov'è.	*Mine doesn't know where it is.*
Di chi è questa felpa?	*Whose is this sweatshirt?*
È mia. La tua è più sporca.	*It's mine. Yours is dirtier.*

When the possessive is used with **essere** alone, as in the examples below, the definite article (**il**, etc.) is often omitted. One of the first phrases Italian children learn is **È mio!** (*It's mine!*).

Di chi è questo libro?	È **mio**.	*It's mine.*
Di chi è questa borsa?	È **tua**.	*It's yours.*
Di chi è questa macchina?	È **sua**.	*It's his.*
Di chi sono questi sandali?	Sono **nostri**.	*They're ours.*
	Sono **vostri**.	*They're yours.*
But ...	Sono **i loro**.	*They're theirs.*

Whether or not the article (**il, la**, etc.) is used, **mio, tuo, suo** still change according to whether the object is masculine or feminine, singular or plural.

The phrase **i tuoi** used without any noun can also mean *your family*, while **i miei** means *my family* and so on ...

3 proprio

Proprio means *one's own* and is used in place of the other possessive adjectives when the subject referred to is an impersonal one, for example *one* or *everyone*.

Non tutti hanno **la propria** macchina.	*Not everyone has their own car.*
Ognuno ama **il proprio** paese.	*Everyone loves his own country.*

It can, however, also be used with another possessive, to reinforce or emphasize the idea of *one's own*.

Marco è contento di vivere **la sua propria** vita.	*Marco is happy to live his own life.*

> **Insight**
>
> **Proprio** (*one's own*) always refers back to an impersonal or
> generic subject such as **ognuno**, **tutti** or impersonal **si**. It
> is not the same as **suo**, which refers to a named or specific
> person. Compare **Tutti amano la propria casa** with **Roberto
> ama la sua casa** or **Gli inglesi amano le loro case**.

4 di *expressing ownership*

English phrases such as *It's Franco's* have to be expressed in Italian
by using **di** (*of*) followed by the person's name.

Questa maglia è **di** Franco.	*This sweater is Franco's.*
Queste scarpe sono **di** Anna.	*These shoes are Anna's.*

To ask who something belongs to, use **di** (*of*) and **chi** (*who*).

Di chi è questa borsetta?	*Whose is this handbag?*
È **di** Cristina.	*It's Cristina's.*
Di chi sono questi soldi?	*Whose is this money?*
Sono **di** Filippo.	*It's Filippo's.*

5 del, della, *etc.*

When there is a noun such as **ragazzo** or **amico**, the **di** combines
with the definite article **il, la** (etc.) to create the forms **del, dello,
dell', della, dei, degli, delle**. You have already seen these forms of
del (which also means *some*) in Unit 3.

Di chi è questa bicicletta?	*Whose is this bicycle?*
È **del** mio amico.	*It's my friend's.*
Di chi sono queste scarpe?	*Whose are these shoes?*
Sono **della** ragazza francese.	*They're the French girl's.*
Di chi sono questi asciugamani?	*Whose are these towels?*
Sono **dell'**albergo.	*They're the hotel's.*
Di chi sono questi libri?	*Whose are these books?*
Sono **dello** studente inglese.	*They're the English student's.*
Di chi sono queste tessere?	*Whose are these passes?*

Sono **dei** ragazzi francesi.	*They're the French kids'.*
Di chi sono questi biglietti?	*Whose are these tickets?*
Sono **degli** studenti stranieri.	*They're the foreign students'.*
Di chi sono queste borse?	*Whose are these bags?*
Sono **delle** ragazze.	*They are the girls'.*

Insight

In Italian, Marco's bag translates as **la borsa di Marco**. While proper names are easy (**la casa di Paolo**), any other reference to people means using the combined forms of **di** and the definite article (**la borsa del ragazzo, i biglietti delle ragazze**).

Language plus

1 Omission of possessive

Italians tend to omit the possessive where the idea of ownership or possession is taken for granted.

Carla parte con **il marito**.   *Carla is leaving with her husband.*
(It is assumed that Carla is leaving with her own husband.)

I bambini alzano **le mani**.   *The children raise their hands.*
(It is assumed that they raise their own hands.)

Arriva **lo zio**.   *Uncle's arriving.*
(It is thought unnecessary to specify whose uncle it is.)

2 Using reflexive pronoun or indirect object pronoun

In Unit 7, we saw how Italian uses a reflexive pronoun, where English would use a possessive, to refer to one's own body or belongings.

Mi metto le scarpe.	*I put my shoes on.*
Si lava i capelli.	*She washes her hair.*

In the same way, the indirect object pronoun is often used when referring to someone else's belongings or even a part of their body.

Ti stiro la camicia?	*Shall I iron your shirt?*
Mamma, Aurelio **mi** sta tirando i capelli!	*Mummy, Aurelio is pulling my hair!*

Insight

While English talks about *my shoes*, *my hat*, *my hands*, Italian tends not to use the possessive adjective, often preferring to use the reflexive pronoun if referring to one's own possessions (**Mi lavo le mani**) or indirect object pronoun if referring to someone else's possessions (**Ti lavo la camicia**).

3 Omitting 'of' with possessive

Italian omits *of* in these expressions.

due miei amici	*two of my friends*
un mio amico	*a friend of mine*

Insight

While English says *two of my friends*, Italian says **due miei amici**. Similarly, **tre mie amiche** (*three of my friends*), **un mio amico** (*a friend of mine*) and **vari nostri amici** (*various friends of ours*).

4 Verb **avere** expressing ownership

Avere (*to have*) can be used to talk about one's possessions. (See **Grammar Appendix** §13.3.)

Ha un cane, signor Bianchi?	*Do you have a dog, signor Bianchi?*
Sì. Si chiama Lillo.	*Yes. He is called Lillo.*

5 quale

Quale (pronoun or adjective) means *which*. In Unit 5, you saw quale used as an adjective, along with a noun.

Quale borsa vuole?	*Which bag do you want?*

You can also use it on its own when asking for information (such as someone's particulars) where in English you would use *what*. Before è (*it is*), it can be elided but should never be followed by an apostrophe.

Singular

Qual è il Suo cognome?	*What is your surname?*
Qual è la Sua data di nascita?	*What is your date of birth?*
Qual è la tua macchina?	*Which is your car?*

Plural

Quali sono i tuoi figli?	*Which are your children?*
Quali sono le tue scarpe?	*Which are your shoes?*
Quali sono i tuoi programmi preferiti?	*What are your favourite programmes?*

Insight

Although **quale** is usually translated as *which* in English, it can just as often mean *what*, particularly in an official context, e.g. when being asked for your name, date of birth or address: **Qual è il Suo indirizzo?**

Language in action

Exercise 1

Chi sono?
Francesco is talking about his family. Can you work out from the family tree on the next page who everyone is? Fill in the gaps with the answers, including their relationship to Francesco, the correct possessive adjective and definite article where needed.

Allora, questo è (**1**) _____ Marco. Questa è (**2**) _____ Marina, e questi sono (**3**) _____ Carlotta e Simone. Questa, invece, è (**4**) _____ Irma, con (**5**) _____ Ugo, e (**6**) _____ Flavia e Diana. (**7**) _____ casa è vicino alla nostra. Ugo quindi è (**8**) _____ e Flavia e Diana sono (**9**) _____. E questo è (**10**) _____ cane, Lucky, che dorme nella stanza di Flavia.

Exercise 2

Complete these sentences with the correct form of the verb (present indicative, imperative or infinitive), and reflexive pronoun.

Esempio: Bambini, **mettetevi** (*mettersi*) le scarpe.

1 Aspettami. Devo solo _____ (mettersi) la giacca.
2 Ho freddo. _____ (mettersi) il maglione.
3 Piove! Esco, ma _____ (mettersi) un impermeabile e porto l'ombrello.
4 Sono stanchissima. Ora _____ (farsi) un bel caffè.
5 Se cadi dalla bici _____ (rompersi) il polso.
6 Alessandro _____ (portarsi) via il portatile. Ne ha bisogno per scrivere il tema.
7 Fa caldo qui dentro. _____ (togliersi) la maglia, sei tutta sudata.

Test yourself

Check your progress! Do you know how to do the following
in Italian?

1 Write the correct form of **mio**.
   Esempio: *la mia* borsa
   a _____ madre
   b _____ cugini
   c _____ scarpe
   d _____ computer
   e _____ marito

2 Write the correct form of **tuo**.
   a _____ cugine
   b _____ zia
   c _____ zio
   d _____ casa
   e _____ moglie

3 Write the correct form of **suo**.
   a _____ macchina
   b _____ figli
   c _____ padre
   d _____ ufficio
   e _____ colleghi

4 Translate these expressions using the correct form of **nostro,
   vostro** or **loro**.
   Esempio: our bed – **il nostro** letto
   a our house
   b your friends
   c your dog
   d their cat
   e their holidays

5 Complete these sentences with the correct form of **suo** or **proprio**.
   a Marco porta la _____ macchina.
   b Ognuno porta il _____ pranzo.
   c Non tutti hanno la _____ casa.
   d Maura accompagna _____ cugina.

6 Use **di, del, della,** etc. to express ownership in these sentences.
   a Questa tessera è _____ studente inglese.
   b Questi biglietti sono _____ mio fratello.
   c Questa bici è _____ mio amico.
   d Questi libri sono _____ miei amici.
   e Queste borsette sono _____ ragazze.
   f Questa giacca è _____ mia collega.
   g Questi soldi sono _____ Giacomo.
   h Questi volantini sono _____ studenti.

7 Say these expressions.
   a *four of my friends*
   b *a friend of his*
   c *a friend of yours*
   d *three of her friends*

8 Choose the correct form of the possessive. Sometimes both are possible.
   a I bambini mettono *la giacca / la loro giacca / le loro giacche*.
   b Giorgio accompagna *la moglie / sua moglie*.
   c Alzate *le mani / le vostre mani / le loro mani* se sapete la risposta.
   d *Mio zio / Lo zio* ha una fabbrica.
   e Portiamo *i libri / i nostri libri*.
   f *Gli amici / I nostri amici* arrivano stasera.

9 Translate these sentences using pronouns.
   Esempio: *I'll wash your sweater.* **Ti lavo la maglia.**
   a *My husband cleans my shoes.*
   b *Gianni cuts my hair.*
   c *Will you wash my car?*
   d *Will you make their breakfast?*

10 Ask someone for this information.
   a Which is your car? (**Lei** form)
   b Which is your boyfriend? (**tu** form)
   c What are your favourite programmes? (**tu** form)
   d What is your date of birth? (**Lei** form)

11

Talking about events and actions in the past

In this unit, you will learn how to:
- **talk about events and actions in the past**
- **talk about events in the past relating to the present**
- **talk about events still going on**

Language points
- **perfect tense (passato prossimo) and avere**
- **perfect tense and essere**
- **verbs which can take both essere and avere in the perfect tense**
- **phrases of time past**
- **reflexive verbs in the perfect tense**
- **negative sentences in the perfect tense**
- **use of present tense with da**
- **months and days**
- **past definite tense (passato remoto)**

Introduction

Look at these sentences referring to past events or actions:

Ma dove sei stato ieri?   *But where were you yesterday?*
Sono stata a casa di Mauro per un   *I was at Mauro's house for a*
   paio di ore.   *   couple of hours.*

Sabato sono andato al mare e ho mangiato un gelato.	*On Saturday, I went to the seaside and I ate an ice-cream.*
Siamo stati in Francia per due mesi.	*We were in France for two months.*
Vivo in Inghilterra da dieci anni.	*I have lived in England for ten years.*
Non lo vedo da cinque giorni.	*I haven't seen him for five days.*
Hai mai visto una casa così brutta?	*Have you ever seen such an ugly house?*
Cristoforo Colombo scoprì l'America nel 1492.	*Christopher Columbus discovered America in 1492.*

Focus on grammar

1 *Perfect tense* (passato prossimo)

In some of the examples above, the perfect tense (**passato prossimo**) is used. It is used when talking about an action which is now over (finished or 'perfect') but has some connection with present events. The perfect is formed using the past participle of the verb (e.g. **mangiato**) with either **avere** or **essere**. It can translate the English perfect tense, (e.g. *I have eaten*) or the English past definite (e.g. *I ate*) in all the contexts listed below.

a No specific occasion mentioned

| **Hai visto** il nuovo film di Benigni? | *Have you seen the new film by Benigni?* |
| **Sei mai stato** in Italia? | *Have you ever been to Italy?* |

b A specific occasion or time mentioned

| Sì, **l'ho visto** la settimana scorsa. | *Yes, I saw it a week ago.* |
| Sì. Ci **sono stato due anni fa**. | *Yes. I went there two years ago.* |

c An action which took place over a longer period of time but is completed

Siamo vissuti a Roma **per dieci anni.**

We lived in Rome for ten years.

Ho lavorato a Milano per due anni. *I worked in Milan for two years.*

2 Forms of past participle

In Italian, the past participles of all **-are** verbs have a regular form ending in **-ato**.

mangiare	*to eat*	**mangiato**
parlare	*to speak*	**parlato**

The past participle of **-ire** verbs is always **-ito**.

dormire	*to sleep*	**dormito**

The past participle of **-ere** verbs can take any one of a number of forms. It might have an **-uto** ending ...

dovere	*to have to*	**dovuto**
potere	*to be able to*	**potuto**

... or it might have a shorter form.

mettere	*to put*	**messo**
vedere	*to see*	**visto**

Many common verbs have a past participle which does not follow any of the patterns above.

dare	*to give*	**dato**
dire	*to say*	**detto**
fare	*to do*	**fatto**
stare	*to be*	**stato**

There is no rule to help you learn all these forms; you just have to remember them! Here are **avere** and **essere** along with some of the more common **-ere** verbs and their past participles. The participles

marked with an asterisk (*) are those that form the perfect tense
with **essere** instead of **avere** (see Sections 3 and 4 below).

avere	*to have*	**avuto**
essere	*to be*	**stato***
chiudere	*to close*	**chiuso**
decidere	*to decide*	**deciso**
dovere	*to have to*	**dovuto**
leggere	*to read*	**letto**
perdere	*to lose*	**perso, perduto**
potere	*to be able to*	**potuto**
prendere	*to take*	**preso**
rimanere	*to remain*	**rimasto***
rispondere	*to reply*	**risposto**
scendere	*to get down*	**sceso***
scrivere	*to write*	**scritto**
tenere	*to hold*	**tenuto**
vedere	*to see*	**visto**
vivere	*to live*	**vissuto***
volere	*to want to*	**voluto**

Insight

To form the perfect tense, you need to know the past
participle of the verb. While it's easy for **-are** and **-ire** verbs,
the past participle of **-ere** verbs is quite variable. If you are
unsure, check the list of irregular verbs at the back of this
book, your dictionary or an online reference source.

3 Perfect tense with **avere**

To form the perfect tense, you use the present tense of the verb
avere (*to have*) with the past participle (**mangiato, dormito,
venduto**, etc.). The verb **avere** changes according to the person who
carried out the action: **ho, hai, ha**, etc., while the participle does
not change.

Ho mangiato un gelato.   *I ate/have eaten an ice-cream.*
Abbiamo dormito per due ore.   *We slept/have slept for two hours.*

Here is the perfect tense of the verb **mangiare** (*to eat*).

ho	mangiato	**abbiamo**	mangiato
hai	mangiato	**avete**	mangiato
ha	mangiato	**hanno**	mangiato

4 Perfect tense with **essere**

Some verbs form the perfect tense using **essere** (*to be*) with the past participle, instead of **avere** (*to have*). In this case, the past participle changes its ending to agree with the subject (the person or thing that has carried out the action), whether masculine or feminine, singular or plural.

Carlo **è andato** in banca.	*Carlo has gone to the bank.*
Anna **è andata** al bar.	*Anna has gone to the café.*
Mario e Maria **sono andati** a scuola.	*Mario and Maria have gone to school.*
Daniela e Franca **sono andate** al cinema.	*Daniela and Franca have gone to the cinema.*

....

sono andato/**a**	**siamo** andati/**e**
sei andato/**a**	**siete** andati/**e**
è andato/**a**	**sono** andati/**e**

....

Insight

When writing about a past event, if you've used a perfect tense with **essere**, check your endings. The past participle has to agree with the subject (the person carrying out the action), whether masculine or feminine, singular or plural. But don't worry about it too much – in spoken Italian, people won't notice so much if you make a mistake!

The verbs which use **essere** rather than **avere** are intransitive; in other words, they do not take an object.

Transitive or intransitive verb?
Try asking the question **Che cosa?** (*What?*) after the verb. If you can answer the question, then the verb is transitive (takes an object). Even if the object is not actually mentioned, it is still a transitive verb. If the question **Che cosa?** does not make sense, then the verb is intransitive (does not take an object). Compare these examples:

Mario parla. Parla ... cosa?

The question can be answered with an object: **Mario parla italiano.**

So **parlare** is a transitive verb and takes **avere.**

Mario parte. Parte... cosa?

Partire cannot take an object, so it is intransitive and takes **essere** in the past tenses. However not all intransitive verbs take **essere!**

Insight
How can you tell if a verb is transitive or intransitive? Read the guidelines above for distinguishing transitive and intransitive verbs. But if you are still uncertain, check your dictionary, which will label the verb **tr.** (**transitivo**) or **intr.** (**intransitivo**). And remember that not all intransitive verbs take **essere** in the perfect tense!

Which verbs take essere?
Verbs taking **essere** can be summarized as follows:

a essere, stare

essere	*to be*	**sono stato/a**
stare	*to be*	**sono stato/a**

Sono stata in chiesa stamattina.

b Verbs of movement or staying still

andare	*to go*	arrivare	*to arrive*
cadere	*to fall*	entrare	*to enter*
partire	*to leave, depart*	restare	*to stay behind, to remain*
rimanere	*to remain, stay behind*	salire	*to go up*
		scendere	*to go down*
scappare	*to run off, escape*	uscire	*to go out*
tornare	*to return*		
venire	*to come*		

Il bambino **è caduto** dall'albero. *The child fell from a tree.*
Gli ospiti **sono venuti** alle otto. *The guests came at eight o'clock.*

c Verbs expressing physical or other change

apparire	*to appear*	crescere	*to grow*
dimagrire	*to get thin*	divenire	*to become*
diventare	*to become*	ingrassare	*to get fat*
invecchiare	*to grow old*	morire	*to die*
nascere	*to be born*	scomparire	*to disappear*

Mia madre **è dimagrita** di 5 kg. *My mother lost 5 kg.*
Io sono **ingrassata** di 2 kg. *I put on 2 kg.*
Sono morto di fame. *I'm starving (lit.: dead with hunger).*
Sono nata il 14 ottobre. *I was born on 14 October.*

d Verbs that are used impersonally or mainly in the third person

accadere	*to happen*
avvenire	*to happen*
bastare	*to be enough*

capitare	*to happen*
convenire	*to suit*
costare	*to cost*
dispiacere	*to displease*
mancare	*to be lacking*
parere	*to appear*
piacere	*to please*
sembrare	*to seem*
servire	*to be useful for*
succedere	*to happen*
valere	*to be worth*
volerci	*to take time*

Quanto **è costato**?	*How much did it cost?*
Ti **è piaciuto** il film?	*Did you like the film?*
Mi **è sembrato** stanco.	*He seemed tired to me.*
Ci **è voluta** un'ora.	*It took an hour.*

See Unit 18 for more details of impersonal verbs.

e Verbs describing weather
In spoken Italian, these verbs can also be used with **avere**.

nevicare *to snow*   piovere *to rain*

Ieri **è piovuto** tantissimo.	*Yesterday, it rained a lot.*
Ieri **ha piovuto** tantissimo.	*Yesterday, it rained a lot.*

5 *Perfect tense with either* **essere** *or* **avere**

Some verbs can be either transitive (taking **avere**) or intransitive (taking **essere**), depending on how they are used. When they are transitive (i.e. they can take an object, even if it is not explicit), they use **avere**. When they are intransitive (i.e. they do not take an object), they use **essere**.

aumentare	*to increase*
cominciare	*to begin*
continuare	*to continue*

diminuire	*to decrease*
finire	*to finish*
migliorare	*to improve*
passare	*to pass, pass by*
scendere	*to descend, come down*

Ho passato il menù a Luca.	*I passed the menu to Luca.*
Sono passata da Gianluca.	*I went by Gianluca's.*
Hanno sceso le scale.	*They came down the stairs.*
Sono scesi per le scale.	*They came down by the stairs.*
Sono scesi dalla macchina.	*They got out of the car.*
I miei figli **hanno cominciato** le vacanze ieri.	*My kids began their holidays yesterday.*
Le vacanze **sono cominciate** ieri.	*The holidays began yesterday.*
Abbiamo finito gli esami una settimana fa.	*We finished the exams a week ago.*
Anche voi **avete finito**?	*Have you finished too?*
Gli esami **sono finiti** la settimana scorsa.	*The exams finished last week.*

Insight

Verbs such as **cominciare, continuare, finire, aumentare, diminuire, migliorare, passare** and **scendere** take **essere** when they are used intransitively and **avere** when they are used transitively. **Aumentare** and **diminuire** are often used with statistics, usually with a perfect tense formed by **essere** (**È aumentato il numero di turisti a Venezia** *The number of tourists in Venice has gone up*).

6 Perfect tense of reflexive verbs

Reflexive verbs (see Unit 7) in the perfect tense need **essere**. The reflexive pronoun (*myself, yourself,* etc.) normally comes before the verb (**mi alzo, mi sono alzato**), while in the infinitive form, the -**si** is attached to the end.

alzarsi	*to get up*	mi sono alzato	*I got up*
sedersi	*to sit down*	mi sono seduto	*I sat down*
vestirsi	*to get dressed*	mi sono vestito	*I got dressed*

As with the other verbs that use **essere**, the participle (**alzato, vestito**, etc.) has to agree with the subject (masculine or feminine, singular or plural).

Giuliano **si è alzato** alle sette.	*Giuliano got up at seven o'clock.*
Maria Grazia **si è alzata** alle otto.	*Maria Grazia got up at eight o'clock.*
I ragazzi **si sono alzati** tardi.	*The boys got up late.*
Le ragazze **si sono alzate** presto.	*The girls got up early.*

Insight

The perfect tense of reflexive verbs is always formed with **essere** because they always have an object (the reflexive pronoun). This means the past participle has to agree with the subject: **mi sono alzata, si sono alzati**. And don't forget the reflexive pronoun **mi, ti**, etc.

7 Expressions of past time

To say how long ago you did something, you use **fa** (*ago*) and the appropriate length of time.

due giorni **fa**	*two days ago*	un anno **fa**	*a year ago*
una settimana **fa**	*a week ago*	poco tempo **fa**	*a short time ago*
un mese **fa**	*a month ago*	pochi giorni **fa**	*a few days ago*
tempo **fa**	*a while ago*		

Due giorni **fa** sono andata dal medico.	*Two days ago, I went to the doctor.*
Un mese **fa** ho comprato una nuova macchina.	*A month ago, I bought a new car.*

To talk about time past, use **scorso**. Scorso is an adjective and has to agree with the noun.

la settimana **scorsa**	*last week*	l'anno **scorso**	*last year*
il mese **scorso**	*last month*	l'estate **scorsa**	*last summer*

L'estate **scorsa** siamo andati in Sardegna.

Last summer, we went to Sardinia.

La settimana **scorsa** ho invitato gli amici a cena.

Last week, I invited my friends to dinner.

Here are some common time phrases referring to the past.

ieri	*yesterday*	stamattina	*this morning*
l'altro ieri	*the day before yesterday*	ieri mattina	*yesterday morning*
oggi	*today*	ieri sera	*yesterday evening*

The days of the week are as follows:

lunedì	*Monday*	venerdì	*Friday*
martedì	*Tuesday*	sabato	*Saturday*
mercoledì	*Wednesday*	domenica	*Sunday*
giovedì	*Thursday*		

The months of the year:

gennaio	*January*	luglio	*July*
febbraio	*February*	agosto	*August*
marzo	*March*	settembre	*September*
aprile	*April*	ottobre	*October*
maggio	*May*	novembre	*November*
giugno	*June*	dicembre	*December*

For ways of expressing dates, see Unit 5.

Insight

Two of the most common words used to express past time
are **fa** and **scorso**. **Scorso** (*last*) is an adjective and has to
agree with the noun: **il mese scorso, la settimana scorsa. Fa**
(*ago*) is an adverb and doesn't change: **una settimana fa, due
giorni fa.**

8 Negative past sentences

When the sentence in the perfect tense is negative, take care over
the positioning of **non** and the other negative words. Italian
negatives usually come in pairs (a double negative) with **non** before
the verb and the other negative element after. Look at the examples
below.

Here, the second negative comes after **avere** or **essere** but before the
participle.

Non sono **mai** stata a Palermo.	*I have never been to Palermo.*
Non abbiamo **ancora** mangiato.	*We haven't eaten yet.*

Here the second negative word comes after the whole verb.

Non ho visto **nessuno** oggi.	*I haven't seen anyone today.*
Non ho fatto **niente** ieri.	*I didn't do anything yesterday.*

For further examples of negative elements and their position with
verbs, see **Grammar appendix** § 9.

9 *Past tense with* **per**

When describing an event or action that went on for a certain
length of time, but is now finished, use the perfect tense with **per**.

Sono andata in palestra per due ore.	*I went to the gym for two hours.*

Ho vissuto a Londra per 15 anni poi   *I lived in London for 15 years, then*
    mi sono sposata e sono tornata   *I got married and went back*
    in Italia.   *to Italy.*

10 *Present tense with* **da**

When the event in question is still going on, use the present tense
with **da**.

Studio l'italiano da cinque anni.   *I have been studying Italian for*
    five years. (lit.: I study Italian
    since five years.)
Sono sposata **da** dieci anni.   *I have been married for ten years.*
Non la **vedo da** tanto tempo.   *I haven't seen her for so long.*

> ### Insight
> **Da or per?** Are you still carrying out an action? Is the action
> still going on? If so, use **da** and the present tense. If the
> action went on for a certain number of years but is now
> finished, use **per** and the perfect tense. The same applies to
> negative statements or questions.

Language plus

1 *The past definite* **(passato remoto)**

As we saw above, the perfect tense (passato prossimo) is the tense
generally used in spoken Italian when talking about an action in
the past, especially if it is somehow related to the present context.

Non **ho** ancora **mangiato**.   *I haven't eaten yet.*
Ieri **è andata** in centro e **ha**   *Yesterday she went to the town*
    comprato una maglia.   *centre and bought a sweater.*

The past definite – also known as the past historic – is used in
most of Italy only to describe a historic event (e.g. the Romans

invading Britain) or a completed action in the past with no link to the present day. Here is an example of the past definite in written Italian.

Maria Stuarda **nacque** nel 1542, **sposò** giovane il futuro Re di Francia e **morì** decapitata nel 1587 per ordine della Regina Elisabetta d'Inghilterra.	*Mary Queen of Scots was born in 1542, married the future King of France when she was very young and was beheaded in 1587 by order of Elizabeth I Queen of England.*

However, speakers in the south will sometimes use the past definite in everyday speech.

Il mese scorso andammo al mare.	*Last month, we went to the seaside.*

Although it is unlikely that you will want to use the past definite, its forms are supplied in the **Grammar Appendix** § 13.1.

2 *Subject pronouns* **io**, **tu**, **lui**, *etc.*

The subject pronouns **io, tu, lui**, etc. are used to emphasize or contrast actions by different people.

Io ho telefonato. **Lui** non ha telefonato.	*I phoned. He didn't phone.*
Io sono stata ad Assisi ma **tu** non ci sei mai stata.	*I have been to Assisi, but you have never been there.*

Insight

In Unit 1, with the present tense, you saw how the subject pronouns **io, tu,** etc. are used only for emphasis or contrast. The verb endings indicate which person is carrying out the action. The same applies to the perfect tense. The subject pronouns should be used only for emphasis.

Language in action

Exercise 1

Le vacanze di Claudia
Read this dialogue between Claudia and Gianna, in which Claudia tells Gianna all about their recent holiday in the country. It didn't please everyone! Try and fill in the gaps in their conversation, using the perfect tense of the verbs supplied and making any necessary changes.

GIANNA	Bentornati dalle vacanze! Come (**1**) _____ (andare)? Tutto bene? Cosa (**2**) _____ (fare) di bello?
CLAUDIA	Sì, (**3**) _____ (essere) una vacanza un po' diversa dal solito ... non (**4**) _____ (andare) al mare quest'anno, (**5**) _____ (prendere) una casa in campagna.
GIANNA	E cosa (**6**) _____ (fare) in campagna?
CLAUDIA	Io (**7**) _____ (fare) delle lunghe passeggiate, Giovanni (**8**) _____ (leggere) molti libri, e non (**9**) _____ (vedere) nessuno. (**10**) _____ (mangiare), (**11**) _____ (cucinare) e (**12**) _____ (dormire).
GIANNA	E i bambini? (**13**) _____ (divertirsi)?
CLAUDIA	No. I bambini (**14**) _____ (lamentarsi) perché per tre settimane non (**15**) _____ (potere) guardare la televisione. (**16**) _____ (giocare) a pallone, (**17**) _____ (andare) in giro in bicicletta, e ci (**18**) _____ (aiutare) a preparare da mangiare.

Notes
• **di bello, di buono, di speciale**
qualcosa **di bello**   *something nice*
qualcosa **di buono**   *something nice (to eat)*
niente **di speciale**   *nothing special*

• **La passeggiata**: This also refers to the nightly promenade up and down the main street, piazza or sea front to be seen in most Italian towns, especially in summer.

Exercise 2

Le vacanze di Claudia (bis)
Now write an account of Claudia's holiday in Italian, in the third person, using all the facts contained in the dialogue.

Esempio: **Claudia e suo marito Giovanni hanno passato le vacanze in campagna ...**

Exercise 3

Viaggio in Scozia
Your Italian friends have just spent seven days touring Scotland. They are very enthusiastic. Carla sends you the itinerary for their tour. Using this as a basis, try to reconstruct the letter she wrote, giving as many details and being as imaginative as possible.

Esempio: **Abbiamo fatto una vacanza bellissima in Scozia. Siamo arrivati a Glasgow. Poi ...**

TOUR PANORAMICO

€400 per pp. inclusa colazione scozzese

Glasgow/Lomond	1 notte	Loch Lomond
Fort William	2 notti	Montagne e Coste
Aviemore	1 notte	Loch Ness & Inverness
Perthshire	1 notte	Distilleria di Whisky, St. Andrews & Golf, Edimburgo
Edimburgo	2 notti	Castello di Edimburgo, Palazzo di Holyrood, Royal Mile, shopping in Princes St

Per agosto supplemento 40 euro

Test yourself

Check your progress! Do you know how to do the following in Italian?

1 Write the past participle of these regular and irregular verbs.
   Esempio: andare *andato*
   a vedere
   b sapere
   c leggere
   d scrivere
   e cercare
   f mangiare
   g capire
   h dire

2 Say whether these verbs are transitive (T) or intransitive (I).
   a leggere
   b saltare
   c volare
   d studiare
   e parlare
   f scendere
   g cominciare
   h piovere

3 Change these sentences from present tense to perfect tense with **avere**.
   a I ragazzi mangiano la pizza.
   b Il poliziotto ci fa la multa.
   c Mia figlia dice delle cose stupide.
   d Mio marito fa il medico.
   e Le mie amiche leggono molti libri.
   f Il nostro insegnante scrive delle poesie.
   g Decidiamo di andare in vacanza.
   h Voglio fare una vacanza al mare.

4 Change these sentences from present tense to perfect tense with **essere**.
   a Io e mia cugina andiamo a Parigi.
   b I ragazzi escono dopo cena.
   c La temperatura scende sotto zero.

d La bambina nasce il 31 dicembre!

e I miei amici escono ma io rimango a casa.

f Torni dalle vacanze stasera?

g Sono a Roma per due giorni.

h Saliamo tutti in macchina.

5 Complete these sentences about the past using **fa** or **scorso**.

a Una settimana _____ sono andata al cinema a vedere un film italiano.

b La settimana _____ è venuto Marco a trovarmi.

c Il mese _____ è arrivata mia cugina da Roma.

d Il treno è partito due minuti _____.

e C'è stato un piccolo problema sabato _____.

6 Complete these sentences using the perfect tense of one of these verbs: **bastare, costare, servire, volerci, invecchiare, scomparire, piovere, sembrare**.

a Quanto _____ quel vestito?

b _____ il latte?

c Sei arrivata adesso? Quanto tempo ti _____?

d Hai visto il professore? _____ tanto!

e Dove sono i bambini? _____ mentre parlavo con Sandro.

f Che tempo! Ieri _____ per due ore.

g _____ la mappa?

h Era pallido in faccia, mi _____ molto stanco.

7 Answer these questions using these negative expressions: **non ... mai, non ... ancora, non ... niente, non ... nessuno, non ... più**. Use each expression only once.

a Hai finito i compiti?   No, _____

b Vai ancora alla classe di flamenco?   No, _____

c Andate al cinema insieme?   No, _____

d Hai visto qualche amico in centro?   No, _____

e Avete mangiato in centro?   No, _____

8 Change the reflexive verbs in these sentences from present tense to perfect tense.

a Le signore si siedono a tavola.

b Il mio amico si veste di nero.

c Io mi sveglio alle sette.

d A che ora ti svegli?

e Vi alzate presto sabato?

f Ci prepariamo per uscire.

g I bambini si vestono da soli.

h Prima di uscire mi lavo, mi vesto e mi trucco. (*fem.*)

9 Complete these sentences with **da** or **per**.

a Sono sposata _____ dieci anni.

b Ho vissuto negli USA _____ venti anni.

c Vivo a Napoli _____ cinque mesi.

d Ho studiato a Londra _____ un mese.

e Non ho visto il nuovo negozio. Non vado in centro _____ tanto tempo.

10 Complete these sentences using the perfect tense of the verb in brackets. Be careful to choose the correct verb – **avere** or **essere**.

a _____ (passare) le nostre vacanze in campagna.

b _____ (aumentare) la temperatura in questi giorni.

c Ho sentito il campanello e _____ (scendere) le scale di corsa!

d Il grande freddo _____ (continuare) per altri dieci giorni.

e I bambini sono a casa, _____ (cominciare) le vacanze scolastiche.

f Quest'anno _____ (diminuire) le spese per le bevande alcoliche.

g La situazione _____ (migliorare) molto negli ultimi dieci anni.

h Marco _____ (finire) i compiti e poi ha guardato la TV.

12

Describing the past

In this unit, you will learn how to:
- *describe how things were in the past*
- *talk about actions or events which happened regularly in the past*
- *talk about actions or events which were in the process of taking place when an event or incident occurred*
- *talk about actions or events which had already taken place when an action or event occurred*
- *talk about actions or events which were about to take place*

Language points
- *imperfect indicative tense* (imperfetto)
- *combination of imperfect tense and perfect tense*
- *imperfect tense to express* **could have, should have**
- *pluperfect tense* (trapassato)
- *past anterior* (trapassato remoto)
- *imperfect tense of* stare *and gerund,* stare per
- *use of imperfect with* da

Introduction

Look at the different ways in which the imperfect is used.

Il cielo era azzurro, e il sole splendeva.	*The sky was blue, and the sun was shining.*

Quando lavoravo a Londra prendevo la metropolitana.	*When I worked in London, I took the Tube.*
Camminava lungo la strada quando ha visto una cosa stranissima.	*He was walking along the street when he saw something very odd.*

And here is an example of how the pluperfect is used:

Eravamo appena entrati quando ha suonato il telefono.	*We had just come in when the telephone rang.*

Focus on grammar

1 *Imperfect* (imperfetto): *the forms*

The imperfect is formed by adding a set of imperfect endings to the stem of the verb. Few verbs have irregular forms in the imperfect.

Verbs ending in **-are**

....

mangiare

mangiavo   mangiavamo
mangiavi   mangiavate
mangiava   mangiavano

....

Verbs ending in -ere

....

leggere

leggevo   leggevamo
leggevi   leggevate
leggeva   leggevano

....

Verbs ending in **-ire**

....

finire

finivo	finivamo
finivi	finivate
finiva	finivano

....

Verbs with slightly unexpected imperfect forms include those with contracted infinitive forms, such as **bere** (**bevevo**), **fare** (**facevo**), **porre** (**ponevo**), **tradurre** (**traducevo**). They derive from the original longer infinitive form (**bevere, facere, ponere, traducere,** etc). The pattern of endings is still the same as those shown above.

....

Insight

Italian irregular verbs come in families. For example, one 'family' of verbs has the contracted infinitive form ending in **-durre** (from the original ending -ducere, from the Latin to lead), such as **condurre** from **conducere**. The imperfect forms all follow the same pattern: **condurre** (**conducevo**), **introdurre** (**introducevo**), **produrre** (**producevo**), **ridurre** (**riducevo**), **tradurre** (**traducevo**), etc.

Another 'family' is based on infinitives whose ending has changed from **ponere** to **porre: disporre, esporre, imporre, proporre, supporre.** The imperfect forms of this family are also based on the original, longer infinitive, e.g. **ponevo**.

....

2 Imperfect: when to use

a State, condition, description

When talking about the past, the perfect tense (**passato prossimo**) is used to talk about an action or an event, while the imperfect tense (**imperfetto**) is used to describe a state or condition.

Nell'Ottocento le case **erano** grandi e difficili da pulire ma tutti **avevano** la cameriera.   *In the 19th century, the houses were big and difficult to clean, but everyone had a maid.*

La ragazza **era** alta, bionda e	*The girl was tall, blonde and had*
aveva gli occhi azzurri;	*blue eyes; she looked Swedish.*
sembrava svedese.	

b Regular event or action in the past

We can also use the imperfect to talk about an action that occurred regularly in the past.

Quando **ero** bambina, **abitavo**	*When I was a child, I lived in*
a Milano. **Frequentavo** una	*Milan. I attended a school*
scuola vicino a casa mia e	*near my house and I went to*
andavo a scuola a piedi.	*school on foot.*
Quando i miei amici **erano** a	*When my friends were in Florence*
Firenze, **pranzavano** in una	*they had lunch in a little*
piccola trattoria e tutti i giorni	*restaurant and every day they*
mangiavano lo stesso piatto.	*ate the same dish.*

c Incomplete event or action in the past

Lastly, the imperfect is used to talk about an action which was never completed (in other words, 'imperfect'), often because another event happened to get in the way. The 'new' event is usually expressed with the perfect tense. You can also think of this combination as a background action (imperfect) and a main action which takes centre stage (perfect).

Camminavo lungo la strada	*I was walking down the road when*
quando mi è **caduto** un	*a brick fell on my head.*
mattone in testa.	
Parlavamo con i nostri amici	*We were talking to our friends*
quando è **arrivato** un vigile	*when along came a traffic*
che ci ha **fatto** la multa perché	*warden who fined us because*
c'**era** divieto di sosta.	*it was a 'no parking' area.*

It is, of course, also possible to have two actions occurring simultaneously over a length of time (*I was eating supper as I watched television*); in this case, we would use two verbs in the imperfect. Neither action is complete:

Guardavo la televisione e **mangiavo** le patatine.

I was watching the television and eating crisps.

Mentre **preparava** la cena, **cantava**.

While she was cooking dinner, she was singing.

Insight

The choice of imperfect or perfect tense is a difficult one for learners of Italian. The imperfect is used to describe something or someone, or to talk about a state, a regular action or event, or an incomplete action or event. The perfect tense is used to describe a one-off action or event, or a complete action or event. However, there are times when the choice is not so clear cut.

d Comparison with English

Do not rely on English usage to determine the correct tense to use in Italian; an English verb in the past such as *I went* can be translated in two different ways. Look at these two examples:

Quando ero piccola, **andavo** a scuola tutti i giorni. (imperfect)

When I was little, I went to school every day.

Ieri **sono andata** al cinema. (perfect)

Yesterday, I went to the cinema.

e Same action, different point of view

Sometimes, the same action or event can be described in two different ways, depending on the point of view of the speaker.

Ieri **faceva** molto caldo e non avevo voglia di mangiare.

Yesterday, it was very hot and I didn't feel like eating.

(The speaker actually experienced the heat and is describing it from a personal/subjective point of view.)

Ieri a Milano **ha fatto** molto caldo. La temperatura è salita a 40 gradi.

Yesterday in Milan, it was very hot. The temperature went up to 40 degrees.

(The TV announcer is stating a fact; she did not experience the heat in person. She is describing the event from an objective point of view.)

Insight

The same action or event can be described in two different ways, depending on the perspective of the speaker. The tense used depends on whether the speaker was involved personally or whether he/she is recounting it from an 'outside' point of view. Don't worry if you get it wrong, you will be understood anyway!

3 *Pluperfect* (**trapassato prossimo**): *the forms*

The pluperfect tense (English: *I had eaten, you had eaten,* etc.) is formed by combining the imperfect of the verb **avere** (**avevo,** etc.) and the past participle of the appropriate verb.

avevo mangiato	avevamo mangiato
avevi mangiato	avevate mangiato
aveva mangiato	avevano mangiato

In the case of verbs that use **essere** (see Unit 11), the imperfect tense of **essere** (**ero,** etc.) is used along with the past participle. The past participle has to agree with the number and gender of the subject.

ero arrivato/a	eravamo arrivati/e
eri arrivato/a	eravate arrivati/e
era arrivato/a	erano arrivati/e

4 Pluperfect: when to use

The pluperfect is used to express an action or event which had (or had not) already taken place.

| Mia moglie non **aveva** mai **visto** Venezia. | My wife had never seen Venice. |

It is often used in a complex sentence to describe a past action or event which had taken place before another action or event, also in the past.

| **Eravamo** appena **arrivati** in Italia quando mio marito si è ammalato. | We had just arrived in Italy when my husband fell ill. |

The pluperfect is often used with one of the following words, some of which are used as time markers:

....

appena	as soon as, no sooner (had ...) than, just
mai	never
non ancora	not yet
già	already
prima	earlier, before
quando	when
dopo che	after
siccome	since
perché	because

....

Avevo appena **cominciato** i miei studi all'Università quando **è morto** mio padre.	I had just begun my course at university when my father died.
I miei cugini non **avevano** mai **visitato** Londra.	My cousins had never visited London.
Non **avevamo** ancora **cominciato** la riunione quando **è andata** via la luce.	We had not yet started the meeting when the lights went off.
Mario **era** già **stato** all'estero molte volte.	Mario had already been abroad many times.
Dopo che tu **eri andata** via, **è venuta** Carla con il fidanzato.	After you had left, Carla came with her boyfriend.

I bambini **erano** stanchi perché
   avevano **fatto** un viaggio
   lungo.

*The children were tired because
   they had had a long journey.*

> **Insight**
> When you write a story or a diary in Italian, you need to
> keep in mind the sequence of actions or events. What came
> first and what came after? The action or event that came first
> will probably be in the pluperfect tense, while the one that
> came later will be in the perfect tense. Using time markers
> will help it make sense!

5 The past anterior (trapassato remoto)

In literary or formal written Italian, when the main verb is in the
past definite (see Unit 11 and **Grammar Appendix** §13.1), the
pluperfect is replaced by the past anterior. The past anterior is
formed by combining the past definite of **avere** or **essere** with the
past participle. Although you are unlikely to use this verb tense
yourself, it's useful to be able to recognize it. The past anterior is
always introduced by the phrases **dopo che, (non) appena, quando.**

Non appena **furono tornati** a casa,
   arrivò un amico da Milano.

*As soon as they had got back
   home, a friend arrived from
   Milan.*

Dopo che **ebbero finito** di studiare,
   uscirono.

*After they had finished studying,
   they went out.*

> **Insight**
> It's not essential for you to learn more advanced language
> structures, such as the past anterior. If, however, you are
> planning to read Italian literature, you will meet a greater
> range of structures and will want to recognize them. But you
> won't actively use all of them in everyday spoken Italian.

Language plus

1 Stare and the gerund

The imperfect tense can be replaced by the imperfect tense of **stare** and the gerund. Unit 6 showed how **stare** is used with the gerund to express the idea of continuous action in the present; in the same way, **stare** can be used in the imperfect tense (**stavo**) with the gerund (**parlando, mettendo, dormendo**) to express the idea of an ongoing action in the past.

Stavamo guardando il telegiornale quando **è andata** via l'elettricità.	*We were watching the news on TV when the electricity was cut off.*
Cosa **stavi facendo** lì per terra?	*What were you doing there on the ground?*

> ### Insight
> **Stare** used with the gerund is a much more 'immediate' way of expressing the past than the plain imperfect verb form. It is a way of speaking about what you were doing at that very moment or about an ongoing action or event. Like all imperfect verb forms, it can express a state or description.

2 stare and per

Stare can be used in the imperfect tense with the preposition **per** to say what you were on the point of doing.

Stava per uscire quando è arrivato il postino.	*She was about to go out when the postman arrived.*
Stavo proprio per telefonarti.	*I was just about to phone you.*

3 Imperfect tense used in polite requests

There are a few special ways in which the imperfect is used (known as 'idiomatic' because they are very much part of the spoken language). One of these is to make a polite request or to ask for something in a less demanding way.

Voleva, signora?	*Can I help you, signora? (lit.: What did you want?)*
Volevo vedere qualche maglia.	*I would like to see a few sweaters. (lit.: I wanted to see a few sweaters.)*

Insight

Voglio, vorrei or volevo? Learn to distinguish between these three verb tenses of **volere: voglio** (present indicative), **volevo** (imperfect indicative), **vorrei** (present conditional). Asking for something using **voglio** can sound quite abrupt (just as *I want … does* in English). Both **volevo** and **vorrei** are more polite ways of asking for something. The same choice applies when asking other people what they want.

---

4 Imperfect tense used to express 'could have', 'should have'

Informally, in spoken Italian, the imperfect can be used to express *could have*, *should have* in place of the more formal past conditional. (See Unit 22 for examples of sentences using the past conditional.)

Potevi telefonarmi.	*You could have phoned me.*
(**Avresti potuto** telefonarmi.)	
Doveva farmi sapere.	*He should have let me know.*
(**Avrebbe dovuto** farmi sapere.)	
Se **venivi**, mi **facevi** un piacere.	*If you had come, you would have done me a favour.*
(Se tu **fossi venuta**, mi **avresti fatto** un piacere.)	

5 *Imperfect used with* **da** *to express the pluperfect*

As we saw in Unit 11, **da** can be used with the present tense to express what one has been doing for some time (and is still doing).

Studio l'italiano **da** tre anni.   *I have been studying Italian for three years (and I am still studying it).*

In the same way, **da** can be used with the imperfect tense to express what one had been doing (and was still doing at the time of speaking).

Imparavo l'italiano **da** tre anni quando il direttore mi ha mandato in Italia.
I had been learning Italian for three years when the manager sent me to Italy.

Eravamo a Oxford già **da** un anno quando abbiamo comprato questa casa.
We had been at Oxford for a year already when we bought this house.

Quando Silvia è venuta a casa mia, non **fumava da** più di un mese.
When Silvia came to my house, she hadn't smoked for over a month.

Compare these examples with the use of **per** to talk about an action or event in the past which is now finished.

Ho lavorato a Napoli **per** dieci anni. *I worked in Naples for ten years.*
Marco è rimasto in Inghilterra **per** cinque mesi.
Marco stayed in England for five months.

_____

Language in action

Exercise 1

Spot the past tenses
Highlight or underline the past tenses used in these two accounts and try to understand the difference between the tenses.

• **Why my mother was angry**

Andavo a casa lunedì sera quando ho incontrato Marco. Marco

andava al bar e così ho deciso di accompagnarlo e prendere qualcosa anch'io. Mia madre intanto mi aspettava a casa e quando sono tornato a casa con tre ore di ritardo, mi ha fatto la predica.

• **My birthday**

Per il mio compleanno, mio marito aveva promesso di portarmi a Parigi. Io non c'ero mai stata. Una mia amica aveva offerto di prendere cura dei bambini. Avevamo già preso i biglietti quando la mia amica si è ammalata e così abbiamo dovuto portare anche i bambini. È stata una gita poco romantica!

Exercise 2

Having carried out Exercise 1, you should be able to decide for yourself which tense to use in this next passage, where infinitives have been given in brackets for you to fill in the correct forms.

(**1**) _____ (conoscere) Gianni da solo cinque mesi quando (**2**) _____ (decidere) che (**3**) _____ (volere) sposarci. Quando (**4**) _____ (dare) la notizia alle nostre famiglie, tutti (**5**) _____ (rimanere) molto sorpresi. (**6**) _____ (ricevere) tanti consigli e tante prediche. Perché (**7**) _____ (sposarsi) così presto? Perché non (**8**) _____ (volere) aspettare? Chi (**9**) _____ (potere) immaginare tutte queste discussioni! Mio fratello (**10**) _____ (sposarsi) un anno prima senza tutte queste storie. Ma la situazione (**11**) _____ (essere) diversa, in quanto lui (**12**) _____ (conoscere) la sua futura moglie da dieci anni; (**13**) _____ (essere) studenti insieme al liceo. Alla fine (**14**) _____ (prendere) la decisione di fidanzarci ma di sposarci solo dopo un anno.

Test yourself

Check your progress! Do you know how to do the following in Italian?

1 Change these sentences from present tense to imperfect tense.
   a Io e mio marito andiamo tutti i giorni alla stesso ristorante.
   b I ragazzi escono la sera e fanno sempre tardi.
   c Il mio ragazzo beve troppo vino.
   d Parlo inglese e italiano e al lavoro traduco testi scientifici.
   e Mio figlio non dice mai la verità, dice solo bugie.
   f La fabbrica produce pezzi di ricambio per automobili.

2 Complete these sentences with either the perfect or imperfect tense of the verb in brackets.
   a Ieri la temperatura _____ (scendere) sotto zero e _____ (cominciare) a nevicare.
   b Mio figlio _____ (nascere) il 14 ottobre quando _____ (abitare) negli Stati Uniti.
   c Ieri sera _____ (volere) uscire con i miei amici ma non _____ (avere) soldi e allora _____ (rimanere) a casa a guardare la TV.
   d I bambini _____ (scappare) via mentre io _____ (parlare) con un'amica.
   e Carmela _____ (essere) molto pallida, forse _____ (stancarsi) troppo ieri sera.
   f Il treno _____ (stare) proprio partendo, quando _____ (arrivare) gli ultimi passeggeri.

3 Change these sentences from present to past, choosing the perfect or imperfect tense as appropriate.
   a Mentre i clienti aspettano la pizza, il cameriere gli porta da bere.
   b Mentre io cucino, mio marito guarda la TV e beve una birra.
   c Mentre mia sorella studia, mio fratello suona la chitarra.
   d Mentre parcheggio la macchina, arriva un vigile.
   e Quando l'aereo comincia ad atterrare, i bambini si mettono a piangere.
   f Parliamo con i nostri amici, quando ci interrompe il professore.

4 Complete these sentences with the pluperfect tense of the verbs in brackets. Watch out for the word order of the time expressions in some cases!

Esempio: Il mio amico ha preso un voto basso perché *non aveva capito* (capire) i verbi irregolari.

a Il mio amico ha fatto un incidente in macchina perché _____ (bere) troppo.

b I nostri amici non _____ (arrivare) ancora in Italia quando la macchina ha cominciato a fare un rumore strano.

c Voi _____ (essere) già in Italia o era la prima volta?

d Noi _____ (arrivare) appena al campeggio quando mio figlio è caduto dalla bicicletta.

e Avevo sonno perché _____ (leggere) un libro fino a mezzanotte.

f Marco, non hai mangiato niente! Ma _____ (mangiare) già prima di cena?

5 Complete the sentences using an appropriate expression of time.

a C'era tanta gente al cinema, per fortuna avevo _____ prenotato i biglietti.

b Studiavo l'italiano da tre anni ma _____ avevo _____ imparato il condizionale.

c Preferivo mettere il cappotto _____ di uscire di casa.

d Mia madre ha portato la pasta _____ noi ci siamo seduti a tavola.

e _____ sono uscita di casa, ha cominciato a nevicare.

f Domani abbiamo l'esame di storia ma _____ ho _____ aperto il libro.

6 Complete the sentence using the imperfect tense of **stare** and the gerund of the verbs in brackets.

a Io _____ (scrivere) una mail quando si è spento il computer da solo.

b Quando sono arrivata a casa sua, il mio ragazzo _____ (riparare) la bici.

c Noi _____ (decidere) se uscire o no, quando ha cominciato a piovere.

d Ho visto che voi _____ (rifare) il soggiorno.

e Cosa _____ (bere) quando ti ho visto al bar?

f I ragazzi _____ (tradurre) un testo dall'italiano in inglese.

7 Complete these sentences using the appropriate form of **stare** in the imperfect tense.

a Ciao Chiara! _____ per andare a prendere i bambini a scuola.

b Ho visto Gianni mentre _____ per prendere l'autobus.

c Eravamo a Roma, _____ per tornare in albergo, quando ci hanno fermato i vigili.

d Scusate, non volevamo disturbare, _____ per uscire?

e Giancarla, _____ per cambiare idea, vero?

8 Complete these sentences with the appropriate form of **volere** in the imperfect tense to make polite requests.

a Signora, _____ vedere qualche maglia?

b Scusi, _____ vedere la borsetta nera in vetrina.

c Signori, cosa _____?

d Dottoressa Giannini, _____ parlarmi?

e Scusi, Professor Baralle, _____ dirLe una cosa urgente.

9 Complete these sentences with the imperfect of the verbs in brackets.

a Luciano _____ (lavorare) all'università da tre anni quando gli hanno dato un contratto permanente.

b _____ (studiare) l'italiano da un anno quando ho fatto l'esame.

c I miei amici non _____ (bere) caffè da mesi e dormivano molto meglio.

d Quando ci siamo sposati, _____ (essere) fidanzati da due anni.

e Quando avete comprato la casa in montagna, _____ (fare) le vacanze nel paese da molti anni?

f Tu prima di vincere la gara, _____ (fare) ciclismo da molto tempo?

10 Complete these sentences using either **da** or **per**.

a Eravamo fidanzati _____ dieci anni quando ci siamo sposati.

b Mi sono trasferita ad aprile. Avevo lavorato nello stesso ufficio _____ venti anni.

c Camilla viveva a Napoli _____ cinque mesi. Era contenta.

d Mi sono iscritta al corso di laurea a settembre. Avevo già studiato a Londra _____ due anni.

e Non avevo notizie della mia amica. Non la vedevo _____ tanto tempo.

13

Talking about the future

In this unit, you will learn how to:
- **talk about future plans**
- **express probability**
- **express or ask about intention(s)**

Language points
- **future tense (futuro)**
- **present tense to express the future**
- **future perfect**
- **future to express probability**
- **future perfect to express probability**
- **phrases of future time**

Introduction

Look at these examples of statements referring to future and present actions or events.

Domani andrò al mercato.	*Tomorrow, I'll go to the market.*
L'anno prossimo mio figlio andrà a Roma.	*Next year, my son will go to Rome.*
Stasera andiamo al cinema.	*Tonight, we're going to the cinema.*
Fra un anno avrete finito di studiare.	*In a year, you will have finished studying.*
Marco e Carla saranno già a casa.	*Marco and Carla will be home already.*

Focus on grammar

1 Expressing the future: future or present tense

In Italian, as in English, the future tense is used to talk about what you are going to do that evening, tomorrow or in the more distant future. And, as in English, the future tense is often replaced by the present tense.

Domani **andrò** a visitare il Museo.	*Tomorrow, I'll go and visit the Museum.*
Domani **vado** a visitare il Museo.	*Tomorrow, I'm going to visit the Museum.*
La settimana prossima **andremo** a Roma.	*Next week, we will go to Rome.*
La settimana prossima **andiamo** a Roma.	*Next week, we're going to Rome.*

Sometimes the future tense contains the idea of a promise.

Te lo **porterò** domani.	*I'll bring you it tomorrow.*
Ti **telefonerò** la settimana prossima.	*I'll call you next week.*

Insight
You can talk about the future using either the future or the present tense. Normally, you would use the present tense for the near future (today, tonight, tomorrow, even next week), but use the future tense for anything beyond that.

2 Forms of the future tense

The future tense is formed by taking the infinitive of the verb (e.g. **parlare**), removing the ending **-are**, **-ere** or **-ire** and adding the future endings. Here are the forms of the future tense:

Verbs ending in -are

parlare
parlerò   parleremo
parlerai   parlerete
parlerà   parleranno

Verbs ending in -ere

leggere
leggerò   leggeremo
leggerai   leggerete
leggerà   leggeranno

Verbs ending in -ire

partire
partirò   partiremo
partirai   partirete
partirà   partiranno

Verbs whose future tense is irregular
Some verbs have a slightly irregular form in the future tense:

• Some verbs drop the initial -e- of the future tense, for example
andare (**andrò**); avere (**avrò**); cadere (**cadrò**); dovere (**dovrò**); potere
(**potrò**); sapere (**saprò**); vedere (**vedrò**); vivere (**vivrò**).

• Some verbs drop the -e- or -i- of the future tense and then change
the stem to **rr**, for example: rimanere (**rimarrò**); tenere (**terrò**);
valere (3rd person form **varrà**); venire (**verrò**); volere (**vorrò**).

• Verbs with a contracted infinitive, for example **bere** and **tradurre**,
also have a double **rr** in the future form (**berrò, tradurrò**).

• Verbs whose infinitive ends in **–ciare** or **-giare** drop the **i** since it is no longer needed to soften the **c** or **g** sound: **cominciare** (**comincerò**); **lasciare** (**lascerò**), **mangiare** (**mangerò**).

• Verbs with infinitive forms ending in **-care** or **-gare** add **h** in order to keep the hard **c** or **g** sound: **cercare** (**cercherò**); **pagare** (**pagherò**).

• The one-syllable verbs **dare**, **dire**, **fare** and **stare** have future tense forms **darò**, **dirò**, **farò**, **starò**.

• The future tense of **essere** is **sarò**.

Insight

Fortunately, there are not very many verbs with an irregular future tense. While the stem or base of the verb changes, the actual future endings remain the same. Watch out for verbs such as **mangiare** and **pagare** which are regular but have spelling changes.

3 Future tense expressing probability

Often in English, you can say *He'll be in London by now*, using a future form to express the present with the meaning of probability. The future in Italian is often used in the same way.

Ormai sarà a Londra.	*He must be in London by now.*
Sarai stanca.	*You must be tired.*
Avrete fame.	*You must be hungry.*

4 Future perfect

The future perfect (future in the past) is used when you talk about a point in the future but referring to what you will have done by that point rather than what you *will do*. It is formed by the future of **avere** or **essere** plus the past participle.

Per martedì **avrò finito** questo libro.	*I will have finished this book by Tuesday.*
La settimana prossima **sarà tornata** in Italia.	*She will have gone back to Italy by next week.*
Si mangia alle 21.00? **Saremo morti** di fame.	*We're eating at 9 p.m.? We will have died from starvation.*

5 Future perfect expressing probability

Like the future, this tense can be used to express probability (what people **will/must** have done by the moment in time at which we are speaking).

Avrà lasciato il numero di telefono, spero.	*She'll have left her phone number, I hope.*
Avrai già **fatto** le valigie, immagino?	*You must have packed already, I imagine.*
Gli **sarà successo** qualcosa.	*Something must have happened to him.*

> ### Insight
> The use of the future tense to express probability or supposition in Italian is very similar to English usage *He must be in London by now* or *He will be in London by now*. Similarly, the future perfect in Italian is used to express the idea *He will have left* or *He must have arrived*.

6 *Future after* **quando** *and* **se**

In English, the future tense is not used after *when* or *if*. In Italian, either the future or the future perfect should be used after **quando** and **se**, when there is a future verb in the main part of the sentence.

| Quando **arriveremo** al mare, i bambini **vorranno** fare subito un bagno. | *When we arrive at the seaside, the children will want to have a swim straightaway.* |
| Se lo **vedrò**, gli **dirò** qualcosa. | *If I see him, I'll say something to him.* |

Quando **arriverete** a Napoli, *When you arrive in Naples, you will*
    dovrete cercare un albergo. *have to look for a hotel.*
Quando **avrò trovato** la lettera, te *When I have found the letter, I'll*
    la **farò** vedere. *show it to you.*

In the last example, the future perfect **avrò trovato** can be replaced
by the future:

Quando **troverò** la lettera, te la *When I find the letter, I'll show it*
    farò vedere. *to you.*

Alternatively both verbs can be in the present tense.

Quando **trovo** la lettera, te la *When I find the letter, I'll show it*
    faccio vedere. *to you.*

Insight

Be careful to use the future tenses (either future or future
perfect) after **quando** and **se**. This doesn't come naturally to
English speakers, since in English the present tense is always
used after *when* or *if*.

Language plus

1 Phrases of time

Here are some of the most common phrases of time used with the
near or distant future.

fra poco	*soon, in a short time*
fra alcuni giorni	*in a few days*
fra qualche giorno	*in a few days*
fra un mese	*in a month*

l'anno prossimo	*next year*
il mese prossimo	*next month*
la settimana prossima	*next week*
martedì prossimo	*next Tuesday*
domenica prossima	*next Sunday*
stasera	*this evening*
domani	*tomorrow*
dopodomani	*the day after tomorrow*
allora	*then, at that time*

Insight

Since Italian does not always use the future tense to talk about the future, the markers of time are important to indicate the future context. **Prossimo** (*next*) can be used to talk about next week, next month or next year.

2 Intention

To say what you intend doing in the future, you can also use:

aver intenzione di	*to intend (doing)*
pensare di	*to think of (doing)*
L'anno prossimo **penso di** lavorare in Italia.	*Next year, I think I might work in Italy.*
L'estate prossima **ho intenzione di** venire a trovarti.	*Next summer, I intend coming to see you* (lit. *find you*).

Insight

There are lots of verbs and phrases which express intention in Italian; many verbs or phrases are followed by di and the infinitive, for example **aver intenzione di, pensare di**. They express intention rather than a definite plan, so sound less certain than using the future tense.

3 Translating the English 'going to'

English frequently uses the verb *to go* to express the future, as in the sentence *He's going to get his degree next year.* In Italian, you cannot use the verb **andare** (*to go*) in this sense. (**Andare** expresses the idea of physically going to a place to do something.) The future tense must be used instead.

La settimana prossima **sarò** a Londra.

Next week, I'm going to be in London.

Language in action

Exercise 1

Some young students are talking about their future plans for next year after they graduate. Write about each student and his/her intentions. The account should be in the third person and based on the information contained in the conversation.

Esempio: *Sandra andrà in Spagna a lavorare, se ...*

LUCA	Cosa farai l'anno prossimo, quando sarai laureata?
SANDRA	Penso di andare a lavorare all'estero. Se non trovo un posto qui, andrò in Spagna. E tu?
LUCA	Mio padre ha un'impresa a Milano. Forse andrò a lavorare con lui. Mi pagherà bene, e non dovrò lavorare troppo.
SANDRA	Vedrai che fra dieci anni avrai già fatto i primi milioni!
LUCA	E tu fra dieci anni avrai già sposato uno spagnolo e avrai fatto tre figli!

Exercise 2

Next year's holidays
Translate this conversation between Luisa and Amelia into English.

LUISA	Dove farete le vacanze l'anno prossimo?
AMELIA	Abbiamo intenzione di andare negli USA. Forse andremo a trovare qualche parente. Mio marito non vuole andare in Sardegna come abbiamo fatto quest'anno.
LUISA	Sarete stufi di fare le vacanze sempre in Sardegna ormai, e sempre allo stesso posto. Avrete visto tutta l'isola, no?
AMELIA	Beh, tutta no, ma forse basterà per adesso!

Exercise 3

Match these halves to make up whole sentences, then complete them with the correct form (present, future or future perfect) of the verbs in brackets.

1 Quando io _____ (*venire*) a cena ...
2 Se tu _____ (*vedere*) Marco ...
3 Appena i bambini _____ (*arrivare*) al mare ...
4 Quando _____ (*fare*) caldo ....
5 Domani sera quando i miei zii _____ (*finire*) di lavorare ...
6 Ad agosto quando io e mio marito _____ (*andare*) in Argentina ...

    a ... _____ (*fare*) un bagno.
    b ... digli che lo _____ (*chiamare*) fra alcuni giorni.
    c ... _____ (*venire*) qui al mare.
    d ... vi _____ (*portare*) un regalo.
    e ... il figlio più piccolo _____ (*rimanere*) qui.
    f ... gli ospiti (*avere*) sete e _____ (*bisognare*) prendere delle bottiglie di acqua minerale.

Test yourself

Check your progress! Do you know how to do the following in Italian?

1 Change these sentences from present to future tense.
   a Vado al mare con la mia famiglia.
   b Partiamo domenica in aereo.
   c I nostri figli leggono molti libri in treno.
   d Puoi portare anche il tuo ragazzo alla festa.
   e Telefona ogni settimana.
   f Vedete dei film italiani a Londra.

2 Answer these questions using the correct form of the future tense and any expression of future time you like.
   Esempio: Hai scritto le cartoline? *No, le scriverò domani.*
   a Hai pagato la bolletta del telefono?   No, la …
   b Hai mangiato i biscotti inglesi?   No, li …
   c Hai cercato delle informazioni sui voli?   No, le …
   d Hai lasciato i documenti per il capo?   No, glieli …
   e Sei andata in centro?   No, ci …
   f Hai fatto i compiti d'italiano?   No, li …

3 Change these sentences from present to future tense.
   a Vengono anche i miei suoceri.
   b Bevo solo acqua.
   c Rimaniamo a casa quest'estate.
   d Ragazzi, tenete d'occhio i bambini?
   e Comincia a fare freddo.
   f Paghi tu la pizza.

4 Answer these questions using the future tense to express probability.
   Esempio: E Marco? (essere a Londra con Josie) *Sarà a Londra con Josie.*
   a E tua madre? (essere da mia sorella)
   b E i bambini? (essere in giardino)
   c Non viene Gino? (avere troppo da fare)
   d Ma gli ospiti mangiano già? (avere fame)
   e Come sta il marito di Suzy? (stare bene ora)

5 Change these sentences from present to future or future perfect tense.

a Gli studenti si iscrivono all'università quando hanno finito il liceo.

b I medici lavorano in ospedale quando si sono qualificati.

c Quando hai pagato con la carta di credito, ti mandano i biglietti a casa.

d Se l'aereo è partito da Roma in orario, i miei genitori arrivano a Londra alle 18.00.

e Quando abbiamo finito di fare le valigie, partiamo per l'aeroporto.

6 Answer these questions using the future perfect to express probability.

Esempio: E Marco? (essere a Londra) *Sarà andato a Londra.*

a Tua madre cos'ha fatto oggi? (andare in centro)

b E i bambini? (giocare in giardino)

c Gino ha finito di lavorare? (finire sicuramente)

d I nostri amici non hanno fame? (mangiare prima di cena)

e Non sono arrivati Carlo e Maura? (perdere il treno)

7 Finish these sentences any way you want, using a future or future perfect tense and **se** or **quando**.

Esempio: Laverò i piatti *quando avremo finito di mangiare.*

a Comprerò una casa in Italia ...

b Cambierò vestito ...

c Telefonerò a Patrizia ...

d Finisco la lettera ...

e Scrivo la mail a mio figlio ...

8 Replace the phrases in bold with a suitable expression of future time, e.g. **la settimana prossima, fra qualche giorno.**

a Siamo a gennaio. **A febbraio** comincio un nuovo lavoro.

b Oggi è mercoledì. **Venerdì** vado al mercato.

c Oggi è il 7 febbraio. **Il 14 febbraio** è San Valentino.

d Sono già le cinque. **Alle cinque e mezzo** devo uscire.

e **Oggi alle sette di sera** vado al cinema.

9 Rewrite these sentences using **aver intenzione di, sperare di** or **pensare di.**

Esempio: Domani andrò in centro a comprare le scarpe.

Domani ho intenzione di andare in centro a comprare le scarpe.

a L'estate prossima verrò a trovarti.

b L'anno prossimo ci sposeremo.

c La settimana prossima i nostri amici partono per la montagna.

d Domenica per pranzo mio marito preparerà un bel arrosto di carne.

e Pagherai la bolletta dell'elettricità domani mattina?

f Affitterete una casa al mare ad agosto?

10 Translate these sentences using the appropriate verb or expression.

a *Tomorrow, I'm going into town.*

b *My sister is going shopping after work.*

c *My sister's going to buy some shoes.*

d *We're going to Naples this weekend.*

e *My son's going to work in London.*

14

Talking about wants and preferences

In this unit, you will learn how to:
- *express a wish or desire for something*
- *express a wish or desire to do something*
- *express a wish for someone else to do something*
- *express a preference*

Language points
- *present tense of* voglio *to express an immediate want*
- volere *used with object or person (*voglio un gelato*)*
- volere *used with infinitive (*voglio andare*)*
- *direct object pronouns* lo, la, li, le
- *pronoun* ne
- *other verbs and infinitive combinations using* a, di
- preferire
- *present conditional* vorrei *to express a wish*
- *idiomatic expressions using* volere *(*voler bene, ci vuole*)*

Introduction

Study these examples of statements expressing a wish, desire or preference, either for yourself or for other people.

Vuole dei biscotti.   *He wants some biscuits.*
Li **vuole** subito.   *He wants them straightaway.*

Vuole che io gli presti dei soldi.	*He wants me to lend him money.*
Vorrei una bistecca con insalata verde.	*I would like a steak with green salad.*
Vorremmo vedere il film di Fellini.	*We would like to see the film by Fellini.*
Carla **preferisce** viaggiare in aereo.	*Carla prefers travelling by plane.*
Preferisco che i ragazzi giochino fuori.	*I prefer the kids to play outside.*

Focus on grammar

1 **Voglio** (etc.) and direct object pronouns

Volere (*to want*) is an irregular verb: it does not follow the regular pattern of -ere verbs (see Unit 5). The forms of the present tense are as follows:

....

voglio	**vogliamo**
vuoi	**volete**
vuole	**vogliono**

....

Volere can be used with an object or a person.

Voglio un panino con salame.	*I want a roll with salami.*
Vuole la mamma.	*He wants his mummy.*

When the original question mentions a named or specific person or object (*la* **mamma**, *il* **medico**, *le* **patatine**), you don't have to repeat the name of the object or person. Instead, you can use the direct object pronouns **lo, la, li, le** (*it/them*) to say *I want it*, *I prefer it*, etc. (In Unit 4, you met **lo, la, li, le** used with ecco.) They normally go before the verb, but there are exceptions to this rule (see Grammar appendix §4.3). Whether you use **lo, la, li** or **le** depends on whether the object in question is masculine or feminine, singular or plural.

Non vuoi il caffè, Sandra?	*Don't you want coffee, Sandra?*
No, non **lo** voglio, grazie.	*No. I don't want it, thanks.*
Vuoi la marmellata?	*Do you want jam?*
Sì, **la** voglio.	*Yes, I want it.*
Volete i fagiolini?	*Do you want green beans?*
No, non **li** vogliamo.	*No, we don't want them.*
Volete le patatine?	*Do you want crisps?*
Sì, **le** vogliamo.	*Yes, we want them.*

> ### Insight
>
> You met **lo, la, li, le** in Unit 4, along with **ecco** (**Eccolo!**
> **Eccoli!**). They can be used with any verb which takes a direct
> object, for example **volere**, as shown above. If you didn't use
> object pronouns, you would have to repeat the person or
> object all the time ('**Vuoi la pizza?**' '**Sì, voglio la pizza.**').

2 Pronoun **ne**

When the original question has **dei, delle,** etc. (*some*) or **un, uno,**
una with the noun, the noun is normally replaced in the answer
with **ne** (*of it, of them*).

Vuole delle melanzane, signora?	*Would you like some aubergines,* *signora?*
Sì, **ne** vorrei un chilo.	*Yes, I would like a kilo (of them).*
Vuoi un biscotto?	*Do you want a biscuit?*
Sì, **ne** vorrei due.	*Yes, I would like two (of them).*

While the direct object pronouns **lo, la, li** and **le** are normally used
to replace a particular or specific person or object (*le* cartoline, *il*
medico), ne is used to replace a non-specific one (*delle* cartoline, *un*
medico). Compare these examples:

C'è il medico?	*Is the doctor here?*
Sì, lo chiamo subito.	*Yes, I'll call him immediately.*
C'è un medico?	*Is there a doctor?*
Sì, ce n'è uno in Via Nomentana.	*Yes, there is one in Via* *Nomentana.*

> ## Insight
>
> English doesn't have to use a phrase such as *of it* or *of them* in this type of sentence. But in Italian, **ne** is normally used whenever you have a quantity in the answer, whether it's a number, a weight or a measure.

3 *Direct object pronouns and* **ne** *with other verbs*

All these pronouns can, of course, be used not just with **volere** but with any verb that takes a direct object and in any tense.

Hai scritto le cartoline?	*Have you written the postcards?*
No, **le** scrivo stasera.	*No, I'll write them tonight.*
Hai visto Luciano al convegno?	*Have you seen Luciano at the conference?*
No, spero di veder**lo** stasera.	*No, I hope to see him tonight.*
Prendi lo zucchero nel caffè?	*Do you take sugar in your coffee?*
Sì, **ne** prendo un cucchiaino.	*Yes, I take one (teaspoonful).*

When direct object pronouns are used with the perfect tense, the past participle changes ending to agree with the pronoun (masculine/feminine, singular/plural). More examples can be found in the **Grammar Appendix** § 4.3. **Lo** and **la** elide to **l'** before the verb **avere** (**l'ho mangiato, l'ho visto**).

Hai mai mangiato la pasta con i tartufi?	*Have you ever eaten pasta with truffles?*
No, non **l'**ho mai mangiata.	*No, I've never eaten it.*
Hai visto i nostri amici?	*Have you seen our friends?*
No, non **li** ho visti.	*No, I haven't seen them.*

> ## Insight
>
> You will often need to use a direct object pronoun with a perfect tense. As well as getting the pronoun right, you have to remember to make the past participle agree with the pronoun: singular or plural, masculine or feminine. Don't forget too that **lo** and **la** become **l'** before the forms of the verb **avere**.

4 **Voglio** *(etc.) and the infinitive*

Voglio can be combined with a verb infinitive to say what one wants to do.

Voglio diventare ricca e famosa.   *I want to become rich and famous.*

Desiderare and **preferire** can also be used in this way.

Desidero iscrivermi al corso.   *I want to enrol for the course.*
Preferiamo mangiare presto.   *We prefer to eat early.*

Insight

In Italian, a common way of combining two verbs (as in English *I want to go*) is a verb in the present/perfect/etc. (e.g. **voglio**) plus an infinitive form (e.g. **andare, prendere**). You can do this easily with verbs such as **volere, desiderare** and **preferire**.

---

5 **Vorrei** *(etc.)*

A less brusque way of saying or asking for what one wants (either with noun object or verb infinitive) is to use the present conditional of **volere** or **desiderare**, the forms of which are given in Unit 20.

Vorremmo una camera matrimoniale con bagno.   *We would like a double room with bathroom.*

Desidererebbero qualcosa da bere?   *Would you like something to drink?*

Vorrei parlare con il direttore, per favore.   *I would like to speak to the manager, please.*

Vorrebbe vedere qualche borsa, signora?   *Would you like to see a few handbags, signora?*

Insight

The present conditional **vorrei** is much more polite than the present simple **voglio**. Similarly, you can use the **tu** or **Lei** form of the present conditional to ask someone a question more politely: **Vorresti/Vorrebbe venire al cinema?** Later, in Unit 20, you'll learn other ways of using the present conditional.

6 Other verbs that can be used with the infinitive

Apart from **volere**, many other verbs can be followed by the infinitive. Sometimes these are joined by the prepositions **a** or **di**, while sometimes they need no preposition at all. Here are some examples:

a No preposition required
Verbs that don't need a preposition include **desiderare** (*to want to*), **osare** (*to dare to*), **potere** (*to be able to*), **preferire** (*to prefer to*), **sapere** (*to know how to*), **volere** (*to want to*).

Preferisco prendere il treno.	*I prefer to take the train.*
Posso venire con voi?	*May I come with you?*
Non **oso** chiedergli niente.	*I don't dare (to) ask him anything.*

b *Verbs requiring a*
Verbs requiring **a** include verbs of beginning, learning and continuing, such as **cominciare a** (*to begin to*), **continuare a** (*to continue to*), **decidersi a** (*to resolve to*), **imparare a** (*to learn to*), **iniziare** (*to begin to*), **mettersi a** (*to set out to, begin to*).

Comincio a capire.	*I'm beginning to understand.*
Impara a fare windsurf.	*He's learning to windsurf.*

c *Verbs requiring di*
Verbs requiring **di** include verbs of ending or giving up, such as **finire di** (*to end*), **smettere di** (*to stop, give up*), and also intention: **decidere di** (*to decide to*), **pensare di** (*to think about*).

Smetto di fumare.	*I'm giving up smoking.*
Finisco di lavorare alle cinque.	*I stop working at 5 p.m.*

A more complete list of verbs and the prepositions that follow them is found in the Grammar appendix § 13.2.

d Infinitive, not gerund

In English, the second verb is often expressed as a gerund (*I stop smoking, I start working*). In Italian, however, the infinitive is always used for this purpose, as in the examples shown above (smetto di *fumare*, comincio a *lavorare*).

> **Insight**
>
> Different verbs have different ways of combining with the infinitive to form sentences. Some verbs (e.g. **volere**, **desiderare**) combine directly, some (e.g. **smettere**, **finire**) are joined by di and some (e.g. **cominciare**, **imparare**) are joined by **a**.

e Verb followed by che and the subjunctive

When two different people are involved, for example when you want someone else to do something (I want him to come), you cannot use the verb and infinitive combination. You use the verb (e.g. **volere**) with che and a verb form known as the subjunctive.

Voglio che Franco venga.	*I want Franco to come.*
Preferisce che paghi io.	*He prefers me to pay.*

For an explanation of the subjunctive verb form, see Unit 17. For other tenses and uses of the subjunctive, see Units 17–22.

> **Insight**
>
> To say what someone wants to do, involving only one person, you can use the verb and infinitive combination (**Voglio andare a letto, Marco vuole mangiare la pizza**). But as soon as someone else is involved, you normally have to use **che** and the subjunctive (**Voglio che Marco vada a letto**).

7 preferire

Preferire (*to prefer*) can be used with an object or person.

Chi preferisci dei due?	*Who do you prefer of the two?*
Preferisco Roberto.	*I prefer Roberto.*
Preferisci la birra o il vino?	*Do you prefer beer or wine?*
Preferisco il vino.	*I prefer wine.*

When **preferire** is used to compare two different objects or persons, the English *to* is translated by **a**.

Preferisco il caffè **al** tè.	*I prefer coffee to tea.*
Preferisco Londra **a** Roma.	*I prefer London to Rome.*

Like **volere** or **desiderare**, the verb **preferire** can be used with a direct object or direct object pronoun.

Come preferisci il caffè?	*How do you prefer your coffee?*
Lo preferisco con latte.	*I prefer it with milk.*

Preferire can also be used with a verb.

Preferisci andare al cinema o pattinare?	*Do you prefer going to the cinema or ice skating?*
Preferisco pattinare.	*I prefer skating.*

Language plus

1 volere

Volere normally forms the perfect tense with **avere** (**ho voluto**). If the verb that follows (e.g. **andare**) forms its perfect tense with **essere**, then **volere** can use either **avere** or **essere**; while **essere** is always correct in this situation, many speakers would use **avere**.

Ho voluto vedere la mostra.   *I wanted to see the exhibition.*
Sono voluto andare a letto presto.   *I wanted to go to bed early.*
(**Ho voluto** andare a letto presto.)

2 ci vuole, ci vogliono, ci mette

Ci vuole means *it takes* (referring to time); for more than one hour, use the plural form **ci vogliono**.

Da Londra a Oxford **ci vuole**   *From London to Oxford, it takes*
   un'ora.   *one hour.*
Da Londra a Edimburgo ci   *From London to Edinburgh, it takes*
   vogliono sei ore in treno.   *six hours by train.*

Ci vuole forms the perfect tense with **essere**.

Da Roma a Reggio Calabria **ci sono** *From Rome to Reggio Calabria, it*
   volute sette ore.   *took seven hours.*

Alternatively, if you want to refer to a specific means of transport or mention a specific person, you can use **ci mette** (**metterci**).

Teresa va tutti i giorni a Napoli. **Ci** *Teresa goes to Naples every day. It*
   mette un'ora.   *takes her an hour.*
Quanto **ci mette** il treno da Roma *How long does the train take from*
   a Parigi?   *Rome to Paris?*
Il treno **ci mette** circa dodici ore. *The train takes about 12 hours.*

> ## Insight
> **Ci vuole** and **ci mette** both refer to time taken, but are used
> in different ways: **ci vuole** is impersonal meaning *it takes*,
> while **metterci** has a particular subject which can be either
> a person or a means of transport (**Io ci metto, il treno ci**
> **mette**).

3 voler bene a

Voler bene a is an expression meaning to love; bene is an adverb and does not change.

A chi **vuoi bene**?	*Who do you love?*
Voglio bene al mio cane.	*I love my dog.*

4 Moods and tenses of volere

Indicative mood: imperfect, perfect
The perfect **ho voluto** and the imperfect **volevo** tend to have slightly different meanings.

Volevo means *I wanted to (but I couldn't)*, while **ho voluto** means *I wanted to (and I did)*.

Volevo andare in banca, ma era chiusa.	*I wanted to go to the bank, but it was shut.*
Ho voluto andare in banca per cambiare soldi.	*I wanted to go to the bank to change money (and I did).*

Conditional mood: present, past
While the present conditional **vorrei** means *I would like*, the past conditional **avrei voluto** means *I would have liked*.

Vorrei andare al cinema.	*I would like to go to the cinema.*
Avrei voluto vedere quel film.	*I would have liked to see that film.*

For more on the conditional mood, see Units 20 and 21.

Insight

The difference between the imperfect tense of **volere** (**volevo**) and the perfect tense (**ho voluto**) is not always obvious to learners. **Volevo** expresses intention, but doesn't mean the action was fulfilled, while **ho voluto** generally means the action was fulfilled.

Language in action

Exercise 1

Which form of **volere** is more appropriate here? Present or conditional? You choose.

1 (*Alla banca*)   Scusi, (volere) aprire un conto studenti.
2 (*A casa*)   Sandro, (volere) venire con me in centro?
3 (*A scuola*)   Professore, (volere) chiederLe un consiglio.
4 (*Al bar*)   Ragazzi, (volere) andare a mangiare la pizza?
5 (*In autobus*)   Signora, (volere) sedersi?
6 (*In un negozio*) Signora, scusi, (volere) vedere quel maglione.
7 (*Fuori*)   Ragazzi, (volere) venire a casa mia stasera?
8 (*A casa*)   Mamma, (volere) telefonare a Chiara.
         Mi passi il telefono?
9 (*A scuola*)   Professore, possiamo finire la lezione in anticipo?
         (Volere) andare a casa a guardare la partita.
10 (*Al mare*)   No, grazie! Non (volere) né orologi né cinture!
         Non compriamo niente.

Exercise 2

Convivere è duro

Sara is telling her friends how unfairly her mother treats her. To make it more challenging for you, we have left out volere every time it occurs. Use the correct form of **volere** (present, imperfect, conditional) to fill in the gaps and reproduce what Sara said.

Mia madre è molto difficile. Io ho 15 anni ma mi tratta come una bambina di 12 anni. Non (**1**) _____ che io esca la sera con i miei amici, oppure mi fa uscire ma (**2**) _____ che torni prima di mezzanotte. Io invece (**3**) _____ andare in discoteca con gli altri e rimanere fino alle due. L'altro giorno (**4**) _____ andare al cinema e ho chiesto dei soldi a mia madre, ma lei non (**5**) _____ farmi andare al cinema da sola. Non (**6**) _____ darmi i soldi. Lei (**7**) _____ avermi sempre con lei.

Test yourself

Check your progress! Do you know how to do the following in Italian?

1 Complete these sentences with the correct forms of the present tense of **volere**.
   a I bambini non _____ andare a letto.
   b Noi _____ andare a mangiare la pizza stasera.
   c Gino, _____ venire con me al cinema domani sera?
   d Ragazzi, dove _____ andare questo finesettimana?
   e Sono stanca, _____ andare a letto.
   f Mio marito _____ comprare un appartamento a Venezia.

2 Answer these questions (sì or no, as you prefer) using **volere** and the appropriate direct object pronoun or **ne**. You can invent the quantities if you answer sì.
   a Vuoi le tagliatelle, Sandra?
   b Bambini, volete il gelato?
   c Signori, volete l'acqua minerale?
   d Vuoi i guanti?
   e Ecco i fichi, vuole anche delle pesche?
   f Signora, vuole un po' di prosciutto?
   g Vuoi zucchero?
   h Volete un po' di vino?

3 Answer these questions using an appropriate tense, a direct object pronoun or **ne**, and the prompt in brackets.
   a Mangiate la pasta tutti i giorni? (due/tre volte alla settimana)
   b Leggete i giornali online? (ogni giorno)
   c Hai pulito lo specchio? (stamattina)
   d Hai venduto la macchina? (sabato scorso ad un mio amico)
   e Hai visto le scarpe di Maura? (quando lei è entrata)
   f Hai comprato dei pomodori per fare il sugo? (cinque chili)
   g Chi fa il letto la mattina? (io)
   h Quanti fichi compri al mercato? (un chilo)

4 Translate these sentences using **volere** with an infinitive.
   a *My son doesn't want to go to bed.*
   b *My husband and I want to buy a house in Tuscany.*
   c *I want to speak Italian.*
   d *Do you want to do the oral exam, Anna?*

e *Our friends want to sell their car.*

f *Do you (two) want to accompany us to the airport?*

5 Write polite requests for these situations using the present conditional **vorrei** etc.

 a *You want to speak to the manager.*

 b *You (two of you) want a double room.*

 c *Ask your colleagues if they would like something to drink.*

 d *Ask a client if she would like to see some houses.*

 e *Ask your friend if he'd like to come to the cinema with you.*

6 Complete these sentences with **a** or **di**.

 a Ci vediamo al cinema. Finisco _____ lavorare alle sei.

 b A scuola i ragazzi imparano _____ parlare una lingua straniera.

 c Abbiamo deciso _____ prenotare una vacanza in Sicilia.

 d I ragazzi si sono messi _____ mangiare alle dieci di sera.

 e Cominciamo _____ mettere in ordine la cucina.

 f Stai proprio male! Perché non smetti _____ fumare?

7 Complete these sentences using **volere** in the perfect tense with **avere** or **essere** as appropriate.

 a I nostri amici _____ vedere la mostra dell'arte indiana.

 b Mio figlio _____ fare l'esame di guida subito.

 c La mia amica Franca _____ venire a Londra in primavera.

 d Domenica scorsa siamo andati a sciare. _____ alzarci presto.

 e Faceva freddo. _____ mettermi la giacca di lana.

 f L'aereo partiva alle cinque di mattina. _____ partire la sera prima e dormire in aeroporto.

8 Translate these sentences using **volere**.

 a *I wanted to eat, but I didn't have time.*

 b *We all went to the pizzeria – we wanted to try the pizza cooked in the wood oven.*

 c *Chiara, do you want to go out tonight?*

 d *She would like to speak to her father.*

 e *I would have liked to go to the cinema.*

 f *Would you like to sit down?*

9 Complete the sentences using either **ci vuole/ci vogliono** or **ci mette**.

 a Quanto tempo _____ da Londra a Napoli in aereo?

 b Da Londra a Napoli in aereo _____ due ore e mezzo.

c Lavori a Londra? Quanto _____ da Oxford a Londra in macchina?

d Dipende dal traffico. A volte _____ solo un'ora.

e Sei tornato? Quanto tempo ti _____ da Salerno a Padova in macchina?

f Tanto! In tutto _____ sette ore, sei ore di guida e un'ora di pausa.

10 Complete these sentences with the correct words to indicate preferences.

a Voi inglesi _____ il tè con latte?

b I vostri amici _____ andare in montagna o al mare?

c Preferisco Roma _____ Napoli.

d Preferisco la pasta _____ riso.

e Preferite la colazione inglese _____ il caffè con la brioche?

15

Describing processes and procedures

In this unit, you will learn how to:
- *say how something is done*
- *say how something ought to be done*
- *give instructions in impersonal form*
- *describe your reactions to something*

Language points
- *passive using* essere *and past participle* (è fatto)
- *passive using* venire (viene fatto)
- *passive using* andare *(va fatto)*
- *passive using* si passivante
- *impersonal* si
- rimanere *and participles*

Introduction

Study these examples of passive constructions and their meanings.

La cena è servita.	*Dinner is served.*
La cena viene servita alle otto.	*Dinner is/gets served at eight o'clock.*
La cena va servita alle otto.	*Dinner should be served at eight o'clock.*

Si serve la cena alle otto.   *Dinner is served (one serves dinner)*
                                    at eight o'clock.

Focus on grammar

1 Active and passive verbs

Normally, the subject of a sentence is the person (or thing) carrying
out the action. This is called an active construction. Sometimes, the
construction is reversed and the person (or thing) is not the 'doer'
but is having something 'done' to him/it. This is called a passive
construction. Here are two examples for contrast:

Active
La cameriera **taglia** il pane per   *The waitress cuts the bread for*
    colazione.   *breakfast.*
Passive
Il pane **viene tagliato** per colazione. *The bread is/gets cut for breakfast.*

In the active example, the waitress is the subject; in this case, the person
carrying out the action. In the passive example, the bread becomes the
subject; in this case, the object having the action done to it.

The passive is less common in everyday speech. It is more often
used in a formal register, in written Italian, in instruction manuals
and sometimes recipes. It is used in scientific papers or reports to
suggest objectivity, since the focus is on the action and not on the
person carrying it out.

Lo sperimento **è stato fatto** al   *The experiment was carried out*
    laboratorio di chimica organica.   *at the laboratory of organic*
                                         chemistry.

In the same way, it can avoid putting the blame on a particular
person.

La collana è stata rubata in casa. *The necklace was stolen in the house*

Insight

While it's important to understand the difference between active and passive, you may not want to use the passive very much. However, you will meet it quite often in written Italian, so you'll find it useful to know its meaning, and distinguish the different meanings of the verbs it can be formed with.

---

2 Passive with **essere**

The passive is formed with **essere** and the past participle, e.g. **parlato, bevuto, capito**. The endings of the past participle have to agree with the subject – the person or thing having the action done to them – i.e. masculine or feminine, singular or plural. (See Unit 11 for the forms of the past participle.) Here are some examples:

I vestiti italiani **sono venduti** in tutto il mondo. — *Italian clothes are sold all over the world.*

La bistecca **è cotta** ai ferri. — *The steak is cooked on the grill.*

3 Passive with **venire**

When the action is carried out regularly, **venire** is often used instead of **essere**.

A Napoli gli spaghetti **vengono mangiati** spesso. — *In Naples, spaghetti is eaten often.*

Il vino **viene bevuto** a tutti i pasti. — *Wine is drunk at all meals.*

4 Passive with **andare**

When something ought to be done, or must be done, **andare** is used in place of **essere**.

Gli spaghetti **vanno cotti** al dente. — *Spaghetti should be cooked 'al dente'.*

Il vino bianco **va servito** fresco.	*White wine should be served chilled.*

5 Passive: range of tenses

The passive verb construction with **essere** has the same wide range of tenses and moods as active verbs. The passive construction with **andare** or **venire** can be used with future and imperfect tenses, and present conditional, but not with compound tenses such as perfect or pluperfect.

- Present

I pasti **sono serviti** in terrazza.	*Meals are served on the terrace.*

- Imperfect

In quei giorni il burro **veniva fatto** in casa.	*In those days, butter was made at home.*

- Future

L'uva non **verrà raccolta** prima di ottobre.	*The grapes will not be picked until October.*

- Conditional

Questo vino **andrebbe servito** fresco.	*This wine should be served chilled.*

- Perfect

Non è **stato fatto** niente.	*Nothing has been done.*

- Pluperfect

La camera non **era stata** ancora **preparata**.	*The room had not yet been prepared.*

- Future perfect

Questa casa **sarà stata** costruita nell'Ottocento.	*This house will have been built in the 19th century.*

The past participle agrees with the subject (masculine/feminine, singular/plural). In the case of the compound tenses – the last three examples shown above – the past participle of **essere** (**stato**) changes as well.

> **Insight**
> You can form the passive with **essere, andare** or **venire**.
> While **essere** is a more general way of expressing the passive,
> **venire** suggests regular actions or events, while **andare**
> suggests the way that things ought to be done. Don't forget
> to make the participle agree.

6 si passivante

Lastly, you can make a passive construction by adding the **si passivante** (literally 'the **si** that makes the verb passive') to the third person singular or plural form of the verb.

If the person or object having the action done to it is singular, the verb is singular.

In classe si parla solo italiano.	*In class, only Italian is spoken (lit. one speaks only Italian).*
A casa mia si mangia spesso il risotto.	*At my house, risotto is often eaten.*

If there is more than one person or object involved, the verb must be plural.

A scuola si parlano dieci lingue diverse.	*At school, ten different languages are spoken.*
D'estate si noleggiano le mountain bike.	*In summer, mountain bikes are rented out.*

> **Insight**
> There is no real equivalent to this construction in English,
> but it is used frequently in Italian, for example on notices,
> leaflets, instructions and recipes: **Qui si parla italiano** (*Italian spoken here*) or **Si noleggiano le biciclette** *Bikes for hire.*

Language plus

1 *Impersonal* **si**

The impersonal **si** construction (**si impersonale**) expresses the formal English *one*. In more colloquial contexts, it is used to express *you* in the general sense or *we*. It is very similar in use to the **si passivante** (see above), but with some important distinctions.

- The impersonal **si** can be used with intransitive verbs.

Si va?	*Shall we go?*
A che ora **si arriva?**	*What time do we get there?*

- The impersonal **si** is used only in the singular.

In Italia **si pranza** all'una.	*In Italy, one dines at one o'clock.*
Non **si sa** mai.	*One never knows./You never know.*
Non **si fa** così.	*One doesn't do that. (That isn't done).*

- Although it uses a singular verb, it always uses a plural adjective or participle.

La sera **si** è sempre **stanchi**.	*In the evening, one is always tired.*

Insight

While English doesn't use *one* much, the Italian **si** form is useful if you don't want to indicate the agent or person responsible, for example to scold someone else's children (**Non si fa così!**) or even just to get your friends moving (**Si va?**).

2 si passivante *used to give instructions*

The **si passivante** construction can be used to explain to someone how to do something, and in this case can be translated in English as *one* or *you.*

Prima **si taglia** la cipolla e **si mette** *First, you cut the onion, you put it*
    nel tegame, poi **si aggiungono**   *in the pan, then you add the*
    i pomodori tagliati a pezzetti   *tomatoes cut into small pieces,*
    e **si lasciano** cuocere per   *and you leave them to cook for*
    mezz'ora.   *half an hour.*

3 ci si

There is an added complication when you use a reflexive verb form (e.g. **si alza, si veste**) with impersonal **si.** To avoid a repetition of **si,** the impersonal **si** combines with the reflexive pronoun **si** to produce **ci si.** Compare these examples:

Si alza.	*He/She gets up./You get up (using*
	Lei form).
Ci si alza.	*One gets up.*
Si veste.	*He/She gets dressed.*
Ci si veste.	*One gets dressed.*
Ci si vede alle cinque?	*Shall we meet at five?*

....

Insight
When you are using a reflexive verb along with the impersonal **si,** you get the combination **ci si.** You might use this when talking about routine in general, rather than your own routine: **ci si alza, ci si veste, ci si vede.**

....

4 rimanere *and past participle/adjective*

As well as using the past participle with **essere, andare** or **venire** to form the passive, you can also use it with **rimanere** (lit.: *to remain*) to express emotion. You can also use an adjective.

Sono rimasto molto contento.	*I was very happy.*
Mia sorella **è rimasta** delusa.	*My sister was disappointed.*
È rimasto ferito nello scontro.	*He was injured in the crash.*

I bambini **sono rimasti** sorpresi.   *The children were surprised.*

Other examples of participles used with rimanere include **impressionato** (*impressed*), **offeso** (*hurt, offended*), **scandalizzato** (*shocked*).

The adverb **male** is also used with **rimanere**.

Siamo rimasti molto **male**.   *We were very hurt.* (not literally)

Italians occasionally use **scioccato** (an English borrowing) for *shocked*.

Insight

While you use **essere** to describe your state of mind (**sono contenta, sono triste**), you use **rimanere** when an event or action has made you become happy/sad/shocked/etc. Of course, both participle and adjective still have to agree (**Sono rimasta molto impressionata, Mio marito è rimasto deluso**).

5 Indirect objects

Turning active sentences into passive is not always possible in Italian. Only direct objects can become the subject of a passive sentence in Italian. In the examples below, the person being given the book is an indirect object (*to him*), so cannot become the subject of a passive sentence. So the second of these three sentences cannot be translated into Italian.

He gives the book.	(Lui) dà il libro.
He is given the book.	Cannot be translated literally.
The book is given to him.	Il libro gli viene dato.

Insight

The passive is a good way to avoid giving credit or blame to any particular person. Don't forget that not all sentences can be turned into passive constructions, only those with a direct object.

Language in action

Exercise 1

Holiday 'musts' at the seaside
Highlight or underline all the constructions using a passive form or si form in this short text about summer in Viareggio in the 1980s!

Si ascoltavano concerti come quello di Gianni Morandi ... al tramonto si visitavano gli studi degli scultori. Il mercoledì si andava al mercato dove si compravano le più belle tovaglie, lenzuola, piatti e bicchieri. Tra i colori preferiti, andava incluso il bianco: camicie bianche, scarpe da tennis bianche ... ecc. L'unica concessione veniva riservata al kaki coloniale che veniva considerato molto di moda.

Exercise 2

How to cook and serve pasta
Even if you don't know how to cook pasta, you can still fill in the gaps using various present tense forms of the passive, either with **andare**, **essere** or **venire**.

In Italia (**1**) _____ (mangiare) molta pasta. La pasta (**2**) _____ (mangiare) all'ora di pranzo, soprattutto al centro e al sud del paese. Al nord, invece, (**3**) _____ (mangiare) più spesso il riso e la polenta. La pasta (**4**) _____ (servire) con sugo di pomodoro o di carne. (**5**) _____ (servire) al dente, e quindi non troppo cotta. A Bologna le tagliatelle (**6**) _____ (servire) spesso con prosciutto e panna mentre in Sicilia gli spaghetti (**7**) _____ (servire) con le melanzane.

And if you want to know more, check out the websites listed in Taking it further.

Test yourself

Check your progress! Do you know how to do the following in Italian?

1 Mark these sentences 'A' for active or 'P' for passive.

a I libri vengono venduti a prezzo scontato.

b Al mercato le pesche costano quattro euro al chilo.

c Al mercato le pesche vengono vendute da maggio fino ad agosto.

d I turisti mandano molte cartoline ai parenti.

e Molte cartoline vengono spedite senza francobollo.

f I bambini si alzano tardi durante le vacanze scolastiche.

2 Transform these sentences from active to passive constructions, using the correct tense of **essere**.

Esempio: Al mercato vendono i fichi freschi. **Al mercato sono venduti i fichi freschi.**

a Al supermercato venderanno il vino.

b Hanno scritto pochi esercizi.

c Sabato hanno festeggiato il compleanno dei gemelli.

d Mettono in ordine le camere.

e Firmano la lettera.

3 Transform these sentences from active to passive constructions, using **venire**.

a In Inghilterra consegnano il giornale a casa.

b In Italia servono il tè al limone.

c Quando abitavo a Londra, consegnavano il latte a casa.

d A Bologna servono le tagliatelle con il ragù bolognese.

e Dopo metteranno i documenti nell'archivio.

4 Transform these sentences from active to passive constructions, using **andare** and the correct form of the verbs in brackets.

a La pasta con i gamberi _____ (servire) senza parmigiano.

b Con il pesce _____ (servire) il vino bianco.

c La cipolla _____ (friggere) prima nell'olio d'oliva.

d La macchinetta da caffè _____ (pulire) regolarmente.

e I compiti _____ (scrivere) ogni giorno.

5 Complete these sentences with a **si passivante** construction using the verb in brackets.

a In centro _____ (affittare) degli appartamenti.

b La domenica _____ (pulire) la casa.

c Qui _____ (parlare) italiano.

d Una volta alla settimana _____ (scrivere) il menù.

e I giornali _____ (vendere) all'edicola.

6 Translate these sentences using the impersonal **si** construction.

a *You never know.*

b *Let's go!*

c *In winter, we are (= one is) sad.*

d *We have (= One has) dinner at 8 p.m.*

e *One travels at night, when it's cool.*

7 Transform these sentences from personal to impersonal si form.

a Ci alziamo sempre alle sette.

b Ci svegliamo molto presto.

c Ci vestiamo di corsa.

d Ci mettiamo in macchina alle 8.30.

e Ci vediamo in centro.

8 Write sentences using the prompts provided and **rimanere**, making the necessary adjustments and agreements.

Esempio: Tu (fem.) – contento – successo del libro? **Sei rimasta contenta del successo del libro?**

a noi – deluso – albergo a Venezia

b nostro figlio – ferito – a scuola

c voi – sorpreso – arrivo dei vostri amici

d io – scandalizzato – tuo comportamento

e i nostri amici – offeso

9 Mark the examples of different types of passive constructions in this text.

Come vengono fatti gli gnocchi di patate? Prima tutti gli ingredienti vengono versati in una grande terrina e vengono mescolati e impastati con le mani rapidamente. L'impasto viene versato sul ripiano del banco da lavoro (worktop) e viene diviso in tanti filoni dello spessore di 2–3 centimetri. Si tagliano e si formano gli gnocchi con le mani o con la forchetta. Poi si mettono su vassoi spolverati di farina e si coprono con un canovaccio (cloth). Gli gnocchi vengono versati in una pentola di acqua salata in ebollizione. Quando salgono in superficie sono pronti. Vanno scolati e conditi con il burro fuso, o con il sugo di pomodoro.

10 Complete this recipe with appropriate forms of **si passivante** and using the following verbs (some may be used twice): **lasciare, mescolare, mettere, sbucciare, soffriggere, tagliare.**

Prima (**a**) _____ la cipolla. Poi (**b**) _____ la cipolla nell'olio d'oliva. Dopo (**c**) _____ e (**d**) _____ i pomodori e (**e**) _____ nel tegame insieme alla cipolla. (**f**) _____ il tutto e (**g**) _____ cuocere mezz'ora a fuoco basso.

16

Talking about likes and dislikes

In this unit, you will learn how to:
- *talk about your likes and dislikes*
- *talk about someone else's likes and dislikes*
- *ask someone about their likes and dislikes*
- *contrast your and someone else's likes and dislikes*

Language points
- **piacere**
- *unstressed indirect object pronouns* mi, ti, gli, *etc.*
- *stressed indirect object pronouns* (a) me, te, lui, *etc.*
- **anche, neanche**

Introduction

Study these examples of how to express likes and dislikes. In each pair of examples, the second one is the more emphatic.

Saying what you like

Mi piace molto Venezia.	*I like Venice a lot.*
A me piace molto Venezia.	*I like Venice a lot.*
Mi piacciono le tagliatelle con salmone e panna.	*I like tagliatelle with salmon and cream.*
A me piacciono le tagliatelle con salmone e panna.	*I like tagliatelle with salmon and cream.*
Mi piace viaggiare.	*I like travelling.*
A me piace viaggiare.	*I like travelling.*

Asking someone else what they like

Ti piace quel ragazzo?	*Do you like that boy?*
A te piace quel ragazzo?	*Do you like that boy?*
Le piacciono i cannelloni?	*Do you like cannelloni?*
A Lei piacciono i cannelloni?	*Do you like cannelloni?*
Vi piace studiare la lingua italiana?	*Do you like studying Italian?*
A voi piace studiare la lingua italiana?	*Do you like studying Italian?*

Saying what others like

A mia figlia piace visitare i musei.	*My daughter likes visiting museums.*
Le piace visitare i musei.	*She likes visiting museums.*
A lei piace visitare i musei.	*She likes visiting museums.*
Non gli piace la pizza.	*He doesn't like pizza.*
A lui non piace la pizza.	*He doesn't like pizza.*

Note: **Cannelloni** and **spaghetti** are plural, as are **lasagne, tagliatelle, rigatoni, maccheroni** and all other forms of pasta.

Focus on grammar

1 piacere: *present tense*

To say that you like something in Italian, use **piacere** (*to please*) with the indirect pronouns **mi, ti, gli,** or their emphatic forms (**a me, a te, a lui,** etc.).

Piacere is like saying 'something is pleasing to me'. This 'something' can be a:

• verb	Mi piace mangiare.	*I like eating.*
• singular noun	Mi piace la pizza.	*I like pizza.*
• plural noun	Mi piacciono i gelati.	*I like ice-creams.*

The forms of **piacere** most often used are **piace** (3rd person singular) and **piacciono** (3rd person plural). The indirect object pronouns **mi, ti, gli**, etc., denote the person who likes or dislikes.

a To say that one likes doing something:

Mi piace fare delle passeggiate.	*I like going for walks.*
Mi piace cucinare.	*I like cooking.*

b To say that one likes a person or object (singular):

Ti piace Giorgio?	*Do you like Giorgio?*
Ti piace questa maglia?	*Do you like this sweater?*
(Questa maglia **ti piace**?)	

c To say that one likes persons or objects (plural):

Le piacciono queste scarpe.	*She likes these shoes.*
(Queste scarpe **le piacciono**.)	

> ### Insight
> **Piacere** is not easy for English speakers to use. English says I like something, whereas Italian says **Mi piace** (Something is pleasing to me), so the subject of the English sentence becomes an indirect object pronoun (**mi, ti, gli**, etc.) or a name preceded by **a** (**A Marco piace ...** *Marco likes ...;* **A Camilla piacciono ...** Camilla likes ...), and the verb matcher the thing/person that is liked, not the person doing the liking.

2 *Indirect object pronouns:* **mi, ti, gli, le, Le, ci, vi, gli**

You met the direct object pronouns **mi, ti, lo, la**, etc. in Unit 4. Luckily, four of the indirect object pronouns (**mi, ti, ci, vi**) share the same forms. Indirect object pronouns also normally come in the same position, i.e. immediately before the verb (**mi piace, ti piacciono**). Here are all the indirect object pronouns:

Singular		Plural	
mi	*to me*	ci	*to us*
ti	*to you*	vi	*to you*
gli	*to him*	gli	*to them**
le	*to her*		
Le	*to you* (formal)		

*An alternative form meaning *to them* is **loro**. This is not common in spoken Italian, although you may see it in written Italian. Unlike the other pronouns, **loro** comes after the verb.

Abbiamo mandato **loro** un invito.   *We sent them an invitation.*

These indirect pronouns are used with any verb where English uses the prepositions *to* or *for* and with many other verbs (see Grammar Appendix §§ 4.1, 4.2).

There are exceptions to the rule that pronouns always come before the verb, and these are also explained in Grammar Appendix § 4.3.

Insight

Italian has many types of pronouns. With piace, you need to use indirect object pronouns. Indirect object pronouns are generally used where in English you would say *to me, to you*, etc., so are also used with any verbs taking **a** (*to*) such as **telefonare, scrivere, mandare, regalare**.

3 piacere: *other tenses*

Piacere has a full range of tenses.

• Imperfect
Gli **piaceva** tanto la cucina italiana.   *He really used to like Italian cooking.*
• Future
Vi **piacerà** molto Firenze.   *You will really like Florence.*

- Present conditional

Mi **piacerebbe** andare a sciare.   *I would like to go skiing.*

- Perfect

Le è **piaciuta** la gita al lago?   *Did you like the trip to the lake?*

- Pluperfect

Gli **era piaciuta** molto Sara.   *He had really liked Sara.*

Note: In the perfect and pluperfect tenses, **piacere** uses **essere**, not **avere** (**è piaciuta**, **era piaciuta**).

Insight

Piacere is used so frequently in the present tense that it is easy to forget that it has a whole range of tenses. The forms of its tenses are all regular, but with the perfect tense it uses **essere** (**è piaciuto**).

---

4 *Stressed pronouns:* **(a) me, (a) te**, *etc.*

a Stressed or unstressed?

To compare likes and dislikes, you can replace the indirect object pronouns shown above with a more emphatic ('stressed') form of indirect object pronoun **me, te, lui**, etc., preceded by preposition **a**. The examples below show both forms:

Unstressed: **Mi** piace il caldo
Stressed: **A me** piace il caldo.   *I like the heat.*

Insight

In English, you can emphasise personal taste simply by the tone of voice: *I like Italian coffee.* You can't do that in Italian, so you have to use a stressed pronoun (**a me**) instead of the normal indirect object pronoun (**mi**).

---

b Forms of stressed object pronouns

Here are all the forms of the stressed object pronouns:

Singular		Plural	
a me	*to me*	a noi	*to us*
a te	*to you*	a voi	*to you*
a lui	*to him*	a loro	*to them*
a lei	*to her*		
a Lei	*to you* (formal)		

c With anche or neanche

The stressed pronouns can be used with **anche** (*also*).

Anche a me piace la pizza.	*I like pizza too.*
Anche a lui piacciono gli studenti inglesi.	*He likes the English students too.*

They can be used with **neanche** (*not even, neither*).

Neanche a noi piacciono i funghi.	*We don't like mushrooms either.*
Neache a loro piace questo tempo.	*They don't like this weather either.*

If **neanche** comes after the verb, use **non** as well.

Non piace **neanche a me** lavare i piatti.	*I don't like washing dishes either.*

In replying to a question, it is not necessary to repeat the verb.

A me piace il mare. E a te?	*I like the seaside. And you?*
Sì. **Anche a me.**	*Yes. Me too.*

Insight

Do you like the same things as your friend? Just use **anche**. And if you both dislike the same things, use **neanche**. Of course, **anche** and **neanche** can also be used with subject pronouns **io, tu, lui,** etc.: **Anch'io mangio troppo** (*I eat too much too*). When used after the verb, **neanche** needs **non** to complete it, in the same way as other negative pairs.

5 Emphatic pronouns used in other contexts

These stressed (emphatic) pronouns can be used not only with **a** but with other prepositions, such as **con, da, di, in, per, su**.

Sono uscita **con lui**.	*I went out with him.*
L'ho fatto **per te**.	*I did it for you.*

This set of pronouns can also be used without any preposition, simply as a more emphatic form of direct object pronoun or for contrast.

Vuole **me** non **te**.	*He wants me not you.*

Insight

The stressed pronouns can be used with any preposition, both simple (**con te, per lui**) and complex (**davanti a noi, di fronte a loro**). In fact, they are the only personal pronouns which can be used after a preposition in this way.

For further information on pronouns, see Grammar Appendix § 4.

Language plus

1 gradire

Another very polite way of offering someone something is to use
gradire.

Gradisci una bibita fresca?   *Would you like a cold drink?*
(**tu** form)
Gradisce una granita di caffè?   *Would you like a coffee granita?*
(**Lei** form)

*una granita di caffè is a coffee ice made with frozen sweetened
coffee.

Insight
> **Gradire** is considered rather old-fashioned. It is really only
> used in a limited context, for example a host offering a drink
> or food to a guest. A guest does not need to reply using
> **gradire**: a simple **Sì grazie** or **No grazie** is enough.

2 piacere *(1st and 2nd person forms)*

You can also use the first and second persons (I, you) with **piacere**
when it has the meaning of *to fancy someone*.

Piaci molto a Giancarlo.   *Giancarlo really likes you.* (lit.: you
           really please him.)

Dimmi, ti **piaccio** veramente?   *Tell me, do you really like me?*
           (lit.: do I really please you?)

3 volere bene, amare

A more common way to express the idea of liking a person is to
use **volere bene a** (*to love, like a lot*) or **amare** (*to love*).

Vuoi bene a Michele?   *Do you love Michele?*
Ti vuole bene?   *Does he love you?*
Amo soltanto mio marito.   *I love only my husband.*

Language in action

Exercise 1

Going to the cinema
Fill in the gaps with the correct form of **piacere** or an indirect object pronoun to say what kind of film Anna, Mara and Anna's husband like watching.

ANNA	Ti (**1**) _____ andare al cinema?
MARA	Sì, mi (**2**) _____ molto. E a te?
ANNA	Sì, anche (**3**) _____ piace.
MARA	Che tipi di film ti (**4**) _____?
ANNA	A (**5**) _____ i film romantici ma a mio marito non (**6**) _____ i film di questo genere.
MARA	E (**7**) _____ che tipi di film (**8**) _____?
ANNA	Nessuno.

Exercise 2

Preferences
What do people like eating? Find out by looking at the illustrations below and answer the questions on people's likes.

Esempio: Cosa piace a Franco?
Gli piacciono le mele.

1 Cosa piace ai bambini?
2 Cosa piace alla mamma?
3 Cosa piace a voi, ragazze?
4 Cosa piace ai ragazzi inglesi ?

5 Cosa piace alla regina d'Inghilterra?
6 Cosa piace agli studenti?
7 Cosa piace agli argentini?

Cosa piace a te? (say what you like!)

1

2

3

4

5

6

7

8

Test yourself

Check your progress! Do you know how to do the following
in Italian?

1 Match the two halves of the sentences containing **piacere** so that they make sense.

a Una volta al mese mi piace   **i** dormire fino a tardi.

b Una volta all'anno ci piace **ii** andare al cinema.

c La domenica mi piace   **iii** passare il finesettimana a Venezia.

d Il sabato sera gli piace   **iv** passare tre settimane al mare.

2 Complete these sentences with the correct form and tense of **piacere**.

a Quando sarai grande, ti _____ essere indipendente.

b Ti _____ vincere la lotteria?

c Quando erano piccoli, ai bambini _____ giocare a pallone.

d È' stata una bella giornata, mi _____ passare una giornata in campagna.

3 Match the two halves of the sentences containing **piacere** so that they make sense.

a Come dolce ci piacciono   **i** Napoli; ci andiamo spesso.

b Come pasta ci piacciono **ii** l'insegnante d'italiano.

c A noi piace   **iii** gli spaghetti con le vongole.

d Agli studenti piace   **iv** i cannoli siciliani.

4 Complete these sentences with the correct form and tense of **piacere**.

a Ieri sera siamo andati da Lina, mi _____ tanto i ravioli fatti in casa.

b Il mese prossimo, andremo a Barga, un paese nella Garfagnana, sono sicura che ti _____.

c Sto leggendo un romanzo di Italo Calvino. Penso che ti _____ questo libro.

d Stiamo bene nella nuova casa ma ci _____ la casa dove stavamo prima.

5 Answer the questions using the appropriate unstressed indirect object pronoun: **mi, ti, gli, le, ci, vi, gli/loro**.

a "La politica interessa ai vostri figli?" "No, non _____ interessa tanto."

b "Vi piace viaggiare in aereo?" "Sì, _____ piace."

c "Ad Emanuela piace stare in Inghilterra?" "Sì, _____ piace."

d "Ti piacciono gli esercizi di grammatica?" "No, non _____ piacciono."

6 Complete these sentences using the stressed pronouns: **me, te, lui, lei, noi, voi, loro.**

a Abbiamo parlato con Marco. Viene al cinema con _____.

b Maura, ha chiamato tuo padre, vuole parlare con _____.

c Vado in centro. Vuoi venire con _____ in macchina?

d L'otto marzo vado da mia madre; questi fiori sono per _____.

7 Choose the appropriate pronoun, either indirect object pronoun (**mi, ti, gli,** etc.) or stressed (**me, te, lui,** etc.), to complete these sentences.

a Lina, questa musica mi piace molto, ma non so se piace anche a _____.

b "Andiamo in treno o in macchina?" "A _____ piace il treno ma decidi tu."

c Gino, _____ piacciono le canzoni di Battisti? A _____ piacciono.

8 Give an appropriate response using **anche.**

a Al mio ragazzo piace molto il risotto! E al tuo?

b Mi piace tanto ballare! E a te?

c A mia moglie piacciono i film romantici. E a tua moglie?

d A mio marito piacciono le macchine sportive. E a tuo marito?

9 Give an appropriate response using **neanche.**

a A molti italiani non interessa molto l'economia mondiale. E agli inglesi?

b Ai miei figli non piace cucinare. E ai tuoi?

c A noi non piacciono i calamari. E a voi?

d A me non interessa studiare. E a te?

10 Complete these sentences with the appropriate form of **amare, piacere** or **volere bene.**

a Mio figlio _____ alla sua sorellina.

b Tutti _____ i nostri figli.

c Anche se sono grassa e brutta, a mio marito _____ così.

d Avevo un cane che si chiamava Lucky, quanto gli _____.

17

Asking for and giving an opinion

In this unit, you will learn how to:
- *express a belief or an opinion*
- *ask someone else's opinion*
- *express a rumour*
- *express a tentative view*

Language points
- *subjunctive mood (present tense)*
- sembrare, parere
- pensare *with* che *and the subjunctive*
- pensare *with* di *and the infinitive*
- *phrases expressing opinion*
- pensare di, *offering an opinion*
- magari

Introduction

There are many ways of expressing an opinion in Italian. One is
to use the indirect object pronouns **mi**, **ti**, **gli** described in Unit 16,
along with **sembrare** or **parere** (*to seem*). Alternatively, you can use
pensare or **credere** (*to think*). With these verbs, you often need to
use a verb form known as the subjunctive, explained below.

Study these examples and their English translation before going on.

Come ti sembra questa proposta?	*What do you think of this proposal? (lit.: How does this proposal seem to you?)*
Questo ragazzo non mi sembra molto intelligente.	*This boy doesn't seem very bright to me.*
Mi pare che sia fattibile.	*It seems to me that it is feasible.*
Credo che sia una buona idea.	*I think it is a good idea.*
Marco pensa che l'albergo sia caro.	*Marco thinks the hotel is expensive.*
Mi sembra di aver già visto questo programma.	*I think I have seen this programme already.*
Mi pare di conoscere questo signore.	*I think I know this gentleman.*
Penso di essere in ritardo.	*I think I am late.*
Crede di aver sbagliato.	*He thinks he has made a mistake.*

Focus on grammar

1 The subjunctive: an introduction

The subjunctive is a 'mood' of the verb used in certain circumstances. The subjunctive is almost extinct in English, but a few remnants of it can be found, for example: *I wish he **were** here*, *If I **were** you*. In Italian, however, it is far from extinct; in fact, it is difficult to express a feeling or opinion, doubt or uncertainty, without using it. Units 17, 18, 19 and 20 illustrate different tenses of the subjunctive and different situations in which they are used.

The subjunctive is rarely found on its own (except for expressing an order: see Unit 9), but is almost always used in a subordinate clause, i.e. a clause or part of a sentence which depends on the main part of the sentence. Most often, the subordinate clause follows the main clause and is introduced by **che** or another joining word. Look at these examples and the English translation.

Normal (indicative) form of the verb	Subjunctive form of the verb
Donatella **è** simpatica.	**Non penso che** Donatella **sia** simpatica.
Donatella is nice.	*I don't think that Donatella is nice.*
Marco **è** antipatico.	**Mi pare che** Marco **sia** antipatico.
Marco is unpleasant.	*I think that Marco is unpleasant.*

Insight

Because the subjunctive is not used in English, it's difficult for English speakers to understand why they should have to learn it. But it is so common in Italian that it is worth investing a little time in learning the forms. If you don't, you will have to find ways of avoiding it, for example when expressing an opinion.

2 Subjunctive: present tense of regular verbs

The present tense of the subjunctive follows the following patterns:

Verbs ending in **-are**

parlare

che	parl**i**	parl**iamo**
	parl**i**	parl**iate**
	parl**i**	parl**ino**

Verbs ending in **-ere**

mettere

che	mett**a**	mett**iamo**
	mett**a**	mett**iate**
	mett**a**	mett**ano**

Verbs ending in -ire

partire

che	parta	partiamo
	parta	partiate
	parta	partano

capire

che	capisca	capiamo
	capisca	capiate
	capisca	capiscano

3 Subjunctive: present tense of irregular verbs

There are several verbs whose present subjunctive form follows a varying pattern. These are listed in the Grammar Appendix § 13.3. Often the **io, tu, lui/lei, loro** forms follow one pattern, while the **noi, voi** forms follow another, for example **andare** has **(che) io vada, (che) noi andiamo**.

Here is the present subjunctive of some of the most common verbs.

Infinitive form		(io)	(noi)
andare	*to go*	vada	andiamo
avere	*to have*	abbia	abbiamo
dare	*to give*	dia	diamo
dire	*to say*	dica	diciamo
dovere	*to have to*	debba	dobbiamo
essere	*to be*	sia	siamo
fare	*to do*	faccia	facciamo
potere	*to be able to*	possa	possiamo
stare	*to be*	stia	stiamo
venire	*to come*	venga	veniamo
volere	*to want to*	voglia	vogliamo

Insight

As with other moods and tenses, the verbs which are most
often irregular are those most frequently used. So it's
worthwhile learning and remembering these verbs, so that
you can use or at least recognize the present subjunctive
forms when you need to.

4 sembrare, parere *used impersonally*

To express an opinion, you can use **sembrare** (to seem) or **parere**
(to appear). These verbs are often used impersonally in the 3rd
person forms **sembra, pare** (*it seems, it appears*), together with
indirect object pronouns **mi, ti, gli** (*to me, to you, to him*, etc.).
They can be used in two different ways.

a *With* **di** *and the infinitive*
If the person expressing the opinion is the same person carrying out
the action, i.e. is the same subject (*I think that I am…*), use **di** and
the infinitive form.

Mi sembra di sognare.	*I think I'm dreaming.*
Gli sembra di conoscere la ragazza.	*He thinks he knows the girl.*

You can also use a past infinitive, combining **avere** or **essere** with a
past participle.

Mi sembra di aver già visto questo film.	*I think I've seen this film already.*
Mi pare di essere arrivata troppo tardi.	*I think I have arrived too late.*

The final e of **avere** or **essere** is often dropped, as in the first
example.

b *Followed by* **che** *and the subjunctive*
If the person expressing the opinion is not the same person
referred to in the dependent clause (I think that he is …), **sembra** is

followed by **che** (that) and a subjunctive form.

Mi sembra che lui **sia** un po' pigro. *I think (that) he is a bit lazy.*
Gli sembra che lei **sia** offesa. *He thinks (that) she is offended.*

Che cannot be omitted (unlike in English, where that can be omitted from this type of sentence).

5 sembrare *used personally*

Sembrare can also be used 'personally', i.e. with a subject, as shown in bold in these examples.

Come ti sembra **il corso**?	How does the course seem to you?
Mi sembra ben organizzato.	It (the course) seems well organized to me.
I bambini mi sembrano stanchi.	The children look tired to me.

Note how Italian uses **come** (*how*) where English would normally say *What (is it) like?*

6 pensare, credere *used to express an opinion*

You can also express an opinion using **pensare** or **credere**. Like **sembrare** and **parere**, when only one person is involved, they can be followed by a simple **di** and the infinitive; when the subject is different, they are followed by **che** and subjunctive.

a *With **di** and infinitive*

Penso di sognare.	*I think I'm dreaming.*
Pensa di vincere.	*He thinks he will win.*

b *With **che** and subjunctive*

Pensa che tu stia sognando.	*He thinks you're dreaming.*
Penso che Venezia sia la città più bella del mondo.	*I think Venice is the most beautiful city in the world.*

> **Insight**
>
> Where the person speaking is the same person carrying out the action, you can avoid the subjunctive by simply using **mi sembra**, **mi pare**, **pensare** or **credere** with **di** and the verb infinitive. But if two different people are involved, you need **che** and the subjunctive.

7 Phrases expressing opinion

Here are some of the most common phrases used for expressing opinion:

a mio parere	*in my opinion*
a mio avviso	*in my opinion*
per me	*in my opinion*
secondo me	*in my opinion*
per quanto mi riguarda	*as far as I am concerned*
per quel che mi riguarda	*as far as I'm concerned*

A mio parere l'albergo è un po' caro.	*In my opinion, the hotel is a bit expensive.*
Per quanto mi riguarda, non vale la pena.	*As far as I am concerned, it's not worth the trouble.*

Obviously anyone can express an opinion, so the same expressions can be used with the full range of possessive adjectives ...

a tuo avviso, a suo avviso, a nostro avviso, a vostro avviso, a loro avviso

... and with the full range of pronouns.

secondo te, secondo lui, secondo lei, secondo Lei, secondo noi, secondo voi, secondo loro

per quanto ti riguarda, per quanto lo/la riguarda, per quanto ci riguarda, per quanto vi riguarda, per quanto li/le riguarda

Insight

These phrases do not need to be followed by **che** and the subjunctive. They are simply a separate phrase, added to the rest of the sentence. So this is a far easier way of expressing an opinion.

Language plus

1 Expressing opinion or rumour (using the conditional)

To express an opinion or voice a rumour, Italian often uses the present conditional (see Unit 20) to express the present tense.

Secondo la stampa, l'Italia **sarebbe** al quinto posto nella graduatoria dei paesi industrializzati.	*According to the press, Italy is in the fifth place in the league table of industrialized nations.*
Secondo i giornali inglesi, la famiglia reale **avrebbe** una nuova carrozza.	*According to the English newspapers, the royal family has a new carriage.*

Insight

For English speakers, this use of the conditional **sarebbe** and **avrebbe** (would be, would have) to express a simple present (*is, has*) may seem strange, but for the press, it is a way of acknowledging that the story is not a confirmed fact but an allegation or rumour; this also avoids possible accusations of getting the facts wrong.

2 sembra di sì, sembra di no

Note the following idiomatic expressions.

Mi sembra **di sì**.	*I think so.*
Mi sembra **di no**.	*I think not./I don't think so.*

Mi pare, penso and **credo** can be used in the same way.

Mi pare di sì./Penso di sì./Credo di sì.	*I think so.*
Mi pare di no./Penso di no./Credo di no.	*I think not./I don't think so.*

Insight

Idiomatic expressions can't always be translated directly into English, but they are worth learning so that you can build up a store of Italian expressions to use in conversation. By learning them as a set phrase, you won't have to worry about getting the verb or pronoun correct, but can just drop them into a conversation. They can make you sound impressively fluent!

3 *Using* **pensare di** *to express an opinion*

To express an opinion about someone or something, use **pensare di** (*to think of*).

Cosa pensi di questa maglietta?	*What do you think of this T-shirt?*
Cosa pensi di questi sandali?	*What do you think of these sandals?*

The correct pronoun to use in place of the noun in each of the sentences above is **ne**.

Cosa **ne** pensi?	*What do you think of it?*
Cosa **ne** pensi?	*What do you think of them?*

Do not confuse **pensare di** (*to express an opinion of something*) with **pensare a** (*to think about something or someone*). Here, you would use **ci** to mean *about it*.

Penso al mio gatto.	*I'm thinking about my cat.*
Non ci pensare più!	*Don't think about it any more!*

Insight

Just changing the preposition can change the whole meaning
of a verb, as in the case of **pensare di** (to have an opinion of)
and **pensare a** (to think about someone or something). In
English, *to think about something* can also mean *to express an
opinion*.

4 Subjunctive: past tenses

The subjunctive has a variety of past tenses.

- Imperfect
Credevo che **fosse** stanco.   *I thought he was tired.*
- Perfect
Credo che **sia arrivato** ieri.   *I think he arrived yesterday.*
- Pluperfect
Credevo che **fosse** già **arrivato**.   *I thought he had already arrived.*

The forms of the imperfect and pluperfect subjunctive are described
in Units 20 and 21 respectively.

5 How to form the perfect subjunctive

To form the perfect tense of the subjunctive, use the present
subjunctive of **avere** (**abbia**, etc.) or **essere** (**sia**, etc.) with the past
participle (e.g. **comprato**).

Non **credo** che lui mi abbia   *I don't think he has bought me a*
comprato un regalo.   *present.*
Non mi pare che lei **sia partita**.   *I don't think she has left.*

6 When to use the perfect subjunctive

The perfect subjunctive is used in a dependent clause to describe
an action which has already taken place. It is generally found
following a main verb in the present or future tense.

| Non credo che il treno sia già partito. | *I don't think the train has left already.* |
| Andremo a Capri a meno che non abbiamo speso tutti i soldi. | *We'll go to Capri unless we have spent all our money.* |

7 magari

Magari can be used as a response when someone is giving an opinion, implying *maybe* or *perhaps*.

| Pensi che i ragazzi verranno? | *Do you think the boys will come?* |
| **Magari!** | *Let's hope so.* |

Magari can express a hope that something might come about, but implies that it is very unlikely to happen:

| Pensate di comprare una nuova macchina? | *Are you thinking of buying a new car?* |
| **Magari!** | *I wish we were!/If only!* |

The many other uses of the subjunctive are covered in Units 18, 19 and 20.

> ## Insight
>
> **Magari** is a very useful word, implying hopes, dreams and cynicism all at the same time. It expresses a wish, while at the same time implying that it is unlikely to be fulfilled. You might meet it followed by an imperfect or pluperfect subjunctive (**Magari vincessi la Lotteria!**), to specify what you wish would happen.

Language in action

Exercise 1

Corso estivo a Oxford
Your friend Cristina wants to send her son Filippo to Oxford to do
an English course. She has found a school that might be suitable.
Offer her your opinion on the various aspects of the summer
school, numbered below, using any of the expressions you have
learned, for example, **pensare, credere, mi sembra, mi pare.**

Esempio: È importante scegliere una scuola seria?
Io **penso** che **sia** molto importante scegliere una scuola seria.

1 Bastano cinquanta sterline di pocket money alla settimana?
2 La scuola è membro dell'ARELS (Association of Recognized
   English Language Schools)?
3 La scuola sta in centro?
4 La scuola ha insegnanti qualificati?
5 Gli insegnanti sono giovani?
6 I ragazzi possono praticare lo sport?
7 I ragazzi devono essere autonomi?
8 La scuola organizza escursioni e attività sociali?
9 I pasti sono inclusi nel prezzo?
10 I ragazzi hanno la possibilità di comprare bibite e merendine?
11 C'è un centro medico?

Exercise 2

How wrong can you be?
Your mother thinks you are a saint. Little does she know... Here is
a list of the things you really do. Now say what your mother thinks
you do!

Esempio: Fumo un pacchetto di sigarette al giorno.
Mia madre ...(non fumare)

Mia madre pensa che io non fumi.

1 Vado a letto dopo le due.
  Mia madre … (*prima di mezzanotte*)
2 In camera mia leggo riviste e ascolto la musica.
  Mia madre … (*studiare*)
3 Ho preso un brutto voto all'esame di storia.
  Mia madre … (*prendere un bel voto*)
4 Sono stata bocciata proprio in inglese.
  Mia madre … (*essere promossa in tutte le materie*)
5 La sera vado al club.
  Mia madre … (*stare a casa della mia amica*)
6 Esco con tanti ragazzi.
  Mia madre … (*non uscire con nessuno*)
7 I miei amici sono tutti pazzi.
  Mia madre … (*essere ragazzi seri*)
8 Prendo sempre la macchina.
  Mia madre … (*andare in autobus*)
9 Mangio un chilo di cioccolato al giorno.
  Mia madre … (*non mangiare mai cose di questo tipo*)
10 Bevo due bottiglie di vino al giorno.
  Mia madre … (*non bere mai bevande alcoliche*)

Test yourself

Check your progress! Do you know how to do the following
in Italian?
1 Complete these sentences using the present subjunctive of the
  regular verbs in brackets.
  a Penso che le vacanze _____ (cominciare) il 20 giugno e
    _____ (finire) il 15 settembre.
  b Pensi che Jane _____ (capire) l'italiano?
  c Mi sembra che gli inglesi non _____ (mangiare) molta pasta.
  d Non credo che i bambini _____ (leggere) molti libri.
  e Mio marito pensa che i ragazzi _____ (dormire) troppo.
2 Complete these sentences using the present subjunctive of the
  irregular verbs in brackets.

a Mi pare che i nostri studenti _____ (essere) molto intelligenti.

b Ti sembra che noi _____ (avere) tempo per fare acquisti?

c Ti pare che noi _____ (dare) troppi soldi ai nostri figli?

d Mia madre non pensa che mio padre _____ (fare) molto in casa.

e Lucia pensa che lei e suo marito non _____ (potere) venire.

3 Match the two halves of the sentences.

a Ho visto le informazioni   **i** e mi pare di aver capito tutto.

b Abbiamo visto il titolo
del film e   **ii** mi sembra di sognare!

c Ho vinto la lotteria –   **iii** ti sembra di conoscerla?

d Guarda quella ragazza
bionda –   **iv** ci sembra di averlo già visto.

4 Match the two halves of the sentences.

a Non penso   **i** che Londra sia una città economica.

b Cristina, pensi   **ii** che la vostra casa sia pulita?

c I miei amici italiani
non pensano   **iii** che tuo padre venga domani?

d Daniela e Antonio, credete   **iv** che il supermercato sia aperto la domenica.

5 Complete these sentences using **sembrare** or **parere** with either **di** or **che** and the verbs in brackets where necessary.

a Mia madre ha chiesto il prezzo e le _____ che sia troppo caro.

b Mi _____ (vedere) il marito di Stella.

c Sono 100 euro. Non vi _____ (spendere) troppo?

d Gli _____ che la macchina sia molto vecchia.

e Ti _____ (avere) tempo da sprecare?

6 Complete these sentences using **pensare** or **credere** with either **di** or **che** and the verbs in brackets where necessary.

a Penso _____ loro _____ (volere) andare a mangiare una pizza.

b Marco pensa _____ (partire) sabato.

c Stella _____ che Marco lavori troppo.

d Credi che ci _____ (essere) posto in macchina?

e I nostri amici pensano _____ (partire) domani mattina.

7 Complete the sentences with appropriate phrases expressing opinion. (There may be more than one suitable answer.)

a A Gianni non piace la televisione italiana. _____ è mediocre.

b Per i nostri genitori l'internet è un mistero. _____ non è essenziale.

c Sono stata due notti in questo albergo. _____ è molto scadente.

d Per _____, io non andrei al mare nel mese di agosto.

8 Write questions for these answers using **pensare di**.

Esempio: Sono proprio belli questi sandali!

Cosa pensi di questi sandali?

a A me piacciono molto queste scarpe.

b Mi piace molto l'Italia.

c Quest'albergo mi sembra buono.

9 Match the two halves of these sentences.

a Secondo La Repubblica,	**i** la squadra italiana avrebbe tanti problemi.
b Secondo il Presidente	**ii** gli inglesi avrebbero tanti del Consiglio, problemi di salute dovuti all'eccesso di alcool.
c Secondo i giornali sportive,	**iii** i magistrati sarebbero tutti comunisti.
d Secondo la televisione inglese,	**iv** il presidente del Consiglio sarebbe disonesto.

10 Complete the sentences using the perfect subjunctive of the verbs in brackets. Be careful with the word order in the first one.

a Penso che le vacanze _____ (cominciare) già.

b Pensi che il capo _____ (capire) la mia richiesta?

c Mi sembra che ci _____ (essere) un errore.

d Non credo che i bambini _____ (fare) i compiti.

e Mio marito pensa che io _____ (spendere) troppo.

f Non credi che loro _____ (dire) la verità?

18

Expressing obligation and need

In this unit, you will learn how to:
- *express an obligation*
- *talk about someone else's obligations*
- *express one's needs*
- *talk about someone else's needs*
- *express a necessity*
- *say what is needed*

Language points
- **dovere**
- **aver bisogno di**
- **bisogna**
- **c'è bisogno di**
- **è necessario/essenziale**, *etc.*
- **occorre, occorrono, ci vogliono**
- *using infinitive or* che *and subjunctive (present tense) after impersonal verbs*

Introduction

The verb **dovere** is used to express duty or obligation (something one has to do) and need (something one needs to do). Other ways to express need in Italian include **bisogna, aver bisogno di, c'è bisogno di**.

Study these examples:

Maria deve studiare di più.	*Maria must study more. (Maria needs to study more.)*
Devo andare a casa. È tardi.	*I must go home. It's late. (I need to go home. It's late.)*
Ho bisogno di andare in bagno.	*I need to go to the bathroom.*
Bisogna pagare il supplemento.	*One must pay a supplement.*
Non c'è bisogno di pagare il supplemento.	*There's no need to pay the supplement.*

Focus on grammar

1 dovere

Dovere is a slightly irregular verb which means *(I) must, (I) have to*. Here are the present tense forms.

....

devo	dobbiamo
devi	dovete
deve	devono

....

In the present indicative tense, **dovere** means *must, have to*.

Devo ritirare I soldi al bancomat.	*I must get some money from the cash machine.*
Dovete guardare i prezzi prima di comprare.	*You must look at the prices before buying.*

In the present conditional (see Unit 20), **dovere** means *should, ought to*.

Dovrei andare a trovare gli amici inglesi.	*I ought to (should) go and visit my English friends.*

Dovresti visitare la cattedrale. *You ought to (should) visit the cathedral.*

To talk about the past, either the imperfect tense or the perfect tense can be used, depending on whether the action happened regularly (imperfect) or once only (perfect).

Quando ero bambina, **dovevo** andare a scuola a piedi. *When I was a child, I had to walk to school.*

Ieri **ho dovuto** comprare una nuova gomma. *Yesterday, I had to buy a new tyre.*

To say what one should have done, use the past conditional (see Unit 21 for forms of the past conditional).

Avresti dovuto telefonargli. *You should have called him.*

Avrei dovuto studiare di più. *I should have studied more.*

Insight

Use the present indicative (**devo, devi, ...**) to say one *must* do something, and the present conditional (**dovrei, dovresti, ...**) to soften the statement, and say one ought to do something. When using past tenses, use the perfect tense (**ho dovuto**) for one action or event, and the imperfect tense (**dovevo**) for something that happened regularly.

2 aver bisogno di

The phrase **aver bisogno di** (to have need of) can be used either with a verb (infinitive form) when talking about an action one has to take, or with a noun, talking about an object or objects one needs; it is normally used in a personalized way, referring to the person carrying out the action. **Avere** changes depending on the person referred to, while **bisogno** does not.

Giorgia **ha bisogno** di telefonare. *Giorgia needs to telephone.*

I ragazzi **hanno bisogno** di una mano.	*The boys need a hand.*
I nostri amici **hanno bisogno** di noi.	*Our friends need us.*
Ho bisogno di un bicchiere di vino.	*I need a glass of wine.*

3 bisogna

Bisogna can only be used with a verb (infinitive form), not an object. It is an impersonal verb with a general or impersonal meaning (one needs, it is necessary). It can be used in two different ways.

a in an impersonalized way, not referring to a particular person, followed by a verb in the infinitive.

Bisogna pagare alla cassa.	*One must pay at the cash desk.*
Bisogna indicare la data di partenza.	*One must indicate the departure date.*

b in a personalized way, referring to the person or people who are to carry out the action, using **che** and the subjunctive (see Unit 17).

Bisogna che tu paghi alla cassa.	*You need to pay at the cash desk.*
Bisogna che Lei indichi la data di partenza.	*You must indicate the departure date. (lit.: It is necessary that you indicate the departure date.)*

> ## Insight
> **Bisogna** is an impersonal verb (*it is necessary*); when used with an infinitive, it does not refer to a particular person. It can, however, be personalized by using **che** and the subjunctive, and referring to a particular person.

4 c'è bisogno di

In certain cases, **bisogna** can be replaced by a similar 'impersonal' phrase **c'è bisogno** (*there is need of*), which can also be used in two different ways.

a in an impersonalized way, followed by **di** and the infinitive.

C'è bisogno di firmare?   *Does one need to sign?*

b referring to a particular person or people, using **che** and the subjunctive.

Non c'è bisogno che Lei firmi.   *There isn't any need for you to sign.*

C'è bisogno can also be used with a noun, to talk about an object or objects one needs:

C'è bisogno di una firma?   *Is a signature needed?*
C'è bisogno di un metodo nuovo.   *A new method is needed.*

Insight
Cè **bisogno di** is an impersonal structure (*there is need*); when used with an infinitive, it does not refer to a particular person. Like **bisogna**, it can be personalized by using **che** and the subjunctive, and referring to a particular person. Unlike **bisogna**, it can also be used with a noun or nouns to say what is needed.

5 è necessario/essenziale

These impersonal expressions formed by **essere** + an adjective can be used in two ways.

a as an impersonal statement, followed directly by the infinitive.

È necessario fare il biglietto.   It is necessary to buy a ticket.

b specifying the person or people involved, using **che** and the subjunctive.

È essenziale che tutti i passeggeri   It is essential that all passengers
  facciano il biglietto.   buy a ticket.

Insight

All the impersonal expressions using **essere** and an adjective can be used not only in the present tense, but also in other tenses such as the imperfect (**era necessario**), future (**sarà necessario**) or present conditional (**sarebbe necessario**). However, the choice of tense for the subjunctive may have to vary to match.

---

6 occorre

Occorre (*it is necessary to*) can be used in the same two ways as the expressions shown above.

a as an impersonal statement, followed directly by the infinitive.

Occorre prendere il treno.   *It's necessary to take the train.*

b specifying the person or people involved, followed by **che** and the subjunctive.

Occorre che voi prendiate il treno   *You must be take the ten o'clock*
  delle dieci.   *train.*

Note: Any of the expressions listed above can, of course, be replaced simply with the verb **dovere**, as illustrated in §1 above.

7 occorre, occorrono, ci vuole, ci vogliono, serve, servono

Occorre/occorrono can also be used with a noun, referring to the object(s) needed. Unlike **aver bisogno di** (see above), **occorre** can be used without reference to a particular person, to make a general statement. If the object needed is singular, use **occorre** (singular); if plural, use the plural **occorrono.**

Per le cartoline **occorre** un francobollo da un euro.	*For postcards, one needs a one-euro stamp.*
Per la festa **occorrono** almeno 25 bottiglie di vino.	*For the party, one needs at least 25 bottles of wine.*

In these last examples, occorre (occorrono) can be replaced by **ci vuole (ci vogliono)** or **serve (servono).**

Per la festa **ci vuole** anche la musica.	*For the party, one needs music, too.*
Per la festa **ci vogliono** almeno 25 bottiglie di vino.	*For the party, one needs at least 25 bottles of wine.*
Per la festa **serve** anche la musica.	*For the party, one needs music, too.*
Per la festa **servono** almeno 25 bottiglie di vino.	*For the party, one needs at least 25 bottles of wine.*

Occorrere and **servire** can be personalized by adding an indirect object pronoun such as **mi, ti, gli,** etc. or the name or job (title) of the person in need.

Mi occorrono cinque francobolli.	*I need five stamps.*
Gli occorre la macchina.	*He needs the car.*
Quante uova **ti occorrono**?	*How many eggs do you need?*
Quanto **ti** serve?	*How much do you need?*
Al direttore **occorrono** le ultime cifre di questo mese.	*The manager needs the latest figures for this month.*

Even **ci vuole/ci vogliono** can be personalized by adding an indirect pronoun, which has to come before the **ci.**

Quanto tempo ti **ci vuole**?	*How long does it take you?*
Mi **ci vogliono** due chili di pomodori.	*I need two kilos of tomatoes.*

> **Insight**
> Out of the three verbs that express need when talking about objects (**occorre**, **ci vuole**, **serve**), the most common are probably **serve** (**servono**) and **ci vuole** (**ci vogliono**). However, **occorre** (**occorrono**) is the one most often found in recipes.

Language plus

1 Other impersonal verbs

As well as those you have seen above, there are many other 'impersonal' verbs, i.e. verbs that are used mainly in the third person (it). Some can be used with the indirect object pronouns **mi**, **ti**, **gli**, etc. (see Unit 16) to 'personalize' them. Most can be used either with the infinitive or with **che** and the subjunctive (see Unit 17). They include **basta** (*it is enough to*), **conviene** (*it is best, it is convenient, it is worth*), **pare**, **sembra** (*it appears, it seems*), **non importa** (*it doesn't matter*).

Look at these examples:

Basta guardare per capire come ha fatto.
One only has to look to see how he did it.

Basta che voi me lo chiediate.
All you have to do is ask me for it.

Conviene prendere il treno.
It's best to take the train.

Ti conviene prendere il treno.
It is best for you to take the train.

Mi pare di sentire qualcosa.
I think I can hear something.

Mi pare che tu non sia convinto.
It seems to me that you aren't convinced.

Non importa avere ragione, meglio essere felici!
Being right doesn't matter, it's better to be happy.

Non importa che tu mi dia I soldi subito.
It's not important for you to give me the money immediately.

Insight

Most of the impersonal verbs you have seen are used in the same way. They can either be followed directly by an infinitive (**Basta guardare!**) or by **che** and the subjunctive (**Basta che tu me lo dica**). If you want to refer to a specific person, you have to use **che** and the subjunctive.

2 *Impersonal phrases with* **essere** *and adjectives*

There are also several impersonal phrases formed by **essere** and various adjectives, such as è **necessario** (see section 5 above). Like the impersonal verbs, most can be used with the infinitive or with **che** and the subjunctive. Here are some examples.

The following phrases can only be used with che and the subjunctive.

È probabile (che)	*It's probable*
È improbabile (che)	*It's unlikely*

The following phrases can be used with the infinitive or with **che** and the subjunctive.

È possible	*It's possible*
È impossibile	*It's impossible*
È necessario	*It's necessary*
È essenziale	*It's essential*
È importante	*It's important*
È facile	*It's easy/it's likely**
È difficile	*It's difficult/it's unlikely**
È utile	*It's useful*
È inutile	*It's useless*
È bello	*It's nice*
È bene	*It's good*
È male	*It's bad*
È meglio	*It's better*
È peggio	*It's worse*
È preferibile	*It's preferable*

È naturale	*It's natural*
È normale	*It's normal*
È strano	*It's strange*

È possibile andare in pullman.	*It's possible to go by coach.*
È importante conservare lo scontrino.	*It is important to keep the receipt.*
È facile sbagliare.	*It's easy to make mistakes.*
È bello stare al mare.	*It's nice being at the seaside.*
È strano vedere Roma d'inverno.	*It's strange seeing Rome in winter.*
È peggio andare in campeggio che dormire in un ostello.	*It's worse camping than sleeping in a hostel.*
È possibile che lui sia ancora in Italia.	*It's possible that he is still in Italy.*
È probabile che noi partiamo sabato.	*It's likely that we'll leave on Saturday.*
È naturale che tu abbia voglia di tornare.	*It's natural that you should want to return.*
È strano che loro non abbiano telefonato.	*It's odd that they haven't telephoned.*
È meglio che Lei non torni tardi.	*It's better that you don't come back late.*

* È **facile** and È **difficile** followed by **che** and the subjunctive can mean *It's likely*, *It's unlikely* rather than their literal meaning:

È facile che ti scotti se non metti la crema.	*It's likely that you will burn if you don't put cream on.*
È difficile che ci siano ritardi.	*It's unlikely that there will be delays.*

Language in action

Exercise 1

At the railway station
Substitute the phrases in bold with a different phrase expressing need.

> **VIAGGIATORE** Un biglietto di andata a ritorno per Roma, per favore. Prima classe.
>
> **IMPIEGATO** A che ora vuole partire?
>
> **VIAGGIATORE** (1) **Devo essere** a Roma per le cinque di sera. Che treno (2) **bisogna prendere**?
>
> **IMPIEGATO** Se Lei (3) **ha bisogno di** essere a Roma per le cinque, (4) **dovrebbe** prendere il treno delle 12.35, che arriva a Roma alle 16.30. È un rapido, però, (5) **bisogna pagare** anche il supplemento.
>
> **VIAGGIATORE** Va bene. Quant'è?
>
> **IMPIEGATO** Sono 22 euro andata e ritorno, compreso il supplemento. (6) **Ha bisogno** di altre informazioni?
>
> **VIAGGIATORE** No, grazie.

Exercise 2

Give some advice to these famous (and less famous) figures. Using any of the expressions in this unit, say what you think they should do, either this week, this year or in general.

1 Il Papa
2 I bambini
3 L'insegnante
4 Tuo marito / tua moglie
5 Il Presidente della Repubblica
6 Il Primo Ministro della Gran Bretagna
7 Il Presidente degli USA
8 Il tuo vicino di casa
9 Tua madre / tuo padre
10 Il giornalaio

Exercise 3

Give practical advice to your friends and family using any of the expressions listed in this unit.

Esempio: Se non vuoi avere freddo, **bisogna che ti metta una maglia.**

1 Ragazzi, se volete giocare a calcio, …
2 Se stai a dieta, …
3 Se hai mal di stomaco, …
4 Se sei raffreddato, …
5 Se vuoi essere autonomo, …

Exercise 4

Agony aunt
You are the agony aunt on a local newspaper. You receive this letter. Write a reply, saying what the correspondent ought to do, and using as many of the expressions you have learned as possible.

Cara Irma

Tra poco nascerà la mia prima bimba e io non so come comportarmi per quanto riguarda gli annunci di nascita. Sui bigliettini si stampa solo il primo nome del bambino o anche eventuali altri nomi? Quando si inviano a parenti e amici? Subito dopo la nascita, oppure in occasione del battesimo, considerando che quest'ultimo potrebbe essere dopo circa due mesi? I confetti quando devono essere offerti? Solo al ricevimento di battesimo o anche prima a chi non vi parteciperà?
(Chiara, Monza)

Cara Chiara,

Ecco alcune regole che ti potranno essere di aiuto. Per gli annunci, non c'è bisogno che voi …

For examples of **confetti** and **bomboniere** given out at Italian weddings and baptisms, look at the websites listed in the **Taking it further** section.

Test yourself

Check your progress! Do you know how to do the following in Italian?

1 Complete the sentences using the correct form of **dovere**.

  a Non _____ lavorare troppo, bisogna passare un po' di tempo con la tua famiglia.

  b Anche le donne lavorano fuori casa, e gli uomini _____ aiutare in casa.

  c _____ andare a letto, domani devo alzarmi alle sei.

  d Quando prendiamo un caffè al bar, _____ pagare alla cassa prima di ordinare.

2 Complete these sentences with the correct form of dovere either in the present indicative (**devo** etc.) or the present conditional (**dovrei** etc.).

  a _____ portare a spasso il cane ma sono stanca.

  b _____ preparare la cena; gli ospiti arrivano tra un'oretta.

  c Domani mio marito _____ alzarsi alle sei perché va a Roma.

  d I nostri amici _____ visitare il centro storico ma forse non hanno tempo.

3 Complete these sentences using **aver bisogno di**.

  a Non ho ancora finito il tema. _____ altri due giorni.

  b Maura, _____ telefonare? Ti presto il cellulare se vuoi.

  c Non possiamo fare tutto da soli; _____ una mano.

  d _____ monete? Ve le posso dare io.

4 Complete these sentences with an appropriate verb, either in the infinitive or using **che** and the subjunctive.

  a Se vuoi partire domani, bisogna che tu me lo _____ .

  b Quando si prende un caffè alla stazione, bisogna _____ alla cassa.

  c Se vuoi metterti il costume da bagno, bisogna _____ a dieta.

  d Se vuoi che io ti prenoti l'albergo, bisogna che tu mi _____ il numero di telefono.

5 Match the two halves of the sentences.

  a Calma, Emanuela,   **i** non c'è bisogno di babysitter.

  b Se non piove   **ii** non c'è bisogno di arrabbiarti.

  c Se usiamo piatti di carta   **iii** non c'è bisogno di lavare i piatti.

  d Se i bambini sono a letto   **iv** non c'è bisogno di impermeabili.

6 Match the two halves of the sentences.

a Ci siamo fermati al garage, perché era necesssario

i che i passeggeri passino per il controllo.

b Prima di imbarcare, è necessario

ii mostrare i documenti.

c Quando si arriva alla frontiera, è necessario

iii che ci siano le infrastrutture.

d Per aumentare il turismo, è necessario

iv fare benzina.

7 Complete these sentences using **occorre, ci vuole** or **serve**. (There may be more than one possibility.)

a Per fare il tiramisu, _____ delle uova.

b Non _____ a niente arrabbiarsi.

c Quando i bambini sono piccoli, _____ molta pazienza.

d Da Roma a Napoli, in macchina _____ due ore.

8 Complete the sentences using **aver bisogno di, bisogna** or **c'è bisogno di.**

a Non _____ di accompagnarmi, prendo un taxi.

b Non _____ spegnere la luce, meglio lasciarla accesa.

c Sto riparando la bicicletta, _____ di un cacciavite.

d _____ di una mano, Sergio?

9 Complete these sentences using **basta, bisogna, conviene, non importa** or **sembra**.

a Se vuoi arrivare la mattina presto, _____ prendere il treno delle sei.

b _____ che lui sia più bravo di te. _____ studiare.

c _____ che il capo lavori meno di noi.

10 Complete these sentences using an appropriate phrase with **essere** and adjective.

a _____ che gli stranieri non parlino l'italiano.

b _____ che Gianni sia già andato a casa.

c _____ che i passeggeri dimentichino qualcosa sul treno.

d _____ avere rimpi anti

19

Expressing emotions and uncertainty

In this unit, you will learn how to:
- *express emotions or feelings*
- *express doubt and uncertainty*
- *express possibility and probability*
- *express a wish and request for others*

Language points
- *subjunctive after verbs of hoping, fearing and other emotions*
- *subjunctive after impersonal verbs and other verbs*
- *subjunctive after certain conjunctions*
- *subjunctive used in other situations*
- *deciding whether to use subjunctive or indicative*

Introduction

In Italian, you use the subjunctive whenever something is a possibility rather than a definite event or a certainty. It is often used after verbs expressing emotion, for example pleasure, hope, fear or sorrow. Compare these examples:

Puoi venire stasera?	*Can you come tonight?*
Spero che tu possa venire.	*I hope you can come.*
Michele è in ritardo.	*Michele is late.*
Temo che Michele sia in ritardo.	*I am afraid Michele is late.*

| Vi siete divertiti. | *You enjoyed yourselves.* |
| Sono contenta che vi siate divertiti. | *I am glad that you enjoyed yourselves.* |

In each of the examples above, the first statement or question contains the 'normal' (indicative) form of the verb; the second has the subjunctive form, used after **spero** (*I hope*), **temo** (*I fear*) and **sono contenta** (*I am glad*).

Focus on grammar

A subjunctive almost always depends on a main verb or verb phrase (the verb in the main part of the sentence) and is normally introduced by **che**. You have seen the subjunctive used after verbs or verb phrases expressing an opinion (Unit 17) and after verbs expressing need or obligation (Unit 18). The following sections demonstrate the range of contexts in which the subjunctive is used. The examples in this unit mainly demonstrate the present tense of the subjunctive; other tenses are covered in Unit 17 (perfect), Unit 20 (imperfect) and Unit 21 (pluperfect).

1 After certain verbs or verb phrases

The subjunctive is used after verbs or verb phrases which express the following:

a Emotions or feelings
Verbs expressing emotion such as **sperare** (*to hope*), **stupirsi** (*to be amazed*), **temere** (*to fear*), **vergognarsi** (*to be ashamed*), **(mi) piace** (*to be pleased*), **(mi) dispiace** (*to regret, be sorry*), **(mi) rincresce** (*to regret*) and verb phrases with **essere**, such as **essere contento** (*to be happy*), **essere arrabbiato** (*to be angry*), **essere sorpreso** (*to be surprised*), **essere stupito** (*to be amazed/astonished*), as well as phrases such as **è un peccato** (*it's a pity*).

Temo che lui **abbia** troppo da fare.	*I'm afraid he has too much to do.*
Mi dispiace che tu **sia** impegnata stasera.	*I'm sorry that you're busy tonight.*
È un peccato che i bambini non **possano** venire.	*It's a pity that the children can't come.*

Insight

The subjunctive is used after most verbs or phrases expressing emotion, whether positive or negative. This applies both to verbs (**vergognarsi, temere, sperare; mi piace, mi dispiace**) and to phrases using **essere** and an adjective (**essere contento, sorpreso, arrabbiato, stupito**).

b Belief, doubt or uncertainty

Verbs expressing belief, such as **credere, pensare, ritenere**, or verbs of doubt such as **dubitare**

Non credo che **costi** troppo.	*I don't think it costs too much.*
Dubito che il treno **parta** in orario.	*I doubt if the train will leave on time.*
Ritengono che **sia** una persona degna di fiducia.	*They maintain that he is a trustworthy person.*

Note, however, that in informal spoken language, verbs such as **credere, pensare, ritenere** are often followed by the normal indicative form, either present or future.

Credo che lui **sia** un parente di Amelia. (more formal)	*I think he's a relative of Amelia.*
Credo che lui **è** un parente di Amelia. (informal)	*I think he's a relative of Amelia.*
Penso che **vadano** a piedi. (formal)	*I think they'll go on foot.*
Penso che **vanno/andranno** a piedi. (informal)	*I think they'll go on foot.*

The use of the subjunctive with **pensare, credere** to express an opinion is covered more fully in Unit 17.

Some verbs, for example **dire, sapere, vedere,** are followed by the subjunctive only when they are negative or when (as in the case of **dicono**) they express hearsay.

So che **ha** una macchina.	*I know she has a car.*
Non so se **abbia** una macchina.	*I don't know if she has a car.*
Dico che **è** bravissimo.	*I say he's very clever.*
Dicono che lei **abbia fatto** vari lifting.	*They say that she has had several face lifts.*
Non dico che **sia** stupido.	*I'm not saying he's stupid.*
Vedo che tuo marito **è** stanco.	*I see that your husband is tired.*
Non vedo perché tu non **possa** farlo da solo.	*I don't see why you can't do it yourself.*

For other uses of **credere, pensare,** see Unit 17.

> **Insight**
>
> It is more difficult to give a rule for the use of the subjunctive after **dire, sapere,** and **vedere** because it is used with these verbs, when they convey uncertainty, as in negative statements or when conveying rumour and hearsay. Similarly, in spoken informal language, **credere** and **pensare** are often used without the subjunctive.

c Possibility, probability

Verbs and verb phrases expressing possibility and probability, such as è **possibile/impossibile,** è **probabile/improbabile/poco probabile** and **può darsi**

Può darsi che te lo **riparino** gratis.	*Maybe they'll repair it for you free of charge.*
È impossibile che lui non **abbia** capito.	*It's impossible for him not to have understood.*

The expressions è **facile/difficile** – as well as meaning *it is easy/ difficult* – can also mean *it is likely/unlikely*.

È facile che gli studenti **sbaglino**.   *It's likely that the students will get things wrong.*

È difficile che gli studenti **capiscano** tutto.   *It's unlikely that the students will understand everything.*

See Unit 18 for a fuller list of impersonal phrases of this type.

d Wishing, requesting
Verbs such as **volere, chiedere, ordinare,** when one wants someone else to do something

Voglio che lui **stia** più attento.   *I want him to be more careful.*

Vorrebbe che i bambini **facessero** meno rumore.   *He would like the children to make less noise.*

The conditional form **vorrei** is always followed by the imperfect tense of the subjunctive, as shown in the last example; both verb forms can be seen in more detail in Unit 20.

e Allowing, forbidding, denying
Verbs such as **permettere** (*to allow*), **vietare** (*to forbid*), **impedire** (*to prevent*) and **negare** (*to deny*)

Non **permette** che i bambini **giochino** in mezzo alla strada.   *She does not allow the children to play in the street.*

Nega che il cane **sia** pericoloso.   *She denies that the dog is dangerous.*

f Waiting, expecting
Verbs such as **aspettare, aspettarsi** (*to wait for, to expect*)

Mi aspetto che tu **sia** puntuale.   *I expect you to be punctual.*

Aspetto che **arrivino** loro per cominciare.   *I am waiting for them to arrive before starting.*

Insight

By now you are probably finding it hard to remember all the verbs which are followed by the subjunctive. With any verb that expresses emotion or uncertainty, it's always best to check. A good dictionary, whether bilingual or Italian only, will indicate whether a verb needs the subjunctive or not.

g Indirect questions

Verbs such as **mi chiedo, mi domando** (*I ask, I wonder why*) used to introduce an indirect question

Mi chiedo perché lui **sia** così nervoso.	*I wonder why he's so edgy.*

h Impersonal verbs or expressions ('it' verbs)

Impersonal verbs (e.g. **bisogna, conviene**) or phrases composed of **essere** and adjective (**è necessario, è essenziale**, etc.)

Bisogna che tu ti **dia** da fare.	*You have to get a move on.*

See also the examples of other impersonal verbs/verb phrases in c above. For a more complete list, see Unit 18.

2 After certain conjunctions

The subjunctive is often introduced by a conjunction, or joining word, which links up the two halves of the sentence, expressing purpose, condition, concession or other circumstance.

perché, affinché	*in order that*
in modo che, in maniera che	*in such a way that*
purché, a condizione che, a patto che	*on condition that*
benché, sebbene	*although*
comunque	*however*
a meno che	*unless*
prima che	*before*

nel caso che, qualora, caso mai	if, in case
nonostante che, malgrado che	despite
come se	as if
senza che	without

Vengo **a condizione che** tu **inviti** anche Edoardo.	I'll come on condition that you ask Edoardo too.
Me ne vado **a meno che** voi non mi **lasciate** in pace.	I'm going unless you leave me in peace.
Se ne va **senza che** lo salutiamo.	He goes off without us saying goodbye to him.
Sposto la macchina **perché** loro **possano** uscire.	I'll move the car so that they can get out.
Nonostante avessimo sonno, non volevamo perdere la festa.	Although we were sleepy, we didn't want to miss the party.
È **come se** non **capisse** niente.	It's as if he didn't understand anything.
Nel caso veniate in Inghilterra, vi lascio il mio indirizzo.	In case you come to England, I'll leave you my address.
Comunque sia la situazione, non possiamo lasciarlo solo.	Whatever the situation is like, we can't leave him alone.

Insight

You often need to use the subjunctive in a complex sentence, for example one which has a main clause and a dependent clause joined to it. Certain conjunctions (joining words) are always followed by the subjunctive. If in doubt, it's always best to check. A good dictionary, whether bilingual or Italian only, will indicate whether a conjunction is normally followed by the subjunctive or not.

3 After a superlative ('the most', etc.)

The subjunctive can be used in a relative clause (**che** clause) which follows a superlative adjective (**la cosa più bella, il libro meno**

interessante), but this is mainly found in more formal language, particularly written. The same applies to its use after **primo** (*first*), **ultimo** (*last*), **unico** and **solo** (*only*).

È la città **più bella** che io conosca.	*It's the most beautiful city I know.*
(È la città più bella che io conosco.)	
È l'**unico** paese che lui non **abbia** mai visitato.	*It's the only country that he's never visited.*
(È l'unico paese che lui non ha mai visitato.)	

4 After certain negatives

After the following negative expressions, the subjunctive is used.

Non è che lui **abbia** tanti soldi.	*It's not that he's got lots of money.*
Non c'è **nessuno che sappia** fare questo.	*There's no one who knows how to do this.*
Non c'è **niente che desideri** di più.	*There is nothing I would like better.*

5 In restricted relative clauses

Clauses like this usually start with **che**. They are general statements which are then 'limited' or 'restricted' by the relative clause, i.e. a clause beginning with **che** (*who, which* or *that*).

a Cerco una ragazza inglese.	*I am looking for an English girl.*
b Cerco una ragazza inglese **che ami i** bambini.	*I'm looking for an English girl who loves children.*
c Mary è una ragazza inglese **che ama** i bambini.	*Mary is an English girl who loves children.*

In (a), there is a generalization: any English girl will do. In (b), a restrictive clause is added: any English girl who loves children; this requires the subjunctive. In (c), a specific girl is mentioned; this example does not require the subjunctive.

Here are some further examples:

d Cerco un navigatore per la
macchina.

*I'm looking for a sat nav for
the car.*

e Cerco un navigatore **che non
costi** troppo.

*I'm looking for a sat nav which
doesn't cost too much.*

f Compro quel navigatore
giapponese **che non costa**
molto.

*I'm buying that Japanese sat nav
that doesn't cost much.*

Example (d) refers to any sat nav for the car. Example (e) refers to
any sat nav that doesn't cost too much. This latter restricted type of
clause needs the subjunctive.

In example (f), a specific sat nav is mentioned, so no subjunctive is
necessary.

Similarly, the subjunctive can be used in a restricted clause after
qualcuno or **qualcosa**.

C'è **qualcuno** che **sappia** parlare
cinese?

*Is there anyone who can speak
Chinese?*

Cerco **qualcosa** che non costi
troppo.

*I'm looking for something that
doesn't cost too much.*

6 After indefinite adjectives, pronouns or adverbs

The subjunctive is also used after indefinite adjectives, pronouns or
adverbs such as these.

....

| qualunque | *whatever, whichever* | chiunque | *whoever* |
| comunque | *however* | qualsiasi | *whatever, whichever* |

....

Qualunque cosa **faccia**, è sempre
mio figlio.

Whatever he does, he's still my son.

Chiunque tu sia, non ti permetto di entrare in casa mia.

Whoever you are, I won't allow you to come in to my house.

Comunque siano le cose, non cambio idea.

However things are, I won't change my mind.

Qualsiasi cosa **organizzi**, sbaglia sempre.

Whatever he organizes, he always makes mistakes.

7 When the subordinate or dependent clause comes before the main clause

When the two parts of the sentence are inverted, the subjunctive is used in the first part after **che**.

Si sa che il progetto non è perfetto.

Everyone knows the plan isn't perfect.

Che il progetto non sia perfetto, si sa già.

That the plan isn't perfect, everyone knows already.

8 As an imperative (order or command)

Normally, the subjunctive is found in a subordinate clause (one that depends on something else), but there are a few situations in which it is found as a main verb, standing on its own, for example as an imperative form. To give a polite request or instruction to someone you are on formal terms with, in Italian, you use the present subjunctive (**Lei** form, plural **Loro**). This is covered in detail in Unit 9.

Venga qui!

Come here!

Faccia presto!

Be quick!

Dica!

Tell me! (*what you want*)

Dicano, signori!

Tell me, ladies and gentlemen.

Insight

The imperative (**Lei** form) is really the only instance when the subjunctive is found as a main verb and not in a dependent clause. Although you don't need to learn all the forms by heart, there are certain key phrases which you will want to use or at least recognize, in a more formal context.

Language plus

How to avoid the subjunctive

If, after reading Units 17, 18 and 19, you prefer to avoid using the subjunctive, note the following:

a Verbs with same subject

Many verbs or verb phrases can be followed directly by the infinitive (**-are**, **-ere**, **-ire**) but only if the person in the main part of the sentence is the same person as in the subordinate (dependent) clause. Some examples of this have already been seen in Units 17 and 18.

Same subject in both parts of sentence:

Io credo **di avere** poche scarpe.   *I think I have few shoes.*

Different subject :

Teresa crede **che io abbia** troppe   *Teresa thinks that I have too many*
   scarpe.   *shoes.*

The same applies to sentences in the past:

Enrico ritiene **di aver reagito** con   *Enrico maintains he reacted*
   calma.   *calmly.*
Gli altri ritengono che Enrico **sia**   *The others maintain Enrico was*
   stato preso dal panico.   *panic-stricken.*

b Impersonal verbs

In the case of impersonal ('*it*' verbs), also listed in Unit 18, the subjunctive can be avoided if it is an impersonal statement that applies to everyone, i.e. if no specific person is mentioned. If, on the other hand, the statement is 'personalized' and a specific person mentioned, then **che** has to be used, followed by the subjunctive.

Impersonal, general statement:

Conviene **partire** presto.   *It's best to leave early.*

Personalized, specific person mentioned:

Conviene **che voi partiate** presto.   *It's best if you leave early.*

Insight

You can't avoid the subjunctive totally, but there are contexts where you can avoid it and use a simpler construction. Apart from the suggestions above, it's also worth remembering that in informal spoken Italian, the subjunctive is sometimes replaced by the normal indicative form. In any case, if you fail to use the subjunctive, Italians will still understand what you are saying.

Language in action

Exercise 1

Highlight all the examples of the subjunctive in the passage below. Then translate it into English, paying particular attention to the way the subjunctive is used.

Animali abbandonati

Vacanze, tempo di abbandoni. Ogni estate si stima che oltre 25.000 cani e migliaia di altri animali domestici vengano lasciati morire. "In Valtellina – spiega Anna Tosi, volontaria del canile Enpa –

riceviamo centinaia di richieste da persone che vogliono che i loro cani vengano tenuti nel nostro Centro." A meno che la situazione non migliori, il randagismo diventerà un pericolo sia per gli uomini che per il bestiame. Qualsiasi provvedimento sia stato varato finora, non ha ottenuto risultati incoraggianti. "La nuova legge appena approvata – aggiunge l'onorevole socialista Dino Mazza – si spera che faccia perdere l'abitudine agli italiani di mettere il cane a dicembre sotto l'albero e ad agosto sull'autostrada." Ma è difficile che questo problema sia risolto facilmente.

Adapted from *Corriere della Sera*

Exercise 2

Complete the gaps in this dialogue with an appropriate subjunctive form:

CHIARA	A che ora partono Michele e Caterina?
LUCIANA	È probabile che (1) _____ verso le sette. I bambini devono salutare i nonni prima di andare via. Almeno Michele vuole che (2) _____ i nonni.
CHIARA	Sono contenta che (3) _____ trovato bel tempo, e che si (4) _____ rilassati un poco.

Exercise 3

Rejoice or sympathize
Say whether you are pleased (sono contento/a), not pleased (mi dispiace), amazed (sono stupito/a, mi stupisce) or indifferent (non mi interessa) at what your friend tells you. Remember that verbs expressing emotion require the subjunctive, either past or present.

Esempio: Ti piace Giorgio? È fidanzato!
Mi dispiace che sia fidanzato.

1 La Scozia ha vinto la partita e gioca contro l'Italia stasera.
2 Domani c'è sciopero. Non ci sono lezioni.

3 Mia madre è caduta. Si è rotta il braccio.
4 Il mio cane è stato investito da una macchina.
5 L'insegnante boccia Giovanni all'esame di storia contemporanea.
6 Stasera mia zia prepara la pasta con le vongole.
7 Mio fratello ha preso in prestito da me un CD e l'ha graffiato.
8 Viene anche la mia ex-ragazza stasera.
9 I miei genitori mi danno cento euro per il mio compleanno.
10 Mio padre mi offre un viaggio a Parigi per festeggiare l'onomastico.
11 Gianna deve stare a dieta perché è ingrassata di cinque chili.
12 Fra me e il calcio, il mio ragazzo preferisce il calcio.

Test yourself

Check your progress! Do you know how to do the following in Italian?

1 Complete these sentences expressing emotion using the present subjunctive form of the verbs in brackets.
  a Mi dispiace che tu non _____ (potere) venire stasera.
  b Sono contenta che loro _____ (sposarsi).
  c Mi stupisco che lui _____ (avere) 40 anni, non li dimostra.
  d Temo che il medico non _____ (essere) molto bravo.

2 Complete these sentences expressing uncertainty using the present subjunctive form of the verbs in brackets.
  a Non credo che il ristorante _____ (essere) aperto la domenica.
  b Dubito che i risultati _____ (essere) soddisfacenti.
  c Il capo ritiene che gli insegnanti _____ (dovere) essere qualificati.
  d Non penso che la carne _____ (fare) bene alla salute.

3 Complete these sentences expressing possibility using the subjunctive form of the verbs in brackets.
  a È' possibile che mia madre _____ (rimanere) in ospedale ancora per un po'.
  b È' impossibile che si _____ (potere) morire di polmonite.
  c Può darsi che lui _____ (preferire) viaggiare in treno.
  d È' probabile che gli uffici _____ (essere) chiusi.

4 Complete these sentences expressing wishes/requests/permission using the subjunctive form of the verbs in brackets.

  a Vogliamo che le nostre famiglie _____ (essere) protette.

  b Chiede che la cucina _____ (venire) pulita ogni sera.

  c Ordina che i cani non _____ (venire) ammessi al ristorante.

  d Permette che i bambini _____ (guardare) la TV fino a mezzanotte.

5 Complete these sentences using the present subjunctive of an appropriate verb from the box.

> andare migliorare risolversi timbrare

  a Bisogna che il problema _____ al più presto possibile.

  b Conviene che i nonni _____ in montagna dove fa fresco.

  c È' necessario che i passeggeri _____ i biglietti.

  d È' importante che l'economia _____ .

6 Match the two halves of the sentences.

  a Prima che tu vada via,   **i** vogliono fare del loro meglio.

  b Nel caso in cui venga rubato il cellulare,   **ii** bisogna chiamare subito la compagnia telefonica.

  c Mangia di notte   **iii** senza che sua madre la veda.

  d Benché gli atleti siano stanchi,   **iv** parliamo del tuo futuro lavoro.

7 Complete these sentences with the appropriate form of the present subjunctive of the verbs in brackets.

  a Non è che l'albergo _____ (essere) lontano, ma i mezzi di trasporto non funzionano.

  b È' l'uomo più brutto che io _____ (conoscere).

  c Non c'è nessuno che mi _____ (potere) aiutare.

8 Choose the correct option.

  a   **i** Vorrei comprare una casa che non sia troppo grande.

      ii Vorrei comprare una casa che non è troppo grande.

  b   **i** Cerco un operaio che possa riparare i tubi del bagno.

      ii Cerco un operaio che può riparare i tubi del bagno.

9 Complete the sentences with **chiunque, comunque, qualunque** or **qualsiasi**.

a _____ sia, non voglio che lui sappia la notizia.

b _____ venga, non posso ospitare nessuno a casa mia.

c _____ motivo abbia, si è comportato in modo vergognoso.

10 Complete these sentences as appropriate. One needs the subjunctive and the other doesn't.

a Non penso che tu …

b Non penso di …

20

Expressing wishes or polite requests

In this unit, you will learn how to:
- *express a wish for yourself*
- *express a wish involving someone else*
- *make a polite request*
- *allow someone to do something*
- *get someone to do something*
- *order, suggest, invite, encourage someone to do something*

Language points
- *conditional* vorrei *to express a wish or request*
- *forms of imperfect subjunctive*
- vorrei che *and imperfect subjunctive*
- *conditional used to express a polite request*
- *other uses of the conditional*
- *other uses of the imperfect subjunctive*
- chiedere, ordinare a qualcuno di
- fare, lasciare *and infinitive*

Introduction

Look at these examples of statements expressing a wish or polite request.

Vorrei mangiare fuori stasera.	*I should like to eat out tonight.*
Vorrei che lui non fosse così ostinato.	*I wish he were not so stubborn.*
Le dispiacerebbe aprire la finestra?	*Would you mind opening the window?*
Ci chiede di non fumare.	*She asks us not to smoke.*

Focus on grammar

1 *Expressing a wish (using* **volere***)*

Units 17, 18 and 19 showed how the subjunctive is used after verbs of emotion, hoping, or fearing; it is also used after verbs of wishing (e.g. **volere**) and requesting (e.g. chiedere) where another person is involved. When expressing a wish for oneself, **voglio** or **vorrei** can be followed directly by the infinitive (see Unit 14 for further examples.) But when expressing a wish that someone else would do something, **voglio** or **vorrei** have to be followed by che then the subjunctive. Look at these two examples.

Domani **voglio lavare** la macchina.	*Tomorrow, I want to wash the car.*
Domani **voglio che** mio marito **lavi** la macchina.	*Tomorrow, I want my husband to wash the car.*

Using the conditional and the subjunctive
Frequently, verbs of wishing are expressed in the present conditional (*I would like*, etc.) and are followed by the imperfect tense of the subjunctive rather than the present tense.

Vorrei che tu mi **portassi** fuori ogni tanto.	*I would like you to take me out every so often.*
Vorrebbe che Lei gli **telefonasse**.	*He would like you to telephone him.*

When a wish is expressed that the action had or hadn't taken place, the pluperfect tense of the subjunctive (see Unit 21) is used.

| **Desidererei** che non **fosse** mai **successa** questa cosa. | *I wish this had never happened.* |
| **Vorrei** che tu non gli **avessi** mai **parlato**. | *I wish you had never spoken to him.* |

Insight

The present conditional and imperfect subjunctive are often found together in the same sentence. While it's possible to find the conditional on its own, the imperfect subjunctive can virtually only be found in a dependent clause. Quite often these two verb forms are found together in a conditional sentence.

2 How to form the conditional (present tense)

The conditional mood in English is expressed by the words *would*, *should*. It is called 'conditional' because the statement will only become fact on condition that something happens. The forms of the present conditional are formed by taking the infinitive (-**are**, -**ere**, -**ire**), dropping the final -**e**, and adding the conditional endings as shown below. The -**are** verbs also change the -**a**- of their stem to -**e**-.

Present conditional endings
-ei, -esti, -ebbe, -emmo, -este, ebbero

Verbs ending in -are

parlare

parler**ei**	parler**emmo**
parler**esti**	parler**este**
parler**ebbe**	parler**ebbero**

Verbs ending in -ere

mettere

metter**ei**	metter**emmo**
metter**esti**	metter**este**
metter**ebbe**	metter**ebbero**

Verbs ending in -ire

partire

part**irei**	partir**emmo**
partir**esti**	partir**este**
partir**ebbe**	partir**ebbero**

The verbs with an irregular conditional form are the same verbs with an irregular future form (see Unit 13) where the stem (the base of the verb) undergoes a change:

- verbs which drop the -e- of the stem, for example: **andare** (**andrei, andresti**); **avere** (**avrei**); **cadere** (**cadrei**); **dovere** (**dovrei**); **potere** (**potrei**); **sapere** (**saprei**); **vedere** (**vedrei**); **vivere** (**vivrei**).

- verbs which drop the -e- or -i- and then undergo a further change, for example: **rimanere** (**rimarrei**); **tenere** (**terrei**); **valere** (3rd person form **varrebbe**); **venire** (**verrei**); **volere** (**vorrei**).

- verbs with a contracted infinitive, for example **bere, tradurre**, have double **rr** (**berrei, tradurrei**).

- verbs whose infinitive ends in -ciare, -giare which drop the **i** since it is no longer needed to soften the **c** or **g**: **cominciare** (**comincerei**); **lasciare** (**lascerei**), **mangiare** (**mangerei**).

- verbs with infinitive forms ending in -care, -gare which add **h** in order to keep the hard **c** or **g** sound: **cercare** (**cercherei**); **pagare** (**pagherei**).

- one-syllable verbs **dare, dire, fare, stare** (**darei, direi, farei, starei**).

- **essere** (**sarei**).

3 When to use the present conditional

a To express a wish

Vorrei un panino con prosciutto.   *I would like a ham sandwich.*

More examples of the present conditional can be found in Unit 14.

b To express a request more politely

Le **dispiacerebbe** passarmi la valigia?	*Would you mind passing me my suitcase?*
Potrei venire più tardi?	*Could I come later?*
Potrebbe prestarmi il suo orario?	*Could you lend me your timetable?*
Mi **farebbe** una cortesia?	*Could you do me a favour?*

The phrase **fare una cortesia** can be replaced by **fare un piacere** or **fare un favore**.

Insight

Of all the uses of the present conditional, the two above are the ones you are most likely to use: expressing a wish or a request politely. You'll find it useful to learn and memorize some common polite phrases with the conditional, for example **Le dispiacerebbe ...? Potrebbe ...? (Mi) farebbe ...?**

---

c To make a statement sound less categorical

Non **saprei** spiegartelo.	*I wouldn't know how to explain it to you.*
Dovrei scrivere delle cartoline.	*I ought to write some postcards.*

Compare this last sentence with:

Devo mandare delle cartoline.	*I must send some postcards.*

d To express rumour, hearsay or report

The conditional mood is often used to tell us what someone said, or what was written in the press. It is translated by a straightforward present indicative in English.

Secondo la stampa, il governo **sarebbe** contrario.	*According to the press, the government is against it.*
Secondo Gianni, Maria **avrebbe** più di 40 anni.	*According to Gianni, Maria is over 40.*

e When a condition is implied or stated

The conditional mood is used when an action is dependent on certain conditions being fulfilled; sometimes these conditions are stated, sometimes they are just implied. (See Unit 22 for further examples of conditional sentences.)

Andrei in vacanza ma non ho soldi.	*I would go on holiday, but I don't have any money.*
Io **partirei** subito.	*I would leave straightaway.*

(In the last example, a condition is implied but not stated, for example, *if I were you, if I were able*.)

Se avessi i soldi, **comprerei** una macchina nuova.	*If I had the money, I would buy a new car.*

f Indirect or reported speech or after a verb of saying, thinking, etc.

Dice che **verrebbe** domani.	*He says he would come tomorrow.*
Penso che **sarebbe** meglio partire presto.	*I think it would be better to leave early.*

For examples of reported speech in the past tense, see Unit 21.

4 How to form the imperfect subjunctive

The imperfect subjunctive is formed by taking the stem of the infinitive – i.e. the infinitive without the final -are, -ere, -ire – then adding the imperfect subjunctive endings, e.g. parlare – **parlassi**. The examples of the subjunctive forms are often shown with **che** since the subjunctive rarely stands on its own. Here are the forms of the imperfect subjunctive for the three main groups of verbs.

---

parlare (che io) parlassi

parl**assi**	parl**assimo**
parl**assi**	parl**aste**
parl**asse**	parl**assero**

---

mettere (che io) mettessi

mett**essi**	mett**essimo**
mett**essi**	mett**este**
mett**esse**	mett**essero**

---

partire (che) io partissi

part**issi**	part**issimo**
part**issi**	part**iste**
part**isse**	part**issero**

Only a few verbs vary from this pattern. They include the following:

bere	*to drink*	(che) io **bevessi**
essere	*to be*	(che) io **fossi**
stare	*to be*	(che) io **stessi**
fare	*to do*	(che) io **facessi**
dire	*to say*	(che) io **dicessi**
dare	*to give*	(che) io **dessi**

---

5 When to use the imperfect subjunctive

The imperfect subjunctive is often used after the following tenses in the main clause: imperfect, present conditional. It can also be used after other tenses: the past definite, the perfect or pluperfect, the past conditional and occasionally the present.

• after the imperfect

Mio marito **aveva** paura che l'albergo **fosse** troppo caro.

My husband was afraid that the hotel was too dear.

• after the present conditional

Sarebbe meglio che tu non mi **chiedessi** questo.

It would be better if you didn't ask me this.

• after the past definite

Il ladro **si lanciò** dalla finestra perché la polizia non lo **prendesse**.

The thief threw himself out of the window so that the police would not catch him.

• after the perfect

La signora ci **ha chiesto** se **ci trovassimo** bene in Italia.

The lady asked us if we were enjoying Italy.

• after the pluperfect

L'insegnante ci **aveva chiesto** se **tenessimo** un diario.

The teacher had asked us if we kept a diary.

• after the past conditional

Non **avrei** mai **pensato** che lui **potesse** fare una cosa del genere.

I should never have thought that he could do a thing like that.

• after the present

Penso che l'autista **avesse** qualche problema.

I think the driver had some problem or other.

Insight

In some of the examples given above, for example those using **chiedere**, the subjunctive form is often replaced by the indicative or 'normal' verb tense, at least in informal and/or spoken language.

In these cases, the choice of whether to use the subjunctive or not is down to register (formal or informal) and context.

Language plus

There are other ways in which you can ask someone to do something without using the subjunctive. Generally, these are combinations of verb and the person being asked and the action that the person is being asked to carry out, with or without prepositions linking these different elements.

1 chiedere a qualcuno di fare qualcosa, insegnare a qualcuno a fare qualcosa

Verbs such as **chiedere** use **a** with the person being given the instruction, then di to link with the infinitive expressing the action the person is being asked to carry out.

Chiedo *al* cameriere *di* portare il menù.	I'll ask the waiter to bring the menu.
I tedeschi **hanno ordinato** *alla* cameriera *di* portare cinque birre.	The Germans ordered the waitress to bring five beers.

You can replace the reference to the person (**al cameriere, alla cameriera**) with an indirect pronoun such as **mi, ti, gli** (see Unit 16). The examples above would then become:

Gli chiedo di portare il menù.

I'll ask him to bring the menu.

I tedeschi **le** hanno ordinato di portare cinque birre.

The Germans ordered her to bring five beers.

Other verbs used in this way include verbs of advising such as **consigliare, dire, suggerire** and verbs of permitting or allowing such as **consentire, permettere.**

Cosa **ci consigli di** fare?

What do you advise us to do?

Non **permette agli** ospiti **di** usare la doccia dopo le otto.

She doesn't allow guests to use the shower after eight o'clock.

Il suo contributo **mi ha consentito di** completare la ricerca.

His contribution allowed me to finish my research.

Il padrone del ristorante **ha detto ai** clienti **di** scegliere quello che volevano.

The owner of the restaurant told the customers to choose what they wanted.

Here are some of the commonest verbs normally linked to the verb infinitive by **di.**

chiedere	*to ask*
comandare	*to command*
consentire	*to allow*
consigliare	*to advise*
dire	*to say, tell*
domandare	*to ask*
impedire	*to prevent*
ordinare	*to order*
permettere	*to permit*
proibire	*to forbid*
promettere	*to promise*
ricordare	*to remind*
suggerire	*to suggest*
vietare	*to forbid*

In addition, a few verbs take an indirect object or indirect object pronoun but are linked to the infinitive by **a.**

Insegno ai bambini **a** nuotare.   *I'm teaching the children to swim.*
Ti insegno a fare il tiramisu.   *I'll teach you to make tiramisu.*

Insight

Verbs and verb infinitives are connected in different ways.
When another person is involved as well (e.g. **il cameriere**),
connections have to be made both with the person and
with the action he/she is carrying out. The most common
combination is **a** with the person (e.g. **cameriere**) and **di**
linking the verb with the infinitive (e.g. **chiedo di portare**):
Chiedo al cameriere di portare il menù.

---

2 invitare qualcuno a fare qualcosa

Some verbs (listed below) are followed directly by the person being
given the instruction or invitation, then by **a** and the infinitive.

Hanno invitato mio marito **a** fare   *They have invited my husband to*
     una conferenza.   *give a lecture.*

With these verbs, the direct object pronoun is used: **mi, ti, lo, la, ci,
vi, li, le** (note the optional agreement of the past participle **invitata**
with the object).

Mi ha invitata a venire al mare   *He invited me to come to the*
     con lui.   *seaside with him.*
Ti ha convinta a comprare quella   *Did he persuade you to buy that*
     borsa?   *bag?*

aiutare	*to help*
costringere	*to force*
convincere	*to persuade*
forzare	*to force*
incoraggiare	*to encourage*
invitare	*to invite*
obbligare	*to oblige*
persuadere	*to persuade*

The verb **pregare** (*to beg*) takes a direct object but is followed by **di**. It is often used in polite requests or invitations.

La prego di seguirmi.   *I beg you to follow me.*

> **Insight**
> Another common combination is the person (e.g. **mia suocera**) as direct object with the verb (e.g. **invito**) and infinitive (e.g. **stare**) linked to the verb by **a**: Invito mia suocera a stare a casa mia.

3 fare, lasciare, sentire, vedere qualcuno fare qualcosa

Other verbs can be followed directly by the person then directly by the infinitive. The pronoun, if used, must be a direct object pronoun.

lasciare fare (*to allow, let, make someone do something*)

La lascia salire sul treno senza   *He lets her get on the train without*
  biglietto.   *a ticket.*
Mi ha fatto salire senza biglietto.   *He let me get on without a ticket.*

sentire (*to hear*), **vedere** (*to see*)

L'ho sentito entrare.   *I heard him come in.*
L'ho visto salire sul treno. *I saw him get on the train.*

Note: A list of some common verbs and the ways in which they connect to the verb infinitive can be found in the Grammar Appendix §13.2.

4 Verb and infinitive/verb with **che** and subjunctive

Finally, look at the difference between the following examples: in column a, the verb is followed directly by the infinitive, while in column b, **che** and the subjunctive are used.

a verb + infinitive	b che + subjunctive
Chiedo a Gianna **di venire** con noi.	Chiedo **che** Gianna **venga** con noi.
I ask Gianna to come with us.	*I ask (someone, not necessarily Gianna herself) that Gianna come with us.*
Marco mi chiede **di pagare**.	Marco chiede **che** io **paghi**.
Marco asks me to pay.	*Marco asks that I pay.*
Non permette a suo marito **di uscire** la sera.	Non permette **che** suo marito **esca** la sera.
She doesn't allow her husband to go out in the evening.	*She doesn't allow that her husband goes out in the evening.*

Language in action

Exercise 1

Expressing a polite request
Ask someone to do something about these situations, using the **Lei** form of the given verb in the present conditional, as in section 3 above.

Esempio: Potrebbe passarmi …? Le dispiacerebbe darmi …?

1 *You need to find the nearest bus stop.*   indicare
2 *The room is very stuffy.*   aprire
3 *Someone has left the door open and there is a draught.* chiudere
4 *You can't reach the sugar; it's near the man opposite.*   passare
5 *You've forgotten your pen and need to fill in a form.*   prestare
6 *You need to know the time.*   dire
7 *Someone's suitcase is blocking your way.*   spostare
8 *You need some help in moving something.*   dare una mano

Exercise 2

In this passage, underline or highlight all the verbs in the subjunctive, as well as the verb, verb phrase, conjunction or other structure that they depend on. Then translate it into English.

Sleeping over at my grandmother's
Era strano quel che succedeva quando dormivo con mia nonna ... quando mi risvegliavo, mi ritrovavo nella stessa posizione ... Penso che mia nonna si svegliasse molto prima di me e mi risistemasse nella stessa posizione, ma era bello immaginare che avessimo dormito in quella posizione per tutta la notte. In ogni caso era bellissimo che lei facesse di tutto per farmelo credere.

From Lara Cardella: *Volevo i pantaloni* (Edizioni Oscar Originals)

Exercise 3

In the following passage, the constructions in bold require the verb following to be in the subjunctive. The infinitive of these verbs is supplied. Work out which form of the subjunctive is required and fill it in.

My past life in Milan
Ogni tanto andavo a casa di Bruno ed **era facile che** (1) _____ (restare) fino alle due di notte a chiacchierare, perché era l'unica persona con cui io (2) _____ (potere) parlare liberamente. Lui **voleva che** io gli (3) _____ (parlare) in inglese, perché stava studiando la lingua, ma io non mi sentivo più a mio agio **nonostante** (4) _____ (essere) la mia madre lingua. Mia madre non sapeva né mi chiedeva mai con chi (5) _____ (uscire) e **lasciava che** io (6) (prendere) la macchina senza farmi domande di nessun tipo.

Test yourself

Check your progress! Do you know how to do the following in Italian?

1 Match the two halves of the sentences.
   - **a** Voglio che
   - **b** Il direttore vuole
   - **c** Vogliamo
   - **d** Vuoi che

   - **i** vendere l'impresa.
   - **ii** ti accompagni?
   - **iii** due biglietti per sabato sera.
   - **iv** tu mi ascolti almeno una volta.

2 Match the two halves of the sentences.
   - **a** Vorrei
   - **b** Mia madre vorrebbe che
   - **c** Vorremmo
   - **d** Vorresti

   - **i** io tornassi in Italia.
   - **ii** andare al cinema con me?
   - **iii** vedere i nostri figli più spesso.
   - **iv** affittare un piccolo appartamento in centro.

3 Complete these sentences with the present conditional of the verbs in brackets.
   - **a** Se abitassimo in Italia, i nostri figli _____ (parlare) italiano.
   - **b** Se avessi i soldi, _____ (comprare) la casa in Toscana.
   - **c** Se potessi, _____ (partire) con lui.
   - **d** Se Gino potesse, _____ (venire) a Napoli.

4 Complete these polite requests with the appropriate verb in the present conditional.
   - **a** Mi _____ un piacere?
   - **b** Mi _____ passare la borsa?
   - **c** Le _____ aprire un po' la finestra?
   - **d** Mi _____ far vedere le scarpe nere?

5 Complete these sentences with an appropriate verb in the present conditional.
   - **a** Se io avessi i soldi, _____ una nuova macchina.
   - **b** Se avessimo più tempo, _____ una vacanza.
   - **c** Se abitassi vicino ai miei genitori, _____ stare con i miei figli.
   - **d** Se tu potessi, _____ lingue?

6 Complete these sentences with an appropriate verb in the imperfect subjunctive.
   - **a** Se tu _____ più attenta, avresti dei voti migliori.
   - **b** Se io _____ in te, cercherei un nuovo posto.

c Se i nostri amici _____ in tempo, potrebbero venire anche loro a teatro.

d Se _____ tempo, potremmo leggere qualche libro.

7 Match the two halves of the sentences so that they make sense.

a Avevamo paura che	**i** tutti i passeggeri scendessero.
b Sarebbe meglio che	**ii** io finissi prima di mezzogiorno.
c Il capo voleva che	**iii** la macchina si fermasse per strada.
d L'autista del pullman chiedeva che	**iv** facessimo tutto noi.

8 Complete the sentences with the appropriate prepositions.

a Chiedi _____ cameriera _____ portarci il menù.

b Mia madre mi permette _____ uscire ma solo il sabato.

c Il capo ci ha ordinato _____ prendere una giornata libera dal lavoro.

9 Complete these sentences with a suitable verb (e.g. **invitare**, **convincere**) and preposition.

a La mia amica mi ha _____ _____ stare a casa sua quest'estate.

b _____ i nostri amici _____ venire con noi al cinema.

c Il fidanzato di Susy l'ha _____ _____ trasferirsi al centro.

10 Complete these sentences using **fare, lasciare**, etc.

a Vieni in macchina con me, ti _____ fare un giro del paese.

b _____ finire questo lavoro, devo finirlo per stasera.

c Marco arriva, l'_____ uscire di casa cinque minuti fa.

d I bambini giocano insieme, meglio _____ giocare.

21

Expressing regrets

In this unit, you will learn how to:
- *express regrets and wishes*
- *say you are sorry*
- *talk about an action which would have taken place (if...)*
- *express rumour or hearsay*
- *use reported speech*

Language points
- *forms of pluperfect subjunctive*
- *uses of pluperfect subjunctive*
- *forms of past conditional*
- *uses of past conditional*

Introduction

When expressing a regret or a wish that the action had or hadn't taken place, the main verb in the present or past conditional is followed by the pluperfect tense of the subjunctive.

Preferirebbe (conditional) che io l'avessi avvertito (pluperfect subjunctive).	*He would prefer me to have warned him.*
Vorrei (conditional) che non fossimo mai venuti (pluperfect subjunctive).	*I wish that we had never come.*

| Avrebbe preferito (past conditional) che la mamma avesse preparato (pluperfect subjunctive) le polpettine. | *He would have preferred his mum to have prepared meatballs.* |

In a simple sentence, involving only the person carrying out the action, the verb, whether in the conditional or past conditional, can be followed directly by the infinitive.

Preferirei non essere qui in questo momento.	*I would prefer not to be here right now.*
Avrebbe voluto non esserci.	*He would have liked not to be there.*
Avremmo voluto vederlo.	*We would like to have seen it.*

Focus on grammar

1 How to form the pluperfect subjunctive

The pluperfect subjunctive is formed by combining the imperfect subjunctive of **avere** or **essere** (whichever the verb normally takes) and the appropriate past participle, e.g. **mangiato, bevuto, partito**. Here, the pluperfect subjunctive is shown following the verb volere to express a regret or a wish for something that could have happened but hasn't.

••

Vorrebbe che ...

avessi mangiato	**avessimo** mangiato
avessi mangiato	**aveste** mangiato
avesse mangiato	**avessero** mangiato

••

Vorrebbe che ...

fossi venuto/a	**fossimo** venuti/e
fossi venuto/a	**foste** venuti/e
fosse venuto/a	**fossero** venuti/e

2 When to use the pluperfect subjunctive

Like the other tenses of the subjunctive, the pluperfect subjunctive is generally used in a dependent clause, after certain verbs or after certain conjunctions. In general, the pluperfect subjunctive is used when the main verb is in a past tense or present or past conditional.

An overview of the different contexts in which the subjunctive is used can also be found in Unit 19. Here are the main contexts in which the pluperfect subjunctive is used:

a After verbs expressing an opinion (see also Unit 17) such as **credere** and **pensare**. Look at these pairs of examples; in the first example of each pair, the pluperfect indicative (the normal verb form) is used; in the second example, the pluperfect subjunctive is used.

With avere

Avevi già **conosciuto** Teresa?	*Had you already met Teresa?*
Pensavo che **tu avessi** già conosciuto Teresa.	*I thought you had already met Teresa.*

With essere

Eri già **stata** a Pompei?	*Had you already been to Pompei?*
Pensavo che **tu fossi** già stata a Pompei.	*I thought you had already been to Pompei.*

> **Insight**
>
> In informal spoken Italian, some speakers replace the
> subjunctive after **pensare** with a plain past tense: **Pensavo
> che eri già stata a Pompei**. This is not correct Italian, but it
> has become quite common.

b After verbs and verb phrases expressing wish or regret, as shown
above, such as **volere, preferire, desiderare**.

Avrei voluto che tu mi **avessi chiesto** il permesso prima di uscire.	*I would have liked you to ask my permission before going out.*
Avremmo preferito che il convegno **fosse stato** a maggio.	*We would have preferred the conference to have been in May.*

> **Insight**
>
> The pluperfect subjunctive represents something which might
> or might not have happened. It is a verb of uncertainty and
> subjectivity, used to express opinion or possibility, rather
> than fact. Even if you'd prefer not to use the subjunctive,
> educated Italian speakers can't really get by without it.

c After verbs and verb phrases expressing emotion, such as **(mi)
piace** (*to be pleased*), **(mi) dispiace** (*to regret, be sorry*), **(mi)
rincresce** (*to regret*), **sperare** (*to hope*), **stupirsi** (*to be amazed*),
temere (*to fear*), **vergognarsi** (*to be ashamed*), and verb phrases
with **essere**, such as **essere contento** (*to be happy*), **essere arrabbiato**
(*to be angry*), **essere sorpreso** (*to be surprised*), **essere stupito** (*to be
astonished*), as well as phrases such as **è un peccato** (*it's a pity*).

Speravo che mio figlio **avesse dato** da mangiare al gatto.	*I hoped that my son had fed the cat.*
Mi dispiaceva che i nostri amici non **fossero venuti**.	*I was sorry that our friends hadn't come.*

Insight

In a complex sentence, wherever verbs expressing emotion (positive or negative) are involved, the subjunctive is generally required. In the examples above, the verb expressing emotion is in the imperfect tense and the pluperfect subjunctive is used in the dependent clause.

d After verbs of doubt, such as **dubitare**, and verbs expressing rumour and hearsay.

Si diceva che lei **avesse sposato** il primo marito solo per i soldi.	*It was said that she had married her first husband only for his money.*
Dubitavo che Gino **fosse stato** direttore dell'impresa, come diceva.	*I doubted whether Gino had been head of the company, as he said.*

Insight

Dire is followed by the subjunctive only when negative or (as in the case of **si dice/dicono**) expressing hearsay.

Dico che è bravissima.	*I say she's very clever.*
Dicevano (Si diceva) che lei **fosse stata** molto furba.	*They said she had been very cunning.*

e After phrases of possibility or probability such as è **possibile/impossibile**, è **probabile/improbabile/poco probabile** and **può darsi**.

Era probabile che mio marito **a vesse bruciato** il sugo di pomodoro.	*It was likely that my husband had burned the tomato sauce.*
Era impossibile che lui **fosse** arrivato in meno tempo di noi.	*It was impossible for him to have got there in less time than us.*

f After verbs of allowing, forbidding, denying, waiting and expecting, such as **permettere** (*to allow*), **vietare** (*to forbid*),

impedire (*to prevent*), **negare** (*to deny*), **aspettare/aspettarsi** (*to wait for, to expect*).

Ci aspettavamo che gli studenti **avessero** festeggiato troppo e che **si fossero** tutti ubriacati.	*We expected that the students would have celebrated too much and would have got drunk.*

g After verbs that introduce an indirect question, such as **chiedere**, **domandare**.

Mi chiedevo perché i nostri cognati **avessero venduto** la casa.	*I wondered why our brother and sister-in-law had sold the house.*

h After impersonal verbs (e.g. **bisogna, conviene**) or verb phrases composed of **essere** and adjective (e.g. **è necessario, è essenziale, è importante**).

Era importante che i passeggeri **avessero fatto** il controllo di passaporti prima di imbarcare.	*It was important for passengers to have gone through passport control before boarding.*
Era essenziale che gli animali **fossero stati** vaccinati prima di essere trasportati.	*It was essential that the animals had been vaccinated before being transported.*

i After certain conjunctions such as **perché** (*in order that*), **in modo che** (*in such a way that*), **a condizione che** (*on condition that*), **benché** (*although*), **a meno che** (*unless*), **prima che** (*before*), **nel caso che** (*if, in case*), **nonostante che** (*despite*), **come se** (*as if*), **senza che** (*without*).

Se n'era andato **senza che** l'**avessimo salutato**.	*He had gone off without us having said goodbye to him.*

Insight

There are many types of conjunction and each of them has
a different relationship with the two parts of the sentence,
whether of concession (**benché**), time (**prima che**) or
condition (**a condizione che**). More examples can be found in
Unit 19.

j After indefinite adjectives, pronouns or adverbs such as
qualunque (*whatever, whichever*), **chiunque** (*whoever*), **comunque**
(*however*), **qualsiasi** (*whatever, whichever*).

Chiunque fosse venuto, non c'era nessuno quando sono arrivata io.	*Whoever had come, there was nobody there when I arrived.*

For a fuller description of all these uses of the subjunctive, see Unit
19.

3 How to form the past conditional

In Unit 20, we saw how the conditional is used to express a wish or
to put a request more politely. The past conditional (English *would
have* or *should have*) is used in a similar way. It is formed in Italian
by combining the conditional of **avere** (or **essere** for certain verbs)
with the past participle (the **-ato, -uto, -ito** form).

Verbs in -are

avrei mangiato	**avremmo** mangiato
avresti mangiato	**avreste** mangiato
avrebbe mangiato	**avrebbero** mangiato

Verbs in -ere

avrei potuto	**avremmo** potuto
avresti potuto	**avreste** potuto
avrebbe potuto	**avrebbero** potuto

Verbs in **-ire**

....

avrei dormito	**avremmo** dormito
avresti dormito	**avreste** dormito
avrebbe dormito	**avrebbero** dormito

....

Verbs that take **essere,** *e.g.* **andare**

....

sarei andato/a	**saremmo** andati/e
saresti andato/a	**sareste** andati/e
sarebbe andato/a	**sarebbero** andati/e

....

In the case of verbs that take **essere**, the past participle has to agree
with the subject (masculine, or feminine, singular or plural).

4 When to use the past conditional

The past conditional – in a similar way to the present conditional
– is used when talking about something that could or would have
happened if certain conditions (explicit or implicit) had been met.
Here are the different contexts in which the past conditional is
used.

a To express a wish or preference

Avrei preferito una granita.   *I would have preferred a granita*
ice. (Condition implied: if it
had been possible)

Avrei voluto una persona più   *I would have liked someone*
esperta.   *more experienced. (Condition*
implied: if it had been possible)

b To make a statement or question sound less categorical or abrupt

Non **avresti avuto** tempo di   *You wouldn't have had time to look*
guardare quella relazione per   *at that report, by any chance?*
caso?

c To express rumour or report

The past conditional is used to say what has been reported by a certain source, e.g. press, TV, where English would use a plain past tense along with a phrase such as *according to*.

Secondo la televisione inglese, gli inglesi **avrebbero speso** di meno sui prodotti alcolici negli ultimi sei mesi.	*According to English television, the English have spent less on alcoholic products in the last six months.*
Secondo fonti ufficiali, 35 persone **sarebbero morte** negli scontri fra le due fazioni.	*According to official sources, 35 people have died in the clashes between the two factions.*

Insight

The use of the past conditional to tell us what has been reported, for example in the press or on television, as in the examples above, is strange to English speakers. In English, a straightforward past tense would be used.

d When a condition is implied or stated

The past conditional is used when the action would have taken place if certain conditions had been fulfilled. Sometimes these conditions are stated; at other times, they are just implied.

Avrei mangiato di più, ma stasera vado a cena fuori.	*I would have eaten more, but I'm going out to dinner tonight.*
Sarei andato in vacanza, ma non avevo i soldi.	*I would have gone on holiday, but I didn't have the money.*
Io non **avrei comprato** quella casa.	*I wouldn't have bought that house.*

(No condition is stated, but the condition implied is: *If it had been me ...*)

Sarei venuta anch'io.	*I would have come too.*

(No condition is stated, but the condition implied is: *If I had known about it.*)

For full details of conditional sentences, see Unit 22.

e Indirect or reported speech, or after a verb of saying, thinking, etc.

In the examples below, English uses the present conditional. Italian, however, after a main verb in the past tense, uses the past conditional.

Mi ha promesso che **avrebbe fatto** benzina.
He promised he would get petrol.

Ha detto che **sarebbe venuto** domani.
He said he would come tomorrow.

> **Insight**
>
> This is another example where English usage is very different from Italian. Where English uses *would*, Italian uses the equivalent of *would have* whenever the main verb is in the past tense.

Language plus

Many common expressions of regret (verbs, verb phrases or just expressions) are followed by the subjunctive. In Unit 19, there is an overview of all the contexts where the subjunctive is used, and in particular the way it is used to express emotion. The different emotions can include happiness, sadness, regret, amazement, envy, fear or shame. Here are just a few examples, including examples using the pluperfect subjunctive.

• **Che peccato!** *What a pity! What a shame!*

Che peccato che lui non **abbia potuto** finire il corso di laurea.
What a pity that he couldn't finish his degree course.

Era veramente **un peccato** che
i nostri amici non **potessero**
venire al matrimonio.

*It was really a shame that our
friends could not come to the
wedding.*

• **Mi dispiace** *I am sorry*

Mi dispiace che non ci **siamo** più
visti.

*I'm sorry that we didn't see each
other again.*

Mi dispiaceva che Luciana **avesse
detto** queste cose.

*I was sorry that Luciana had said
these things.*

• **Sono desolato** *I'm really sorry*

Sono desolato che lui non ti **abbia**
più **telefonato**.

*I'm really sorry that he hasn't rung
you any more.*

Eravamo desolati che il nostro
cane **si fosse smarrito**.

*We were upset that our dog had
gone missing.*

• **Magari** *I wish! /If only …*

Magari avessimo vinto la lotteria!

If only we had won the lottery …

Magari ci fossimo sposati!

If only we had got married …

(See also Unit 17 for other examples of Magari.)

Insight

Remember that the pluperfect subjunctive is the tense used to
express things that never happened, things that might have
happened and things that you wish had happened (or not).

Language in action

Exercise 1

Nando is having car problems. Fill in the gaps, this time with the correct form of the subjunctive, either imperfect, perfect or pluperfect tense, and make any necessary adjustments.

ANDREA	Ciao, Nando, pensavo che tu (**1**) _____ (partire) per la Spagna.
NANDO	No, invece abbiamo avuto dei problemi con la macchina. Il meccanico ci aveva fatto la manutenzione e ha detto che era tutto a posto ma è impossibile che (**2**) la _____ (controllare) per bene, perché dopo neanche duecento metri si è fermata e non è più partita. Magari non (**3**) la _____ (portare) mai da lui!
ANDREA	Ma vi fidavate di questo meccanico? Lo conoscevate già?
NANDO	Noi veramente non sapevamo se (**4**) _____ (essere) bravo o no. Dei nostri amici avevano portato la macchina da lui, e ci avevano detto che era bravo, benché (**5**) _____ (fare) pagare un prezzo un po' salato. E poi ci ha riparato la macchina subito, senza che (**6**) _____ (dovere) aspettare.
ANDREA	Era meglio invece se (**7**) _____ (aspettare)!

Exercise 2

Soggiorno a Venezia

Read this brief account of a holiday in Venice that didn't go according to plan. Highlight all the subjunctive forms and the verbs or other constructions that they depend on. Then translate the whole passage into English, paying particular attention to the subjunctives.

La vita è piena di sbagli. Avevamo prenotato l'albergo a Venezia su consiglio di un'amica. Non sapevamo che lei non fosse mai stata a Venezia, e che il nome dell'albergo l'avesse trovato su una vecchia guida turistica. Sarà stato bello cinquanta anni fa, ma non più. E il ristorante poi ...! Morivamo di sete! Nonostante avessimo detto al cameriere tre volte di portare del vino rosso, ci ha portato solo acqua minerale. Peccato poi che il cuoco abbia dimenticato di togliere lo spago prima di servire l'arrosto ... mi chiedevo poi perché mio marito avesse deciso di mangiarlo, ma lui, poveretto, aveva pensato che il cuoco avesse preparato una specialità tipica e che lo spago ne fosse una parte essenziale. Avremmo mangiato meglio alla mensa degli studenti – e avremmo anche speso di meno.

Test yourself

Check your progress! Do you know how to do the following in Italian?

1 Complete the sentences with the correct form of the pluperfect subjunctive. Watch the word order in the first one!
   a Sei arrivata adesso? Pensavo che tu _____ (arrivare) già.
   b L'insegnante voleva che i ragazzi _____ (leggere) il libro prima dell'esame.
   c Mi dispiaceva che voi _____ (venire) senza avvertirmi.
   d Mio padre sperava che noi _____ (finire) i preparativi per il matrimonio.

2 Complete the sentences with the correct form of the past conditional.
   a Io _____ (preferire) il pesce ma era finito.
   b Marco _____ (venire) ma ha un altro impegno.
   c La banca ci _____ (prestare) i soldi.
   d _____ (essere) felici di accettare il vostro invito ma non ci siamo in quel periodo.

3 Match the two halves of the sentences expressing emotion.
   a Speravo che   **i** il gatto avesse mangiato il canarino della vicina di casa.

b Ero contenta che   **ii** la macchina si fosse fermata dopo solo 500 metri.

c Ero rimasta stupita che   **iii** mio marito fosse venuto con me in Italia.

d Gli dispiaceva che   **iv** i miei amici avessero preparato la cena.

4 Complete these sentences with the correct verb form of the pluperfect subjunctive. Be careful with the word order in the second one.

    a Era impossibile che loro non _____ (ricevere) il pacco.

    b Era probabile che i bambini non _____ (essere) mai al mare e che non _____ (vedere) mai la sabbia.

    c Era possibile che voi _____ (arrivare) dopo di noi.

5 Answer the questions using **si diceva** or **dicevano** with the correct pluperfect subjunctive form.

    a È' vero che la principessa si era fidanzata di nascosto?
    Si diceva che ....

    b È' vero che la mozzarella era stata contaminata dall'acqua?
    Dicevano che ...

6 Match the two halves of the sentences, so that they makes sense.

    a Non riuscivo a mangiare niente   **i** nel caso Gino non l'avesse preso stamattina.

    b Andavamo in giro scalzi   **ii** benché avessi avuto fame prima.

    c Abbiamo preso il pane   **iii** come se mia madre non ci avesse mai comprato le scarpe.

7 Answer the questions, saying you would have done but you didn't have enough money.

    Esempio: Sei andata in vacanza quest'estate?
    Ci sarei andata ma non avevo i soldi.

    a Siete andati a sciare quest'inverno?

    b Avete comprato una nuova macchina?

    c Hai comprato qualcosa di nuovo per la casa?

8 Complete the sentences with the correct form of the past conditional.

    a Secondo il presidente della banca, l'economia mondiale _____ (migliorare).

b Secondo il giornalista, il presidente del consiglio _____ (nascondere) i fatti.

c Secondo la polizia, i due politici _____ (avere) dei problemi finanziari.

d Secondo la mia amica, _____ (stare) gli ultimi a consegnare i compiti.

9 Match the two halves of these sentences with indirect or reported speech.

a Mio marito mi ha detto che **i** avrebbero consegnato il frigorifero domani sera.

b L'idraulico ha promesso che **ii** mi avrebbe comprato dei fiori.

c Hanno promesso che **iii** sarebbe venuto domani mattina.

10 Match the two halves of the sentences expressing regret.

a Eravamo desolati che **i** voi aveste avuto tanti problemi di salute.

b Mi dispiaceva che **ii** i nostri figli fossero andati a vivere nel Canada.

c Magari **iii** avessero tagliato tutti gli alberi vicino a casa nostra.

d Era un peccato che **iv** mio figlio si fosse sposato con un'italiana.

22

Expressing conditions

In this unit, you will learn how to:
- **express a condition that can be met or a statement of fact**
- **express a condition unlikely to be met**
- **express a condition that can no longer be met**

Language points
- **se *with present/future/past tenses (condition that can be met)***
- **se *with imperfect subjunctive and present conditional (condition unlikely to be met)***
- **se *with pluperfect subjunctive and past conditional (condition that can no longer be met)***
- **phrases that express a condition (a condizione che, a meno che, *etc.)***

Introduction

Study these different examples of conditional sentences before reading the grammar explanations.

Se ho tempo, scrivo delle cartoline.	*If I have time, I write postcards.*
Se verrà Marco, andremo al cinema.	*If Marco comes, we will go to the cinema.*
Se fossi ricca, comprerei una Ferrari.	*If I were rich, I would buy a Ferrari.*
Se avessimo tempo, andremmo a visitare la cattedrale.	*If we had time, we would go and visit the cathedral.*

Se fossi andata in Italia, avrei imparato l'italiano.	*If I had gone to Italy, I would have learned Italian.*
Se avessimo comprato la guida, non avremmo avuto tanti problemi per trovare un buon ristorante.	*If we had bought the guide, we would not have had so many problems finding a good restaurant.*

Focus on grammar

1 Conditional sentences: introduction

When we start a sentence with *if* in English, we are setting out a condition. This can be one of many kinds:

• A straightforward statement of fact or a condition which can easily be met

If you stay up late, you will be tired tomorrow.
If we have time, we will go and see the Duomo.

• A condition unlikely ever to be met

If I were to become rich, I would buy a Rolls Royce.

• A condition that can no longer be met, because the time or opportunity has passed

If I had married Giovanni, I would have had an Italian mother-in-law.

In Italian, the condition or hypothesis is introduced by **se**. You can now look at how the different types of conditional sentence are expressed in Italian.

2 Expressing a real possibility

Where the conditions are likely to be met or are a straightforward statement of facts, the normal indicative verb form is used both for the main verb and for the verb introduced by **se**, in one of these tenses.

• **Present tense**

Se Lei mi **dà** cinquanta euro, io Le **do** il resto.	*If you give me 50 euros, I'll give you the change.*

• **Future tense**

Se **andrete** a Roma, **potrete** vedere il Colosseo.	*If you go to Rome, you will be able to see the Colosseum.*

• **Past tense**

Se **aveva** paura, non lo **dimostrava**.	*If she was afraid, she didn't show it.*

• **Combination of present and future tenses**

Se non **fai** il bravo, non **andrai** al mare domani.	*If you don't behave, you won't go to the seaside tomorrow.*

• **Combination of perfect and future perfect tenses**

Se **hai parlato** con lui, **avrai capito** come stanno le cose.	*If you have spoken to him, you will have understood how things are.*

• **Combination of present and imperative**

Se **vieni, fammi** sapere.	*If you come, let me know.*

Insight

In this type of conditional sentence (a condition that is likely to be met), a wide variety of tenses can be used. The main point to remember is that these sentences don't need the subjunctive. Since they are practically a statement of fact, they use the 'normal' indicative tenses.

3 Expressing a condition unlikely to be met

Where the condition expressed is unlikely to be fulfilled, the main clause (the action or event which would or wouldn't happen) uses the present conditional, while the se clause uses the imperfect subjunctive, to express a condition unlikely to come true.

Se l'albergo non **fosse** così caro, **resteremmo** più di una notte.	*If the hotel were less expensive, we would stay more than one night.*
Se **avessimo** più soldi, **andremmo** a mangiare al ristorante.	*If we had more money, we would go and eat in a restaurant.*
Gli italiani non **farebbero** tanti incidenti se **guidassero** con più attenzione.	*The Italians wouldn't have so many accidents if they drove more carefully.*

Insight

This type of conditional sentence (a condition that is unlikely to be met) normally uses the conditional and the subjunctive: the present conditional in the main clause to say what would (or wouldn't) happen, and the imperfect subjunctive in the se clause to supply the condition.

4 Expressing a condition that can no longer be met

When the condition or hypothesis expressed cannot now be fulfilled because the opportunity has passed, the main clause (the action or event which would have happened) uses the past conditional, while the se clause uses the pluperfect subjunctive.

- **Se** clause

Se io non **avessi perso** il portafoglio ...	*If I had not lost my wallet ...*

- Main clause

... non **avrei avuto** tutti questi problemi.	*... I wouldn't have had all these problems.*

- **Se** clause and main clause

Se fossimo venuti in treno, **saremmo arrivati** prima.	*If we had come by train, we would have got here sooner.*
Se tu avessi guidato con più prudenza, non **saremmo andati** a finire contro il muro.	*If you had driven more carefully, we would not have ended up crashing into the wall.*

> ### Insight
> This type of conditional sentence (a condition that can no longer be met) normally uses the conditional and the subjunctive: the past conditional in the main clause to say what would have (or wouldn't have) happened, and the pluperfect subjunctive in the **se** clause to supply the condition. It can best be summed up by the words *If only...*

The past conditional can also be used after a gerund (**-ando** or **-endo**) which implies the idea of *if*.

Sapendo questo, **non sarei andata** con lui.	*If I had known this, I wouldn't have gone with him.*

It is also possible to have a combination of pluperfect subjunctive in the **se** clause and a present conditional in the main clause.

Se io **fossi rimasta** in Italia, **sarei** più contenta ora.	*If I had stayed in Italy, I would be happier now.*

5 Phrases expressing condition

A few conjunctions (joining words) that express condition are:

a condizione che	*on condition that*
a meno che (non)	*unless*
purché	*provided that*
nel caso che	*in the event that*

All these conjunctions are followed by a verb in the subjunctive (see Unit 17 for forms of the present subjunctive).

Io ti accompagno **a condizione che tu paghi** la benzina.	*I'll go with you on condition that you pay for the petrol.*
Potete uscire **purché non rientriate** tardi.	*You can go out so long as you don't come back late.*

A meno che is followed by **non**.

Possiamo andare al mare **a meno che** tu **non preferisca** andare in campagna.	*We can go to the seaside unless you prefer to go to the country.*

....

Insight

If you prefer to avoid the subjunctive, it's useful to know that the first two sentences above can be expressed far more simply by using **se** and a plain indicative tense (**Se paghi tu la benzina ...** , **Se non rientrate tardi ...**) rather than a conjunction with the subjunctive.

....

Language plus

Conditional sentence using the imperfect

In informal spoken Italian, in a sentence such as those shown in §4 above, where the conditions cannot now be met, both past conditional and pluperfect subjunctive are replaced by a simple imperfect indicative.

Se lo **avessi saputo**, non **sarei venuta** stasera.	*If I had known, I wouldn't have come this evening.*
(Se lo **sapevo**, non **venivo** stasera.)	

Sometimes only the **se** clause is replaced by an imperfect.

Se **sapevo**, non **sarei venuta** stasera.	*If I had known, I wouldn't have come this evening.*

Insight

The choice of verb form depends on the context and register (formal or informal). In informal spoken Italian, it is quite common to use a plain imperfect indicative tense in place of the past conditional or the pluperfect subjunctive or both.

Anche se

Anche se (*even if*) can also be used to express a condition, most frequently one unlikely to be met.

Anche se tu fossi l'ultimo uomo sulla Terra, non ti sposerei mai.	*Even if you were the last man on Earth, I would never marry you.*

Anche se can also be followed by a plain indicative tense.

Anche se i nostri amici vengono, non si fermeranno a mangiare.	*Even if our friends come, they won't stay to eat.*

Language in action

Exercise 1

Next time ...

Supply the missing half! Conditional sentences are generally a pair formed by a **se** clause and a main clause, but in this dialogue, one of each pair is missing. Using the verbs in the box below, try and complete the sentence by making up the missing half. Some verbs may be used more than once.

---

essere fare invitare venire

CARLA	Ciao, Maria. Come mai non sei venuta stasera?
MARIA	(**1**) _____ se non avessi avuto tante altre cose da fare.
CARLA	Peccato. Se tu (**2**) _____ , ti avrei fatto conoscere mio cugino.
MARIA	Pazienza! Sarà per la prossima volta. Se lui (**3**) _____ per Natale, fammi sapere.
CARLA	Non mancherò. Intanto se tu non (**4**) _____ sempre così impegnata ti inviterei a cena.
MARIA	Se mi (**5**) _____ , accetto volentieri!

Note: **Pazienza!** N*ever mind! Can't be helped.* (lit.: *Patience!*)

Exercise 2

Still time ...

In this set of examples, there is still the chance to change your destiny!

1 Se mia madre sapesse cucinare, _____ (*mangiare meglio*)
2 Se mio padre fosse meno rigido, _____ (*uscire tutte le sere, fare quello che voglio*)

3 Se vivessimo in una casa più grande, _____ (*avere una camera tutta mia*)

4 Se tu abitassi più vicino a casa mia, _____ (*vederci più spesso*)

5 Se mio fratello fosse vegetariano, _____ (*non mangiare la carne*)

Exercise 3

If only ...

What might have happened if you or your friends had done things differently? Some suggestions are supplied, but you are free to make up your own endings.

1 Se io avessi sposato un italiano, _____
(*rimanere in Italia, parlare italiano meglio, avere una vita più felice*)

2 Se noi avessimo studiato i verbi, _____
(*essere più bravi, avere un voto migliore*)

3 Se tu fossi andata all'università, _____
(*divertirsi, trovare un lavoro migliore*)

4 Se lei avesse messo il vestito più bello, _____
(*conoscere l'uomo dei suoi sogni ...*)

5 Se lui non avesse bevuto tanto, _____
(*andare a finire contro un muro, distruggere la macchina*)

Test yourself

Check your progress! Do you know how to do the following in Italian?

1 Complete the sentences expressing conditions likely to be met with the appropriate forms of the verbs in brackets.

a Se _____ (uscire), _____ (chiudere) bene la porta.

b Se _____ (venire) anche Gianni e Carla, _____ (essere) in dieci.

c Se ti _____ (rubare) la borsetta con le carte di credito, _____ (rimanere) senza soldi.

2 Complete the sentences expressing statements of fact with the appropriate forms of the verbs in brackets.

  a Se non andiamo subito in centro, _____ (trovare) i negozi già chiusi.

  b Se continui a mangiare tanto, _____ (mettere) dieci chili.

  c Se i bambini non stanno un po' all'ombra, _____ (prendere) un colpo di sole.

3 Complete the sentences expressing conditions that are unlikely to be met with the appropriate forms of the verbs in brackets.

  a Se tu non _____ (lavorare), _____ (potere) passare più tempo con i bambini.

  b Se tuo marito _____ (essere) meno egoista, _____ (potere) darti una mano in cucina.

  c Se noi _____ (avere) più tempo, _____ (potere) fare un viaggio più lungo.

4 Complete the sentences expressing conditions that can no longer be met with the appropriate forms of the verbs in brackets.

  a Se tu _____ (venire) alla festa, ti _____ (divertirsi).

  b Se Gino _____ (guidare) con più attenzione, non _____ (fare) un incidente.

  c Se noi _____ (passare) più tempo in Italia, _____ (imparare) l'italiano.

5 Rewrite these sentences, replacing the subjunctive and conditional forms with a plain imperfect indicative.

  a Se tu avessi mangiato di meno, non saresti ingrassata poi tanto.

  b Se tu fossi venuta alla festa, ti avrei presentato i miei amici.

  c Se i ragazzi avessero studiato, avrebbero preso voti migliori.

6 Complete these sentences using the gerund of **avere**, **comprare** or **sapere**.

  a _____ tanti soldi da spendere, potremmo comprare dei mobili antichi.

  b _____ a che ora arrivano i nostri parenti, potremmo preparare il pranzo.

  c _____ tante scarpe in Italia, avrei avuto la valigia sovrappeso.

7 Complete these sentences with appropriate conjunctions.

  a Ti porto io _____ tu non abbia voglia di andare da sola.

  b Potete venire al concerto _____ stiate zitti.

c Andiamo al mare _____ rimangano dei soldi a fine mese.

And finally, since this is the last unit of the book, see if you can do the following:

8 Find the following forms of these irregular verbs by looking up the verb table in the Grammar Appendix.

  a perfect tense of **chiedere**

  b perfect tense of **essere**

9 Find the meanings of these grammatical terms by looking up the Glossary.

  a transitive verb

  b invariable noun

10 Find where you would look for information on these grammar topics by looking up the Index.

  a the present subjunctive

  b direct object pronouns

Congratulations on completing *Essential Italian grammar*!

I hope you've enjoyed using the book as much as my own students do! Please feel free to contact me by mail c/o Hodder Headline Ltd, 338 Euston Road, London NW1 3BH, or by e-mail. I have a page on the Open University website (www.open.ac.uk), which you can access via the Search facility. My e-mail address is a.proudfoot@open.ac.uk. I welcome comments on the book, suggestions for improvement, and any general comments or queries you may have about learning Italian.

Buono studio!

Anna Proudfoot

Taking it further

There are branches of the Italian Cultural Institute (**Istituto Italiano di Cultura**) throughout the world, hosting events focused on Italian culture, including art, literature and film. Some Institutes also organize Italian language courses, both weekly and at weekends, and can provide information on courses at language schools in Italy. Enter 'Italian Cultural Institute' into any good Internet search engine.

If you are studying or planning to study at university, don't forget that a language degree course is not the only way to keep up your Italian. Many courses nowadays offer the chance to spend a period abroad through the Erasmus–Socrates scheme.

Why not take the chance to improve your Italian by spending a fortnight or a month in Italy on a language course? There are lots of language schools and summer schools in Italy, some in famous cities such as Florence or Siena, others in smaller places or at the seaside. The Italian Cultural Institute can usually advise. And with low-cost flights to all areas of Italy, there has never been a better time to visit **il Bel Paese**.

Italy online

The Internet is a useful source of information on Italy and Italian events. Here are just a few useful websites for Italian learners. Some offer practical advice, others are there for fun! Websites come and go so, although we have checked them all before publication, don't be surprised if some have disappeared.

Search engines

Why not use an Italian search engine?

www.virgilio.it

www.yahoo.it

www.google.it

Don't forget to type in the keyword in Italian!

Language learning sites

There are quite a few useful sites for language learners:

Online dictionaries, etc.

www.alphadictionary.com/directory/Languages/Romance/Italian
(Links to online dictionaries)

Other resources for Italian learners

www.bbc.co.uk/languages/italian (BBC language resources, Italian)

www.oggi-domani.com (Italian online course for beginners)

highered.mcgraw-hill.com/sites/0072415517 (Italian exercises for
beginners)

www.locuta.com/eclass.html (Italian grammar resource)

forum.wordreference.com/forumdisplay.php?f=26 (Italian
language-learning forum)

web.uvic.ca/hispanital/italian/italian100/index.htm (Italian exercises from University of Victoria)

www.iluss.it (a non-profit organization which promotes Italian language and culture abroad)

www.learnitalianpod.com/category/beginner (50 five-minute podcasts for beginners in Italian with lots of repetition, download free)

www.initalia.rai.it/default.asp (RAI site for Italian learners)

www.slf.ruhr-uni-bochum.de/etandem/etindex-en.html (e-tandem project, find a study partner in Italy)

Information on Italy and Italian regions

www.enit.it (Italian government tourist board)

www.mediasoft.it (links to a range of Italian resources)

www.censis.it (facts and figures on Italy)

www.istat.it (facts and figures on Italy)

www.LifeinItaly.com (Italian news, art, fashion, culture, weather and property, in English)

http://www.italia-magazine.com/ (online magazine in English covering property, holidays, food, culture and people in Italy)

www.italymag.co.uk (online magazine in English covering property, holidays, culture, food and language in Italy. Registered users can take part in the forum)

Information on Naples

www.dentronapoli.it

www.itb.it/metroNA/fsm_1.htm (the Circumvesuviana railway timetables for Pompei)

Why not choose your favourite city and make your own list of websites?

Italian newspapers

www.repubblica.it (La Repubblica)

www.corriere.it (Corriere della Sera)

www.lastampa.it (La Stampa)

www.ilmessaggero.it (Il Messaggero)

Italian TV and Radio

www.rai.it (RAI TV, the state TV channels)

www.educational.rai.it (RAI TV educational channel)

www.flysat.com/tv-it.php (details of Italian TV channels available via Satellite, including details for UK)

wwitv.com/portal.htm (gateway to television websites worldwide. Includes links to Italian TV websites both terrestrial and satellite with live streaming TV clips in Italian including the weather)

www.qsl.net/g3yrc/radio-online/Europe/Italy.htm (Italy online radio stations)

www.italiamia.com/music_radio.html (Italian radio stations)

Italian food

www.pasta.it (everything you always wanted to know about pasta)

www.cookaround.com/yabbse1/forum.php (Italian cooking forum, in Italian)

www.buttalapasta.it (Italian food)

Miscellaneous

www.bomboniere.com (buy *confetti* and *bomboniere* for weddings, etc. online)

www.ilmiogatto.net (for cat lovers)

www.alfemminile.com/world/communaute/forum/forumo.asp (women's online forum)

Key to the exercises

Unit 1

1 4 a la mia amica inglese b un turista tedesco c uno studente inglese
2 1 Mi chiamo Tracey Jones. Sono inglese, di Milton Keynes. Sono studentessa.
   2 Mi chiamo Massimiliano Lusardi. Sono italiano, di Genova. Sono studente.
   3 Mi chiamo Dottor Barnes / Joe Barnes. Sono di Oxford ma sono gallese. Sono professore universitario.
   4 Mi chiamo Camilla Pennino. Sono italiana, di Roma. Sono medico.
3 1 tedesco 2 gallese 3 scozzesi 4 irlandese 5 italiani 6 austriaci 7 americani 8 inglesi

Test yourself

1 Sono Anna./Mi chiamo Anna.
2 a Come ti chiami?
   b Come si chiama?
3 Sono di Milano.
4 Sono italiano /a / inglese / scozzese / etc.
5 a E tu, di che nazionalità sei?
   b E Lei, di che nazionalità è?
6 a Di dove sei?
   b Di dov'è?
7 Sono sposata. Mio marito si chiama Giorgio.
8 Marco è sposato?
9 a E tu, che lavoro fai?
   b E Lei, che lavoro fa?
10 a Professore/Professoressa b Avvocato c Ingegnere

Unit 2

1 a un cornetto b una birra c una brioche d un toast e un bicchiere di acqua minerale f un caffè g un cappuccino h un'aranciata i una limonata j una spremuta k un aperitivo l un digestivo

2 a due cornetti b due birre c due brioche d due toast e due bicchieri di acqua minerale f due caffè g due cappuccini h due aranciate i due limonate j due spremute k due aperitivi l due digestivi

3 1 Due cappuccini e un cornetto, per favore.
  2 Un aperitivo, un'aranciata e due toast, per piacere.
  3 Un caffè, una spremuta e due cornetti, per favore.
  4 Una birra, una coca cola e un bicchiere di acqua minerale, per piacere.
  5 Due caffè e un bicchiere di acqua, per favore.
  6 Due coni, per piacere.

Test yourself

1 Vorrei due paste e due cappuccini/due caffè.

2 Che cos'e? Che cosa sono?

3 a È' un telefonino.
  b È' una bibita analcolica.
  c Sono paste di mandorla.
  d Sono panini con formaggio.

4 Chi è? Chi sono?

5 a È uno studente inglese.
  b È uno stilista italiano.
  c Sono turisti inglesi.
  d Sono amici italiani.

6 a uno spuntino b un caffè c una spremuta di arancia d un'aranciata e uno studente f un'automobile

7 a due aperitivi b due paste c due giornali d due lezioni e due programmi f due artiste (female) g due bar h due caffè

8 a Questi sono Carlos e Gianni.
  b Queste sono Maura e Teresa.
  c Questa è mia madre.
  d Questo è mio marito.

9 a una ragazza inglese b un aperitivo analcolico c una birra fresca d paste di mandorla sarde e gnocchi buoni f panini grandi

10 a uno studente italiano
   b una tavola rotonda
   c un'automobile italiana
   d una signora anziana
   e una casa piccola / una piccola casa

Unit 3

1 a dei salatini / alcuni salatini / qualche salatino / un po' di salatini
  b delle pizzette / alcune pizzette / qualche pizzetta / un po' di pizzette
  c dell'aranciata / un po' di aranciata
  d dell'acqua frizzante / un po' di acqua frizzante
  e delle patatine / alcune patatine / qualche patatina / un po' di patatine
  f degli spuntini / alcuni spuntini / qualche spuntino / un po' di spuntini
  g del vino / un po' di vino
  h dei liquori / alcuni liquori / qualche liquore / un po' di liquori
  i dei pasticcini / alcuni pasticcini / qualche pasticcino / un po' di pasticcini
  j delle bibite / alcune bibite / qualche bibita / un po' di bibite
  k della birra / un po' di birra
  l del gelato / un po' di gelato
  m degli stuzzicchini / alcuni stuzzicchini / qualche stuzzicchino / un po' di stuzzicchini
  n degli aperitivi / alcuni aperitivi / qualche aperitivo / un po' di aperitivi
  o delle bevande alcoliche / alcune bevande alcoliche / qualche bevanda alcolica / un po' di bevande alcoliche
  p dei dolci / alcuni dolci / qualche dolce / un po' di dolci
  q dei grissini / alcuni grissini / qualche grissino / un po' di grissini
  r della coca cola / un po' di coca cola
  s delle bevande analcoliche / alcune bevande analcoliche / qualche bevanda analcolica / un po' di bevande analcoliche
  t delle uova sode / alcune uova sode / qualche uovo sodo / un po' di uova sode

2 1 Ce ne sono dieci. 2 Ce n'è un litro. 3 Ce ne sono sei. 4 Ce n'è un chilo. 5 Ce ne sono due.

Test yourself

1 a C' è una toilette/un bagno?
  b C' è un telefono?
2 a Ce n'è una al primo piano.
  b Ce n'è uno al bar.
3 a Ci sono delle pesche?

b Ci sono dei panini?

4 a Ce ne sono due chili.

b Ci sono (dei) panini con prosciutto e formaggio.

5 a dei panini b alcuni panini c un po' di panini d qualche panino

6 a Non c'è un treno per Milano.

b Non c'è una bottiglia di vino in casa.

7 a Ci sono studenti inglesi in albergo/nell'albergo?

b Ci sono dei giornali italiani?

8 a Non ci sono amici alla festa.

b Non ci sono programmi interessanti alla TV.

9 a C'è qualcosa da mangiare?

b C'è qualcuno?

10 a Non c'è niente da mangiare.

b Non c'è nessuno.

Unit 4

1 1 nel 2 nell'; in 3 nel 4 nel/in 5 nel 6 nel 7 alla 8 nella 9 sullo; nello 10 nel

2 1 Sono in Via Roma, vicino all'Orto Botanico.

2 È in Piazza del Duomo, vicino alla Torre Pendente.

3 Sono in Via Alessandro Volta, vicino al Museo di Storia Naturale.

4 È in Via Nicola Pisano, vicino alle cliniche universitarie.

5 È in Via Antonio Rosmini, vicino allo Stadio Garibaldi.

6 È in Piazza Manin, vicino al Battistero.

Test yourself

1 a Dov'è la stazione?

b Dove sono gli studenti inglesi?

2 a La stazione è in fondo a questa strada.

b Gli studenti inglesi sono al bar.

3 a le pianiste b i camerieri c le chiavi d gli spuntini e gli alberghi f le aranciate

4 a l'automobile rossa b la bibita fresca c gli alberghi costosi d il programma interessante e gli specialisti bravi f le scarpe nuove

5 a in città b in giardino c a scuola d in campagna e a casa

6 a dal medico b allo sportello c al cinema d nello stadio e nel ristorante f negli alberi

7 in primo piano, in mezzo, lontano, in alto, in basso
8 a davanti a b di fronte a c a sinistra di d in fondo a e vicino a
9 a Eccomi b Eccola c Eccolo d Eccoli e Eccoti
10 a Ceniamo da Maura.
  b Compro panini alla salumeria.
  c Mio marito rientra dal lavoro alle 20.00.
  d Viene da Napoli.

Unit 5

1 1 Preferisco quella in campagna/in città.
   2 Prendo quella economica/cara.
   3 Metto quelli sportivi/eleganti.
   4 Compro quelle con tacco alto/senza tacco.
   5 Invito quelli italiani/quelli inglesi.
   6 Prendo quello con prosciutto/con formaggio.
   7 Mangio quelli alle nocciole/al cioccolato.
   8 Bevo quello rosso/bianco.
   9 Leggo quello inglese/italiano.
  10 Vedo quelli comici/romantici.
2 1 Quell'aranciata è tiepida.
   2 Quel palazzo è lontano.
   3 Quegli studenti sono stupidi.
   4 Quell'albergo è scadente/economico.
   5 Quei giornalisti sono disonesti.
   6 Quella bottiglia è vuota.
   7 Quel film è noioso.
   8 Quel museo è aperto.
   9 Quello straniero è antipatico.
  10 Quello specialista è giovane.

Test yourself
1 a questo biglietto b queste scarpe c questa gonna d questi sandali
2 a quello scontrino b quell'agendino c quella pensione d quel
   ristorante e quelle scarpe f quegli stuzzicchini g quei sandali h quegli
   alberghi
3 a quanti panini b quante sigarette c quanta pasta d quante lasagne
   e quanto zucchero

4　a abito　b abiti　c abitiamo　d abitano
5　a prendo　b prende　c prendete　d prendono
6　dieci, undici, dodici, tredici, quattordici, quindici, sedici, diciassette, diciotto, diciannove, venti
7　a venticinque　b trentotto　c centoventotto
　　d millequattrocentocinquanta　e dieci virgola cinque
8　a dieci euro　b cento euro　c duemila euro　d un milione di euro
9　a il trentun agosto　b l'otto gennaio　c il primo marzo
10　a　Sono le ventuno e quindici./Sono le nove e un quarto.
　　b　Sono le cinque e mezzo.
　　c　È' l'una.
　　d　È' mezzanotte.
　　e　Sono le sedici e quarantacinque./Sono le quattro e quarantacinque./ Sono le cinque meno un quarto.

Unit 6

1　Il signor Ruzzini comincia a lavorare alle otto e quindici. Abita a Pisa ma lavora a Firenze. Ogni giorno prende il treno. Parte alle sette e arriva alle otto.

2　La signora Giannini lavora in centro. Comincia alle otto e trenta e finisce alle sette. Quando torna a casa, è stanca morta. Suo marito non lavora ma resta a casa con la bambina. La sera lei e suo marito guardano la TV.

3　stiamo uscendo　usciamo; Sto venendo　Vengo; Mi sto mettendo　Mi metto; Stai scherzando!　Scherzi!

4　1　Noi **andiamo** in Argentina. Voi **andate** in Sardegna, come sempre?
　　2　**Partiamo da** Oxford il 19 agosto di sera. **Arriviamo a** Buenos Aires il 20. E **torniamo a** Oxford il 5 settembre.
　　3　Malcolm **lavora** come medico. Alex **lavora** a Londra. Fa molta musica, ha molti amici, va al cinema la sera.
　　4　Anna è sempre al lavoro. **Torna** a casa solo per la cena. È molto stressata. **Scrive** sempre libri. **Finisce il** libro di grammatica prima delle vacanze, spero!

5　1　Sto preparando/facendo un tè.
　　2　Sto andando a noleggiare la macchina.
　　3　Stiamo portando il cane a spasso/portandolo a spasso.
　　4　Sto riparando la radio./Sto riparandola.

5 Sto scrivendo un romanzo.

6 Mi sto tagliando le unghie.

7 Sto partendo.

8 Sto bevendo un caffè.

9 Sto facendo una foto della nuova casa.

10 Sto traducendo una lettera.

Test yourself

1 a finisci b finisce c finiamo d finiscono

2 a dormo b dorme c dormite d dormono

3 a Dove abiti?

   b Dove lavora?

   c Dove studiate?

4 a Come arrivi a scuola?

   b Come sta tua madre?

   c Come va il lavoro?

   d Com'è Londra?

   e Come sono le lasagne?

5 a A che ora comincia il film?

   b A che ora chiude il supermercato?

   c A che ora finisci di lavorare?

6 a Mia madre sta cucinando.

   b Mio marito sta lavorando.

   c Noi stiamo cenando.

   d Voi cosa state facendo?

7 a oggi pomeriggio/questo pomeriggio b stamattina c stasera d oggi

8 a ieri mattina b l'altro ieri/l'altroieri c la settimana scorsa d ieri sera

9 a domani b dopodomani c la settimana prossima d domani sera

10 a ubriaco fradicio b bagnato fradicio c pieno zeppo d piano piano

Unit 7

1 *Sample answer*

Piero e Maddalena, perché non andate a **farvi** la doccia? Su, cercate di **sbrigarvi**! Poi **mettetevi** i vestiti puliti e **pettinatevi** un pochino. Bevete il latte, mangiate i biscotti poi andate a lavarvi i denti. **Mettetevi** le scarpe e la giacca, che fa freddo. / Serafino, vai a fare la doccia, sbrigati! **Mettiti** la camicia bianca e la cravatta azzurra. Bevi il caffè, mangia qualcosa! **Mettiti** il cappello!

2 1 Preferisco farmi prima la doccia.

   2 Preferisco prendere prima il caffè.

   3 Preferisco mettermi prima i calzini.

   4 Preferisco pettinarmi prima.

   5 Preferisco lavarmi prima i capelli.

   6 Preferisco fare prima colazione.

3 Sample answer

La mattina mio marito si alza prima di me e mi prepara il caffè. Io mi alzo dopo, mi faccio la doccia, mi lavo i capelli, mi vesto e poi mi preparo ad uscire. Dopo colazione, mi trucco, mi lavo i denti, mi metto le scarpe, mi pettino un'altra volta poi esco. Mio marito invece si fa la doccia, si veste, si lava i denti, si pettina e si fa la barba. Poi si mette le scarpe ed esce.

Test yourself

1 Esempi: Mi alzo alle sette, faccio un caffè, mi faccio la doccia, mi vesto, mi trucco.

2 Esempi: I bambini si alzano alle otto, si fanno la doccia, si vestono, fanno colazione, si mettono le scarpe, vanno a scuola.

3 a Davide si mette la giacca.

  b Carlo e Maura si mettono il cappotto.

  c I bambini si mettono i guanti.

  d Io mi metto i pantaloni.

  e Tu ti metti la maglia.

4 a Luisa deve truccarsi.

  b Devi prepararti?

  c Preferiamo vestirci prima di cena.

  d Preferite mettervi il cappotto pesante?

  e Gli studenti preferiscono prepararsi dopo.

5 a una volta al giorno b due volte alla settimana c una volta al mese d una volta all'anno e spesso f raramente g qualche volta h ogni tanto

6 a prima di te b dopo di lui c dalle dieci alle quattordici/due d poi e dopo/più tardi

7 a rapidamente b bene c facilmente d meglio

8 a in maniera educata/in modo educato b in maniera sgarbata/in modo sgarbato c in maniera brusca/in modo brusco d con entusiasmo/in maniera entusiasta

9 a Mettetevi le scarpe!
  b Mettiamoci la giacca!
  c Lavati i capelli!
  d Truccati per la festa.
  e Preparatevi adesso.
10 Chi va piano va sano e va lontano.

Unit 8

1 1 posso 2 possono 3 puoi 4 possiamo 5 potete 6 può
2 1 Può comprare un vestito nuovo.
   2 Può venire dopo.
   3 Possono andare al cinema.
   4 Potete/Possiamo fare lo scambio di casa.
   5 Puoi andare a luglio.
   6 Possiamo/Potete andare domani.
   7 Posso accompagnarti se vuoi.
   8 Potete venire con noi, se volete.
3 1 sappiamo 2 sanno 3 sai 4 Potete 5 Sapete 6 potete 7 so 8 sa
   9 potete 10 può 11 può 12 potete 13 potete 14 puoi 15 puoi 16 sai

Test yourself

1 a puoi b può c possiamo d potete e possono
2 a Posso andare in bagno?
   b Posso vedere le foto?
   c Posso parlare con il direttore?
3 a potrebbe b può c potete sapete d puoi
4 a Si può b È possibile/Si può c Si può d È possibile/Si può
5 a sai b sa c sappiamo d sapete e sanno
6 a possono b posso c sai d sa; può
7 a ii b ii c i d i
8 a Potresti/Potrebbe farmi un piacere?
   b Mi potresti potrebbe passare il sale?
   c Potresti/Potrebbe chiudere la finestra?
9 a Potrei passare domani.
   b Potrei telefonare più tardi.
   c Potrei darti una mano.
10 a è in grado b ce la faccio c ne posso più d Ce la facciamo

Unit 9

1 Sample answer
Vai a vedere i chiostri di Santa Chiara. Cerca di visitare anche il Palazzo
Reale e il Museo nazionale dove ci sono molti oggetti trovati a Pompei. Se
la tua ragazza vuole comprare vestiti, andate al Vomero o a Via Toledo,
dove ci sono dei negozi molto eleganti. Assaggia le sfogliatelle e bevi un po'
di limoncello. Per l'alloggio, prenota una camera al Majestic. Oppure, se
preferisci, spendi meno e vai al Terminus, vicino alla stazione ferroviaria.
Prova a visitare i posti interessanti anche fuori città, ad esempio,
Capri. Prendi l'aliscafo per arrivarci. Oppure vai a Sorrento – prendi la
Circumvesuviana, è un piccolo treno che parte da Piazza Garibaldi.

2 Sample answer

Turista   Senta, scusi! Come arrivo alla Biblioteca Bodleiana?

Tu   Dunque ... uscendo dal Museo, giri a destra, vada diritto per
questa strada, che si chiama St Aldates, poi al semaforo giri
a destra, questa è la High Street, continui per 200 metri, e
dopo la University Church (la Chiesa di St Mary the Virgin),
volti a sinistra ... attraversi la piazza della Radcliffe Camera
e l'entrata alla Biblioteca Bodleiana è proprio di fronte.

Turista   Ah, grazie. Lei è molto gentile.

Test yourself

1 a Senti questo!   b Parla lentamente/piano!   c Finisci i compiti!

2 a Prenda una pasta!   b Mi porti il conto!   c Pulisca la tavola!

3 a Usciamo!   b Andiamo in pizzeria!   c Mettiamo il divano vicino alla
finestra!

4 a Mettetevi i guanti!   b Finite i compiti!   c Studiate i verbi!

5 a   Tagliare i pomodori.

   b   Riscaldare l'olio di oliva.

   c   Far bollire l'acqua per la pasta.

6 a   Ragazzi, non mangiate tutti i cioccolatini.

   b   Maura, non dimenticare l'appuntamento.

   c   Dottor Di Giacomo, non si preoccupi.

7 a Fà!   b Date!   c Dica!   d Sappia!   e Stai!   f Venga!

8 a Mangiala!   b Passalo!   c Non berlo!

9 a Lo prenda!   b Li mangi!   c Non la beva!

10 a Compratelo!   b Scrivetele!   c Pulitele!

Unit 10

1 1 mio fratello 2 sua moglie 3 i loro figli 4 mia sorella 5 suo marito
   6 le loro figlie 7 La loro 8 mio cognato 9 le mie nipoti 10 il loro cane
2 1 mettermi 2 Mi metto 3 mi metto 4 mi faccio 5 ti rompi 6 si porta
   7 Togliti

Test yourself

1 a mia madre b i miei cugini c le mie scarpe d il mio computer
   e mio marito
2 a le tue cugine b tua zia c tuo zio d la tua casa e tua moglie
3 a la sua macchina b i suoi figli c suo padre d il suo ufficio
   e i suoi colleghi
4 a la nostra casa b i vostri amici c il vostro cane d il loro gatto
   e le loro vacanze
5 a sua b proprio c propria d sua
6 a dello b di c del d dei e delle f della g di h degli
7 a quattro miei amici/quattro mie amiche
   b un suo amico/una sua amica
   c un tuo amico/una tua amica
   d tre suoi amici/tre sue amiche
8 a la giacca b la moglie/sua moglie c le mani d Mio zio e i libri/i nostri
   libri f I nostri amici
9 a Mio marito mi pulisce le scarpe.
   b Gianni mi taglia i capelli.
   c Mi lavi la macchina?
   d Gli fai la colazione?
10 a Qual è la Sua macchina?
   b Qual è il tuo ragazzo?
   c Quali sono i tuoi programmi preferiti?
   d Qual è la Sua data di nascita?

Unit 11

1 1 è andata 2 avete fatto 3 è stata 4 siamo andati 5 abbiamo preso
   6 avete fatto 7 ho fatto 8 ha letto 9 abbiamo visto 10 Abbiamo
   mangiato 11 (abbiamo) cucinato 12 (abbiamo) dormito 13 Si sono
   divertiti 14 si sono lamentati 15 hanno potuto 16 Hanno giocato

17 sono andati   18 hanno aiutato

2 Sample answer
Claudia e suo marito Giovanni hanno passato le vacanze in campagna. Non hanno fatto niente di speciale ma si sono riposati. Claudia ha fatto delle lunghe passeggiate, suo marito ha letto molti libri, e hanno cucinato, mangiato e dormito. I bambini si sono lamentati. Si sono annoiati perché non hanno potuto guardare la televisione.

3 Sample answer
Carissima Daniela
Abbiamo fatto una vacanza bellissima in Scozia. Ci siamo fermati prima a Glasgow, nell'albergo Royal Hotel, in pieno centro. Il giorno dopo siamo andati a Loch Lomond, un lago bellissimo circondato di montagne. Poi siamo andati sempre con il pullman a Fort William, più al nord. Lì abbiamo visto le montagne e le coste, certi colori stupendi e pochi turisti, per fortuna. Dopo due notti al Castle Hotel di Fort William, ci siamo trasferiti ad Aviemore, posto di villeggiatura invernale. Aviemore è stata la base per una gita a Loch Ness e ad Inverness. Grande delusione – non abbiamo visto il mostro di Loch Ness. Il giorno dopo siamo andati nel Perthshire dove abbiamo fatto una visita ad una distilleria dove fanno il whisky Famous Grouse (quello che beve tuo padre). Lo stesso giorno siamo andati al famoso campo di golf a St Andrews che è piaciuto molto a mio marito, appassionato di golf. L'ultima tappa è stata la più bella perché abbiamo passato due notti nella capitale, Edimburgo. Abbiamo visto il castello e il palazzo di Holyrood e abbiamo anche fatto un po' di shopping: maglie di cashmire e qualche kilt! Il viaggio in totale è costato quasi 400 euro a testa, più i voli, ma è valsa proprio la pena, dovresti andarci anche tu!

Test yourself

1 a visto b saputo c letto d scritto e cercato f mangiato g capito
  h detto

2 a T b I c I d T e T f T g T h I

3 a I ragazzi hanno mangiato la pizza.
  b Il poliziotto ci ha fatto la multa.
  c Mia figlia ha detto delle cose stupide.
  d Mio marito ha fatto il medico.
  e Le mie amiche hanno letto molti libri.

f Il nostro insegnante ha scritto delle poesie.

g Abbiamo deciso di andare in vacanza.

h Ho voluto fare una vacanza al mare.

4 a Io e mia cugina siamo andati a Parigi.

b I ragazzi sono usciti dopo cena.

c La temperatura è scesa sotto zero.

d La bambina è nata il 31 dicembre!

e I miei amici sono usciti ma io sono rimasto/a a casa.

f Sei tornato/a dalle vacanze stasera?

g Sono stato/a a Roma per due giorni.

h Siamo saliti tutti in macchina.

5 a fa b scorsa c scorso d fa e scorso

6 a è costato b È' bastato c ci è voluto d È' invecchiato e Sono scomparsi f è piovuto g È' servita h è sembrato

7 a No, non li ho ancora finiti.

b No, non ci vado più.

c No, non ci andiamo mai.

d No, non ho visto nessuno.

e No, non abbiamo mangiato niente.

8 a Le signore si sono sedute a tavola.

b Il mio amico si è vestito di nero.

c Io mi sono svegliato/a alle sette.

d A che ora ti sei svegliato/a?

e Vi siete alzati/e presto sabato?

f Ci siamo preparati/e per uscire.

g I bambini si sono vestiti da soli.

h Prima di uscire mi sono lavata, mi sono vestita e mi sono truccata.

9 a da b per c da d per e da

10 a Abbiamo passato b È' aumentata c ho sceso d ha continuato e hanno cominciato f sono diminuite g è migliorata h ha finito

Unit 12

1 **Why my mother was angry**

Andavo a casa lunedì sera quando **ho incontrato** Marco. Marco **andava** al bar e così **ho deciso** di accompagnarlo e prendere qualcosa anch'io. Mia madre intanto mi **aspettava** a casa e quando **sono tornato** a casa con tre ore di ritardo, mi **ha fatto** la predica.

(All the examples of the perfect tense represent one event or action.
Andavo, **andava** and **aspettava** are examples of an incomplete action.)
My birthday
Per il mio compleanno, mio marito **aveva promesso** di portarmi a
Parigi. Io non **c'ero mai stata**. Una mia amica **aveva offerto** di prendere
cura dei bambini. **Avevamo già preso** i biglietti quando la mia amica **si
è ammalata** e così **abbiamo dovuto** portare anche i bambini. **È stata** una
gita poco romantica!
(All the examples of the perfect tense represent one action or event. The
pluperfect tense represents actions already completed – or not – before
the main action takes place.)

2   1 Conoscevo   2 abbiamo deciso   3 volevamo   4 abbiamo dato   5 sono
rimasti   6 Abbiamo ricevuto   7 ci sposavamo   8 volevamo   9 poteva
10 si era sposato   11 era   12 conosceva   13 erano stati
14 abbiamo preso

Test yourself

1   a   Io e mio marito andavamo tutti i giorni alla stesso ristorante.
    b   I ragazzi uscivano la sera e facevano sempre tardi.
    c   Il mio ragazzo beveva troppo vino.
    d   Parlavo inglese e italiano e al lavoro traducevo testi scientifici.
    e   Mio figlio non diceva mai la verità, diceva solo bugie.
    f   La fabbrica produceva pezzi di ricambio per automobili.

2   a è scesa; ha cominciato   b è nato; abitavamo   c volevo; avevo; sono
    rimasto/a   d sono scappati; parlavo   e era; si è stancata   f stava; sono
    arrivati

3   a   Mentre i clienti aspettavano la pizza, il cameriere gli ha portato
        da bere.
    b   Mentre io cucinavo, mio marito guardava la TV e beveva una birra.
    c   Mentre mia sorella studiava, mio fratello suonava la chitarra.
    d   Mentre parcheggiavo la macchina, è arrivato un vigile.
    e   Quando l'aereo ha cominciato ad atterrare, i bambini si sono messi
        a piangere.
    f   Parlavamo con i nostri amici, quando ci ha interrotto il professore.

4   a aveva bevuto   b erano ancora arrivati   c eravate già stati   d eravamo
    appena arrivati   e avevo letto   f avevi già mangiato

5   a già   b non … mai   c prima   d dopo che   e Appena   f non … ancora

6   a stavo scrivendo   b stava riparando   c stavamo decidendo   d stavate

rifacendo e stavi bevendo f stavano traducendo
7 a Stavo b stava c stavamo d stavate e stavi
8 a voleva b volevo c volevate d voleva e volevo
9 a lavorava b Studiavo c bevevano d eravamo e facevate f facevi
10 a da b per c da d per e da

Unit 13

1 *Sample answer*
Sandra forse andrà in Spagna a lavorare quando sarà laureata. Luca
forse andrà a lavorare con suo padre, che lo pagherà bene. Non dovrà
lavorare troppo, e fra dieci anni forse avrà fatto i primi milioni. Fra
dieci anni Sandra forse avrà sposato uno spagnolo e avrà fatto tre figli.

2 Luisa   Where are you going on holiday next year?
   Amelia We intend to go to the USA. Maybe we'll go and see some
           relatives. My husband doesn't want to go to Sardinia like we
           did this year.
   Luisa   You must be fed up of always going to Sardinia by now, and
           always to the same place. You must have seen the whole
           island, haven't you?
   Amelia Well, not all, but maybe it'll be enough for now!

3 1d Quando io **verrò** a cena, vi **porterò** un regalo.
   2b Se tu **vedrai** Marco, digli che lo chiamerò fra alcuni giorni.
   3a Appena i bambini **arriveranno** al mare, **faranno** un bagno.
   4f Quando **farà** caldo, gli ospiti **avranno** sete e bisognerà prendere delle
   bottiglie di acqua minerale.
   5c Domani sera quando **finiranno** di lavorare, i miei zii **verranno** qui
   al mare.
   6e Ad agosto quando io e mio marito **andremo** in Argentina, il figlio
   più piccolo **rimarrà** qui.

Test yourself

1 a Andrò al mare con la mia famiglia.
   b Partiremo domenica in aereo.
   c I nostri figli leggeranno molti libri in treno.
   d Potrai portare anche il tuo ragazzo alla festa.
   e Telefonerà ogni settimana.
   f Vedrete dei film italiani a Londra.

2 a No, la pagherò domani.

  b No, li mangerò domani.

  c No, le cercherò domani.

  d No, glieli lascerò domani.

  e No, ci andrò domani.

  f No, li farò domani.

3 a Verranno anche i miei suoceri.

  b Berrò solo acqua.

  c Rimarremo a casa quest'estate.

  d Ragazzi, terrete d'occhio i bambini?

  e Comincerà a fare freddo.

  f Pagherai tu la pizza.

4 a Sarà da mia sorella.

  b Saranno in giardino.

  c Avrà troppo da fare.

  d Avranno fame.

  e Starà bene ora.

5 a Gli studenti si iscriveranno all'università quando avranno finito il liceo.

  b I medici lavoreranno in ospedale quando si saranno qualificati.

  c Quando avrai pagato con la carta di credito, ti manderanno i biglietti a casa.

  d Se l'aereo sarà partito da Roma in orario, i miei genitori arriveranno a Londra alle 18.00.

  e Quando avremo finito di fare le valigie, partiremo per l'aeroporto.

6 a Sarà andata in centro.

  b Avranno giocato in giardino.

  c Avrà finito sicuramente.

  d Avranno mangiato prima di cena.

  e Avranno perso il treno.

7 a Comprerò una casa in Italia quando avrò dei soldi.

  b Cambierò vestito quando tornerò a casa.

  c Telefonerò a Patrizia quando lei sarà a casa.

  d Finisco la lettera quando avrò mangiato.

  e Scrivo la email a mio figlio quando avrò acceso il computer.

8 a Il mese prossimo comincio un nuovo lavoro.

  b Fra due giorni vado al mercato.

  c Fra una settimana /La settimana prossima è San Valentino.

d Fra mezz'ora devo uscire.

e Stasera vado al cinema.

9 a L'estate prossima spero di /ho intenzione di venire a trovarti.

b L'anno prossimo abbiamo intenzione di sposarci.

c La settimana prossima i nostri amici pensano di partire per la montagna.

d Domenica per pranzo mio marito pensa di preparare un bel arrosto di carne.

e Hai intenzione di pagare la bolletta dell'elettricità domani mattina?

f Avete intenzione di affittare/Pensate di affittare una casa al mare ad agosto?

10 a Domani vado in centro.

b Mia sorella va a fare la spesa dopo il lavoro.

c Mia sorella va a comprare delle scarpe/comprerà delle scarpe.

d Andiamo a Napoli questo finesettimana.

e Mio figlio lavorerà a Londra.

Unit 14

1 1 vorrei 2 vuoi 3 vorrei 4 volete 5 vuole 6 vorrei 7 volete 8 voglio 9 Vogliamo 10 vogliamo

2 1 vuole 2 vuole 3 vorrei 4 volevo 5 voleva 6 ha voluto 7 vorrebbe

Test yourself

1 a vogliono b vogliamo c vuoi d volete e voglio f vuole

2 a Sì, le voglio./No, non le voglio.

b Sì, lo vogliamo./No, non lo vogliamo.

c Sì, grazie, la vogliamo./No, grazie, non la vogliamo.

d Sì, li voglio./No, non li voglio.

e Sì, ne vorrei un chilo./No, non ne vorrei.

f Sì, ne vorrei un etto./No, non ne vorrei.

g Sì, ne vorrei un cucchiaino./No, non ne voglio.

h Sì, ne vogliamo due bicchieri./No, non ne vogliamo.

3 a No, la mangiamo due o tre volte alla settimana.

b Sì, li leggiamo ogni giorno.

c Sì, l'ho pulito stamattina.

d Sì, l'ho venduta sabato scorso ad un mio amico.

e Sì, le ho viste quando lei è entrata.

f Sì, ne ho comprati cinque chili.

g Lo faccio io.

h Ne compro un chilo.

4 a Mio figlio non vuole andare a letto.

   b Io e mio marito vogliamo comprare una casa in Toscana.

   c Voglio parlare italiano.

   d Vuoi fare l'esame orale, Anna?

   e I nostri amici vogliono vendere la macchina.

   f Volete accompagnarci in aeroporto?

5 a Vorrei parlare con il direttore.

   b Vorremmo una camera matrimoniale.

   c Vorreste qualcosa da bere?

   d Vorrebbe vedere qualche casa?

   e Vorresti venire al cinema?

6 a di b a c di d a e a f di

7 a hanno voluto b ha voluto c è' voluta/ha voluto d Abbiamo voluto
   e Ho voluto f Siamo voluti/Abbiamo voluto

8 a Volevo mangiare ma non avevo tempo.

   b Siamo andati tutti in pizzeria – abbiamo voluto provare la pizza
   cotta nel forno a legna.

   c Chiara, vuoi uscire stasera?

   d Vorrebbe parlare con suo padre.

   e Avrei voluto andare al cinema.

   f Vuole sedersi?

9 a ci vuole b ci vogliono c ci metti d ci metto e ci è voluto f ci sono
   volute

10 a preferite b preferiscono c a d al e o

Unit 15

1 Si ascoltavano concerti come quello di Gianni Morandi ... al tramonto
   si visitavano gli studi degli scultori. Il mercoledì si andava al mercato
   dove si compravano le più belle tovaglie, lenzuola, piatti e bicchieri.
   Tra i colori preferiti, andava incluso il bianco: camicie bianche, scarpe
   da tennis bianche ... ecc. L'unica concessione veniva riservata al kaki
   coloniale che veniva considerato molto di moda.

2 1 si mangia 2 viene mangiata 3 si mangiano 4 viene servita
   5 Va servita 6 vengono servite 7 vengono serviti

Test yourself

1   a P   b A   c P   d A   e P   f A
2   a   Al supermercato verrà venduto il vino.
    b   Sono stati scritti pochi esercizi.
    c   Sabato è stato festeggiato il compleanno dei gemelli.
    d   Sono state messe in ordine le camere.
    e   È' firmata la lettera.
3   a   In Inghilterra il giornale viene consegnato a casa.
    b   In Italia il tè viene servito al limone.
    c   Quando abitavo a Londra, il latte veniva consegnato a casa.
    d   A Bologna le tagliatelle vengono servite con il ragù bolognese.
    e   Dopo i documenti verranno messi nell'archivio.
4   a va servita   b va servito   c va fritta   d va pulita   e vanno scritti
5   a si affittano   b si pulisce   c si parla   d si scrive   e si vendono
6   a   Non si sa mai.
    b   Si va!
    c   D'inverno si è tristi.
    d   Si cena alle otto/20.00.
    e   Si viaggia di notte quando fa fresco.
7   a   Ci si alza sempre alle sette.
    b   Ci si sveglia molto presto.
    c   Ci si veste di corsa.
    d   Ci si mette in macchina alle 8.30.
    e   Ci si vede in centro.
8   a   Siamo rimasti delusi dall'albergo a Venezia.
    b   Nostro figlio è rimasto ferito a scuola.
    c   Siete rimasti sorpresi dall'arrivo dei vostri amici.
    d   Sono rimasto scandalizzato dal tuo comportamento.
    e   I nostri amici sono rimasti offesi.
9   Come **vengono fatti** gli gnocchi di patate? Prima tutti gli ingredienti
    vengono versati in una grande terrina e **vengono mescolati e impastati**
    con le mani rapidamente. L'impasto viene versato sul ripiano del banco
    da lavoro e **viene diviso** in tanti filoni dello spessore di 2–3 centimetri.
    Si tagliano e **si formano** gli gnocchi con le mani o con la forchetta.
    Poi **si mettono** su vassoi spolverati di farina e si coprono con un
    canovaccio. Gli gnocchi **vengono versati** in una pentola di acqua salata
    in ebollizione. Quando salgono in superficie sono pronti. **Vanno scolati
    e conditi** con il burro fuso, o con il sugo di pomodoro.

10 a si taglia b si soffrigge c si sbucciano d si tagliano e si mettono
   f Si mescola g si lascia

Unit 16

1 1 piace 2 piace 3 a me 4 piacciono 5 me piacciono 6 piacciono
   7 a lui 8 piacciono
2 1 Gli piace il pane con la marmellata.
   2 Le piace l'insalata verde.
   3 Ci piacciono le patate fritte.
   4 Gli piacciono gli hamburger.
   5 Le piacciono le patate.
   6 Gli piace la pasta.
   7 Gli piace la carne.
   8 Mi piace la pizza./Mi piacciono i gelati./ecc.

Test yourself

1 a iii b iv c i d ii
2 a piacerà b piacerebbe c piaceva d è piaciuto
3 a iv b iii c i d ii
4 a sono piaciuti b piacerà c piacerebbe d piaceva
5 a gli b ci c le d mi
6 a noi b te c me d lei
7 a te b me c me
8 a Anche al mio.
   b Anche a me.
   c Anche a mia moglie.
   d Anche a mio marito
9 a Neanche agli inglesi.
   b Neanche ai miei.
   c Neanche a noi.
   d Neanche a me.
10 a vuole bene b amiamo c piaccio d volevo bene

Unit 17

1 1 Io penso che bastino cinquanta sterline.
   2 Credo che la scuola sia membro dell'ARELS.

3 Mi sembra che la scuola stia in centro.

4 Penso che la scuola abbia insegnanti qualificati.

5 Credo che gli insegnanti siano giovani.

6 Mi sembra che i ragazzi possano praticare lo sport.

7 Credo che i ragazzi debbano essere autonomi.

8 Penso che la scuola organizzi escursioni e attività sociali.

9 Mi pare che i pasti siano inclusi nel prezzo.

10 Mi sembra che i ragazzi abbiano la possibilità di comprare bibite e merendine.

11 Penso che ci sia un centro medico.

2 1 Mia madre pensa che io vada a letto prima di mezzanotte.

2 Mia madre crede che io studi.

3 Mia madre pensa che io abbia preso un bel voto.

4 Mia madre crede che io sia stata promossa in tutte le materie.

5 Mia madre pensa che la sera io stia a casa della mia amica.

6 Mia madre crede che io non esca con nessuno.

7 Mia madre pensa che i miei amici siano ragazzi seri.

8 Mia madre crede che io vada in autobus.

9 Mia madre pensa che io non mangi mai cose di questo tipo.

10 Mia madre crede che io non beva mai bevande alcoliche.

Test yourself

1 a comincino; finiscano b capisca c mangino d leggano e dormano

2 a siano b abbiamo c diamo d faccia e possano

3 a i b iv c ii d iii

4 a iv b iii c i d ii

5 a sembra/pare b sembra/pare di aver visto c sembra/pare di spendere d sembra/pare e sembra/pare di avere

6 a che, vogliano b di partire c pensa d sia e di partire

7 a A suo parere/Secondo lui b A loro avviso/Secondo loro c A mio avviso/Secondo me d quanto mi riguarda

A mio avviso (etc.) can be replaced by **a mio parere** (etc.) in a, b and c.

8 a Cosa pensi di queste scarpe?

b Cosa pensi dell'Italia?

c Cosa pensi di quest'albergo?

9 a iv b iii c i d ii

10 a siano già cominciate b abbia capito c sia stato d abbiano fatto e abbia speso f abbiano detto

Unit 18

1   1 Bisogna che io sia 2 devo prendere 3 deve essere 4 bisogna che
prenda 5 deve pagare 6 Le servoro

2 /3   Make sure you use as many of the expressions covered in this unit as
possible. Check your answers with a friend or your tutor.

4   *Sample answer*
Cara Chiara
Ecco alcune regole che ti potranno essere di aiuto. Per gli annunci, non
c'è bisogno che voi mandiate bigliettini. Dovete invece avvertire gli
amici e i parenti stretti telefonicamente. Se però avete molti parenti e
amici in altre città, bisogna che comunichiate la notizia per posta. In
questo caso è essenziale far stampare dei bigliettini. Bisogna mandarli
dopo la nascita, quando rientrerai a casa dall'ospedale. Sul cartoncino,
bisogna che mettiate tutti i nomi del bambino, se non sono più di tre.
I confetti, invece, bisogna darli solamente in occasione del battesimo.
Bisogna che questi siano celesti per un maschietto e rosa per una
femminuccia.

Test yourself

1 a devi b devono c Devo d dobbiamo
2 a Dovrei b Devo c deve d dovrebbero
3 a Ho bisogno di b hai bisogno di c abbiamo bisogno di d Avete
bisogno di
4 a dica b pagare c stare d dia
5 a ii b iv c iii d i
6 a iv b i c ii d iii
7 a occorrono/ci vogliono b serve   c ci vuole d ci vogliono
8 a c'è bisogno b bisogna c ho bisogno d Hai bisogno
9 a bisogna b Non importa; Basta c Mi sembra
10 a È normale b È possibile c È facile d È inutile

Unit 19

1   Vacanze, tempo di abbandoni. Ogni estate si stima che oltre 25.000
cani e migliaia di altri animali domestici **vengano** lasciati morire.
"In Valtellina – spiega Anna Tosi, volontaria del canile Enpa –
riceviamo centinaia di richieste da persone che vogliono che i loro

cani **vengano** tenuti nel nostro Centro." A meno che la situazione non **migliori**, il randagismo diventerà un pericolo sia per gli uomini che per il bestiame. Qualsiasi provvedimento **sia stato varato** finora, non ha ottenuto risultati incoraggianti. "La nuova legge appena approvata – aggiunge l'onorevole socialista Dino Mazza – si spera che **faccia** perdere l'abitudine agli italiani di mettere il cane a dicembre sotto l'albero e ad agosto sull'autostrada." Ma è difficile che questo problema **sia risolto** facilmente.

Holidays, a time when animals are abandoned. Every summer, it is estimated that over 25,000 dogs and thousands of other pets are left to die. 'In the Valtellina,' explains Anna Tosi, a voluntary worker at the Enpa kennels, 'we receive hundreds of requests from people who want their dogs to be looked after in our Centre.' Unless the situation improves, the stray dog problem will become a danger both to man and livestock. The measures taken up to now have not achieved encouraging results. 'It is to be hoped that the new law just approved', adds the socialist MP Dino Mazza, 'will get the Italians to kick their habit of putting a dog under the tree at Christmas and out on the motorway in August.' But it is unlikely that this problem will be solved easily.

2 1 partano 2 salutino 3 abbiano 4 siano
3 Sample answers
  1 Sono contenta che la Scozia abbia vinto la partita e che giochi contro l'Italia stasera.
  2 Mi dispiace che ci sia sciopero. Ma sono contenta che non ci siano lezioni.
  3 Mi dispiace che tua madre sia caduta e che si sia rotta il braccio.
  4 Mi dispiace/Sono desolata che il tuo cane sia stato investito da una macchina.
  5 Non sono stupita che l'insegnante bocci Giovanni all'esame di storia contemporanea.
  6 Sono contenta che stasera tua zia prepari la pasta con le vongole.
  7 Mi dispiace che tuo fratello abbia preso in prestito da te un CD e che l'abbia graffiato.
  8 Sono stupita che venga anche la tua ex-ragazza stasera.
  9 Sono contenta che i tuoi genitori ti diano cento euro per il tuo compleanno.
  10 Sono contenta che tuo padre ti offra un viaggio a Parigi per

festeggiare l'onomastico.

11 Mi stupisce che Gianna debba stare a dieta.

12 Mi dispiace che fra te e il calcio, il tuo ragazzo preferisca il calcio.

Test yourself

1 a possa b si sposino c abbia d sia
2 a sia b siano c debbano d faccia
3 a rimanga b possa c preferisca d siano
4 a siano b venga c vengano d guardino
5 a si risolva b vadano c timbrino d migliori
6 a iv b ii c iii d i
7 a sia b conosca c possa
8 a i b i
9 a Comunque b Chiunque c Qualunque/Qualsiasi
10 The first needs the subjunctive, for example:
  Non penso che tu abbia molto tempo.
  Non penso di avere molto tempo.

Unit 20

1 1 Mi potrebbe indicare la fermata più vicina?
   2 Le dispiacerebbe aprire la finestra?
   3 Le dispiacerebbe chiudere la porta?
   4 Le dispiacerebbe passarmi lo zucchero?/Potrebbe passarmi lo zucchero?
   5 Le dispiacerebbe prestarmi la penna?/Mi potrebbe prestare la penna?
   6 Mi potrebbe dire l'ora?
   7 Le dispiacerebbe spostare la valigia?/Potrebbe spostare la valigia?
   8 Mi potrebbe dare una mano?

2 Era strano quel che succedeva quando dormivo con mia nonna ...
   quando mi risvegliavo, mi ritrovavo nella stessa posizione ... **Penso che
   mia nonna si svegliasse** molto prima di me e mi **risistemasse** nella stessa
   posizione, ma **era bello immaginare che avessimo dormito** in quella
   posizione per tutta la notte. In ogni caso **era bellissimo che** lei **facesse** di
   tutto per farmelo credere.
   *It was strange what happened when I slept in my grandmother's bed ...
   when I woke up, I found myself in exactly the same position... I think
   that my grandmother woke up a good bit before me and put me back in
   the same position, but it was nice to imagine that we had slept in that*

*position for the whole night. Anyway, it was really nice that she did
everything possible to make me believe it.*

3   1 restassimo   2 potessi   3 parlassi   4 fosse   5 uscissi   6 prendessi

Test yourself

1 a iv   b i   c iii   d ii
2 a iv   b i   c iii   d ii
3 a parlerebbero   b comprerei   c partirei   d verrebbe
4 a farebbe   b potrebbe   c dispiacerebbe   d potrebbe
5 a comprerei   b faremmo   c potrebbero   d studieresti
6 a stessi   b fossi   c facessero   d avessimo
7 a iii   b iv   c ii   d i
8 a alla; di   b di   c di
9 a invitato a   b Invitiamo; a   c convinta a
10 a faccio   b Lasciami   c ho visto   d lasciarli

Unit 21

1   1 fossi già partito   2 l'abbia controllata   3 l'avessimo mai portata   4
fosse   5 avesse fatto   6 dovessimo   7 aveste aspettato

2   La vita è piena di sbagli. Avevamo prenotato l'albergo a Venezia su
consiglio di un'amica. Non **sapevamo che** lei non **fosse** mai stata a
Venezia, e **che** il nome dell'albergo **l'avesse trovato** su una vecchia guida
turistica. Sarà stato bello cinquanta anni fa, ma non più. E il ristorante
poi …! Morivamo di sete! **Nonostante avessimo detto** al cameriere
tre volte di portare del vino rosso, ci ha portato solo acqua minerale.
Peccato poi che il cuoco **abbia dimenticato** di togliere lo spago prima
di servire l'arrosto … mi chiedevo poi perché mio marito avesse deciso
di mangiarlo, ma lui, poveretto, **aveva pensato che** il cuoco **avesse
preparato** una specialità tipica e **che** lo spago ne **fosse** una parte
essenziale. Avremmo mangiato meglio alla mensa degli studenti – e
avremmo anche speso di meno.
*Life is full of mistakes. We had booked the hotel in Venice on the
advice of a friend. We didn't know that she had never been to Venice,
but had found the name in an old guide book. It might have been nice
50 years ago, but no longer. And the restaurant …! We were dying of
thirst. Despite the fact that we had asked the waiter three times to bring
us some red wine, he brought us only mineral water. A pity, too, that*

*the chef forgot to take off the string around the roast before serving it.
I wondered why my husband had decided to eat it, but he, poor thing,
had thought the chef had prepared some typical local speciality and
that the string was an essential part of it. We would have eaten better at
the student canteen, and we would have spent less, too.*

Test yourself

1 a fossi già arrivata b avessero letto c foste venuti d avessimo finito
2 a avrei preferito b sarebbe venuto c avrebbe prestato d Saremmo stati
3 a iv b iii c ii d i
4 a avessero ricevuto b fossero mai stati; avessero mai visto c foste arrivati
5 a Si diceva che la principessa si fosse fidanzata di nascosto.
   b Dicevano che la mozzarella fosse stata contaminata dall'acqua.
6 a ii b iii c i
7 a Ci saremmo andati ma non avevamo i soldi.
   b Ne avremmo comprato una ma non avevamo i soldi.
   c Avrei comprato qualcosa ma non avevo i soldi.
8 a sarebbe migliorata b avrebbe nascosto c avrebbero avuto
   d saremmo stati
9 a ii b iii c i
10 a ii b i c iv d iii

Unit 22

1 1 Sarei venuta 2 fossi venuta 3 viene 4 fossi 5 inviti
2 1 ... mangeremmo meglio.
   2 ... potrei uscire tutte le sere./potrei fare quello che voglio.
   3 ... avrei una camera tutta mia.
   4 ... ci vedremmo più spesso./ci potremmo vedere più spesso.
   5 ... non mangerebbe la carne.
3 Sample answers
   1 ... sarei rimasta in Italia./avrei parlato italiano meglio./avrei avuto
   una vita più felice.
   2 ... saremmo più bravi./avremmo avuto un voto migliore.
   3 ... ti saresti divertita./avresti trovato un lavoro migliore.
   4 ... avrebbe conosciuto l'uomo dei suoi sogni.
   5 ... non sarebbe andato a finire contro un muro./non avrebbe
   distrutto la macchina.

Test yourself

1 a esci; chiudi b vengono; siamo c rubano; rimani
2 a troveremo b metterai c prenderanno
3 a lavorassi; potresti b fosse; potrebbe c avessimo; potremmo
4 a fossi venuta; saresti divertita b avesse guidato; avrebbe fatto c
   avessimo passato; avremmo imparato
5 a Se tu mangiavi di meno, non ingrassavi poi tanto.
   b Se tu venivi alla festa, ti presentavo i miei amici.
   c Se i ragazzi studiavano, prendevano voti migliori.
6 a Avendo b Sapendo c Comprando
7 a a meno che b a condizione che c purché
8 a ho chiesto b sono stato
9 a a verb which can be used with an object
   b a noun which has the same form in singular and plural
10 a see Verbs, then Subjunctive (present)
   b see Pronouns, then Direct object

Grammar appendix

This section of the book covers only those points that have not been covered in the units, or that have been mentioned only in passing. It includes a list of irregular verbs and a list of verb links, for easy reference (§§ 13.3 and 13.2 respectively).

1 Nouns with irregular plurals

Nouns with regular plurals and a few nouns with irregular plurals are illustrated in Unit 2. Here, we show only those nouns which do not follow those patterns and which have not been illustrated in Unit 2.

1.1 Invariable plural forms (nouns with the same form in both singular and plural)

Nouns ending in -i
These are mainly feminine:

| la cris**i** | *crisis* | le cris**i** | *crises* |

But note:

| il brindis**i** | *toast* | i brindis**i** | *toasts* |
| (e.g. to bride and groom) | | | |

Feminine nouns ending in -ie

| la ser**ie** | *series* | le ser**ie** | *series* |

But note:

| la mog**lie** | *wife* | le mog**li** | *wives* |

Abbreviated words

la bici(cletta)	*bike*	le bici	*bikes*
il cinema(tografo)	*cinema*	i cinema	*cinemas*

Words borrowed from other languages (mainly ending in a consonant)

il night	*nightclub*	i night	*nightclubs*
il computer	*computer*	i computer	*computers*

1.2 Irregular and other plural forms

Nouns with masculine singular ending in -o, but feminine plural ending in -a

il paio	*pair*	le paia	*pairs*
l'uovo	*egg*	le uova	*eggs*
il migliaio	*thousand*	le migliaia	*thousands*

Nouns with masculine singular ending in -o, and alternative plurals (masculine ending in -i, feminine ending in -a)

These nouns have a regular masculine plural ending in -i and an irregular feminine plural ending in -a. Often the regular plural has a figurative meaning, while the irregular plural has a literal meaning.

i braccio	*arm*	le braccia	*arms (of a person)*
i bracci	*arms (e.g. of a (chandelier)*		

In some cases, there is no difference in meaning, but the irregular form is more common:

il lenzuolo	*sheet*	le lenzuola	*sheets*
		i lenzuoli	*sheets*

Masculine nouns ending in -co, -go

Nouns where the stress falls on the second-to-last syllable form their plural in -chi or -ghi, keeping the hard g sound.

| il luo**go** | *place* | i luo**ghi** | *places* |
| il fi**co** | *fig* | i fi**chi** | *figs* |

Unfortunately, there are many exceptions:

| l'ami**co** | *friend* | gli ami**ci** | *friends* |

Words where the stress generally falls before the second-to-last syllable form their plural in -**ci** and -**gi** with a soft **g**.

| l'aspara**go** | *asparagus* | gli aspara**gi** | *asparagus* |
| il medi**co** | *doctor* | i medi**ci** | *doctors* |

But again, there are very many exceptions.

| il catalo**go** | *catalogues* | i catalo**ghi** | *catalogues* |

Feminine nouns ending in -ca, -ga
These form their plural in -**che** and –**ghe**.

| l'ami**ca** | *friend* | le ami**che** | *friends* |

Feminine nouns ending in -cia, -gia
These have a plural ending -**cie** or -**gie** if there is a vowel before the -**cia** or –**gia**.

| la farmac**ia** | *chemist's* | le farmac**ie** | *chemists* |
| la valig**ia** | *suitcase* | le valig**ie** | *suitcases* |

They have plural ending -**ce** or -**ge** if there is a consonant before the -**cia** or –**gia**.

| la spiagg**ia** | *beach* | le spiag**ge** | *beaches* |
| la manc**ia** | *tip* | le man**ce** | *tips* |

Masculine nouns ending in –io
If the stress falls on the **i**, the **i** is doubled.

| lo **zio** | _uncle_ | gli **zii** | _uncles_ |

Otherwise, it is not.

| lo stud**io** | _study_ | gli stud**i** | _studies_ |

Compound nouns

Nouns made up of two different words stuck together sometimes have irregular plural forms.

| il capostazione | _station master_ | i capistazione | _station masters_ |
| il fuoribordo | _motor boat_ | i fuoribordo | _motor boats_ |

Since the rules – and the exceptions – are numerous, it is safer to use a good dictionary to check the plural of such nouns.

---

2 Adjectives extra

The following adjectives can take different forms when they come directly before a noun: **bello, buono, grande, santo.**

bello

Bello has the same forms as the definite article **il, lo, la,** etc.

un **bel** ragazzo	_a nice-looking boy_
una **bella** casa in campagna	_a beautiful house in the country_
un **bello** specchio antico	_a beautiful antique mirror_
Hanno ricevuto dei **bei** regali.	_They received some lovely presents._
Hai fatto delle belle foto.	_You've taken some lovely photos._
... una casa con dei **begli** alberi intorno	_... a house with beautiful trees around_

buono

In the singular, **buono** has the same forms as the indefinite article **un, uno, una,** etc.

un **buon** ristorante	*a good restaurant*
un **buono** studente	*a good student*
una **buona** persona	*a good person*
una **buon**'idea	*a good idea*

grande

Before masculine singular nouns, **grande** can have a shortened
form, but this is optional.

| un **grande** capitano / un **gran** | *a great captain* |
| capitano | |

Do not use the shortened form if the noun starts with a vowel,
with **gn, pn, ps, s, x, z, s** + consonant, or **y** or **i** followed by another
vowel.

| un **grande** albergo | *a great hotel* |
| un **grande** scultore | *a great sculptor* |

santo

Finally, **santo** (feminine **santa**) meaning *holy*, *saint* can have a
shortened form before a masculine singular name, unless it begins
with **gn, pn, ps, s, x, z, s** + consonant or **y** or **i** followed by another
vowel.

San Marco
Santo Stefano
Santa Lucia

It can drop the final **-o/-a** vowel before a name beginning with a
vowel.

Sant'Ambrogio
Sant'Anna

3 Comparison

3.1 Comparative adjectives

Più, meno

Comparative adjectives are formed using **più** (*more*) or **meno** (*less*). When making a comparison between two people, two objects or two other elements, *than* is expressed by **di**, or by **che** if it comes directly between the two elements compared.

Oggi ti amo più **di** ieri, meno **di** domani.	*Today I love you more than yesterday, less than tomorrow.*
Lui è meno bravo **di** te.	*He is less clever than you.*
Marco è più simpatico **di** Giuliano.	*Marco is nicer than Giuliano.*
Fa meno freddo oggi **che** ieri.	*It is less cold today than yesterday.*
Oggigiorno si mangia più pesce **che** carne.	*Nowadays, one eats more fish than meat.*

Di (than) can combine with il, lo, la, etc.

Gli italiani sono più simpatici **degli** inglesi.	*The Italians are nicer than the English.*

buono – più buono – migliore

Buono (*good*) has two comparative forms: **più buono** and **migliore**. There is little difference in meaning, but while **più buono** is often used for food and drink, **migliore** is normally used in a more general context.

I gelati francesi sono **buoni**, ma i gelati italiani sono **più buoni**.	*French ice-creams are good, but Italian ice-creams are better.*
Con l'antenna parabolica, la qualità della trasmissione è **migliore**.	*With a satellite dish. the quality of transmission is better.*

cattivo – più cattivo – peggiore

Cattivo (*bad*) has two comparative forms: **più cattivo** and **peggiore**. There is little difference in meaning, but while **più cattivo** is often used for food and drink, **peggiore** is normally used in a more general context.

| Questo vino è **cattivo**, ma l'altro è ancora **più cattivo**. | *This wine is bad, but the other is even worse.* |
| Questa pensione **non** è **buona**, ma l'altra è **peggiore**. | *This hotel isn't good, but the other is worse.* |

grande – più grande – maggiore

Grande (*big*) also has two comparative forms: **più grande** and **maggiore**. While **più grande** can be used to refer either to physical size or age difference, **maggiore** generally refers to age difference or to an abstract quality, but not to physical size.

Milano è **più grande** di Torino.	*Milan is bigger than Turin.*
La mia sorella **maggiore** (or **più grande**) si chiama Rosa.	*My older sister is called Rosa.*
Per gli studenti, lo sport è un tema di **maggiore** interesse.	*For the students, sport is a topic of greater interest.*

piccolo – più piccolo – minore

Piccolo (*small*) also has two comparative forms: **più piccolo** and **minore**. While **più piccolo** can be used to refer either to physical size or age difference, **minore** generally refers to age difference or to an abstract quality, rather than physical size.

La nostra camera è **più piccola** della vostra.	*Our room is smaller than yours.*
Il suo fratello **minore** si chiamava Luca.	*His younger brother was called Luca.*
Questo episodio è di **minore** importanza.	*This incident is of lesser importance.*

Plural forms

Both **maggiore** and **minore** have plural forms: **maggiori**, **minori**.

3.2 Relationship of equality: adjectives

tanto … quanto; così … come
To compare two things of equal qualities, use **tanto … quanto** or **così … come**. Così and **tanto** can be omitted from the sentence without changing the meaning.

Una pensione può essere **tanto** comoda **quanto** l'albergo di lusso.

A guest house can be just as comfortable as a luxury hotel.

3.3 Superlative adjectives

Most and *least* are expressed using **il più** and **il meno** with the adjective and often followed by **di** where English would use *in.*

È il ristorante **meno caro** della città.

It's the least expensive restaurant in town.

È **la** chiesa **più** bella di Venezia.

It's the most beautiful church in Venice.

The more common adjectives can also come before the noun.

È **il più** bel ragazzo della classe.

He's the best-looking boy in the class.

buono, cattivo, grande, piccolo
Buono, cattivo, grande, piccolo all have two different forms of superlative, each with slightly different meanings (see comparative forms above).

Gli incidenti stradali sono **la maggiore** causa di morte in Italia.

Road accidents are the biggest (greatest) cause of death in Italy.

La FIAT 500 è **la** macchina **più piccola** di tutte.

The 500 is the smallest car of all. (physical size)

Superlative with no comparison implied
To express a superlative quality, when no comparison is being made, use **molto, estremamente** or **veramente** with the adjective.

I bambini erano **veramente** stanchi.

The kids were really tired.

Or add the suffix **-issimo** onto the end.

Questi fiori sono **bellissimi**. *These flowers are very beautiful.*

In addition to their regular superlative forms ending in **-issimo**, **buono**, **cattivo**, **grande** and **piccolo** have alternative superlative forms, respectively **ottimo**, **pessimo**, **massimo** and **minimo**. Like other adjectives, all change their ending to agree with the noun.

Ottime queste tagliatelle! *Excellent, this tagliatelle!*
È **pessimo** questo albergo. *This hotel is rubbish.*
È il **massimo**! *That's really the best! (sometimes used ironically)*

Non ha fatto il **minimo** sforzo. *He didn't make the slightest effort.*
Non ho la **minima** idea. *I haven't got a clue.*

3.4 Comparative adverbs

più, meno
As with adjectives, comparisons can be made using **più** (*more*) and **meno** (*less*) along with the appropriate adverb.

Gianfranco cammina **più velocemente** di me. *Gianfranco walks faster than me.*

Gianfranco cammina **meno velocemente** di Filippo. *Gianfranco walks less quickly than Filippo.*

bene, male, molto, poco
These four adverbs have irregular comparative forms **meglio**, **peggio**, **più**, **meno**, respectively.

Giuliana guida **bene**, ma Mariangela guida **meglio**. *Giuliana drives well, but Mariangela drives better.*
Franco cucina **male**, ma Giovanni cucina **peggio**. *Franco cooks badly, but Giovanni cooks worse.*
Marco studia **molto**, ma Monica studia **di più**. *Marco studies a lot, but Monica studies more.*

| Arabella lavora **poco**, ma Marina lavora **di meno**. | *Arabella works little, but Marina works less.* |

3.5 Relationship of equality: adverbs

tanto ... quanto; così ... come
You have already seen these pairs used with adjectives. Their use with adverbs is similar. **Così** and **tanto** can be omitted from the sentence without changing the meaning.

| Sandra guida **così** male **come** sua sorella. | *Sandra drives just as badly as her sister.* |

3.6 Superlative adverbs

il più possibile/molto/-issimamente
There are several ways to form superlative adverbs. Sometimes, no comparison is implied. Study these examples.

Guidava **molto lentamente**.	*He drove very slowly.*
Guidava **lentissimamente**.	*He drove very slowly.*
Guidava **il più lentamente possibile**.	*He drove very slowly/as slowly as possible.*
Guidava **il più lentamente di tutti**.	*He drove the slowest of everyone.*
Lo vedo **il meno possibile**.	*I see him as little as possible.*

bene, male, molto, poco
These adverbs have a normal superlative form ending in -issimo.

Ha sciato **benissimo**.	*She skied very well.*
L'ha fatto **malissimo**.	*He did it very badly.*
Ho mangiato **moltissimo**.	*I've eaten loads.*
Hai studiato **pochissimo**.	*You've studied very little.*

Their irregular superlative forms **il meglio, il peggio, il più, il meno** respectively can also be used as a relative superlative (i.e. comparing with someone else's efforts).

Ha fatto **il meglio** possibile.   *He did as best he could.*
Ha studiato **il più** possibile.   *He studied as much as possible.*
Cerca di camminare **il**   *Try to walk as little as possible.*
    meno possibile.

The forms **il meglio, il peggio** can also be used as nouns (the best,
the worst).

Ha dato **il meglio** di se stessa.   *She gave the best of herself.*
Non sai ancora **il peggio**.   *You don't know the worst.*

---

4 Pronouns

There are several types of pronouns. The most important group
is that of personal pronouns, including direct object, indirect
object, subject pronouns and stressed pronouns. The direct object
pronouns are illustrated in Units 4 and 14. Here, we explain other
types of pronouns.

4.1 Indirect object pronouns

The forms **mi, ti, gli, le, Le, ci, vi, gli/loro** are used with any verb
that takes an indirect object.

Verbs of *giving*, *lending*, etc. such as **dare, prestare, portare**

Vi porto il conto?   *Shall I bring (to) you the bill?*
Ti ha dato il resto?   *Did he give (to) you the change?*

Or expressing the idea of doing something for someone.

Mi compreresti il giornale?   *Would you buy the newspaper for
                                                 me?*
Ti preparo un caffè?   *Shall I make (for) you a coffee?*

4.2 Combined object pronouns

Look what happens when a direct object **lo, la, li, le,** etc. (see Unit 14) meets an indirect object **mi, ti, gli, le,** etc. The indirect object pronouns come first and change form slightly. **Mi, ti, ci, vi** become **me, te, ce, ve** before a direct object pronoun, to produce **me lo, te lo,** etc. **Gli, le, Le** combine with the direct object pronouns to form a single word **glielo** (etc.).

Indirect	Direct	Combined
mi	lo	me lo
ti	lo	te lo
gli	lo	glielo
le	lo	glielo
Le	lo	glielo
ci	lo	ce lo
vi	lo	ve lo
gli	lo	glielo

The pattern is the same whether the direct object pronoun is **lo, la, li** or **le** (for example **me li, me le,** etc.). The exception to the pattern is **loro,** which comes after the verb and does not combine with the other pronouns.

Use of combined pronouns
Here are examples of how they are used:

Come si apre questa bottiglia?	*How does one open this bottle?*
Te la apro io.	*I'll open it for you.*
I ragazzi hanno lasciato questo libro.	*The kids have left behind this book.*
Glielo mandiamo per posta.	*We'll mail it to them.*

Glielo can mean *it to him* or *it to her* or *it to them*. To avoid any confusion or ambiguity, you can use **a lui, a lei, a loro.**

Lo mando **a lui**.	*I send it to him.*
Lo mando **a lei**.	*I send it to her.*
Lo mando **a loro**.	*I send it to them.*

4.3 Position of pronouns

Normally the pronouns come before the verb, but this is not true in all cases:

After the infinitive
The pronouns come after and are joined onto the end of the infinitive (the -**are**, -**ere**, -**ire** form).

Sono andata in centro per **comprarla**.	*I went to the centre to buy it.*
Ho deciso di **spedirgli** una cartolina.	*I've decided to send him a postcard.*
Mi ha telefonato per **chiedermelo**.	*He rang me to ask me for it.*

With the modal auxiliary verbs **volere, dovere, sapere, potere, preferire**
With these verbs, the object pronouns can either be joined to the end of the infinitive, as above, or come before both verbs.

Lo puoi comprare in centro.	*You can buy it in town.*
or Puoi comprar**lo** in centro.	
Voglio parlar**gli** chiaro.	*I want to speak clearly to him.*
or **Gli** voglio parlare chiaro.	
Deve dir**glielo** appena possibile.	*She must tell him (it) as soon as possible.*
or **Glielo** deve dire appena possibile.	

With the gerund (-**ando**, -**endo** *form*)
The object pronouns are joined to the end of the gerund.

| Telefonando**ti** di sera, risparmio parecchio. | *By phoning you in the evening, I save a lot.* |

| Riparando**telo** gratis, ti faccio un grande favore. | *Repairing it for you free, I'm doing you a big favour.* |

With **stare** and the gerund, the object pronouns can be joined to the end of the gerund, as above, *or* can come before **stare**.

| **Lo** stavo guardando ora. *or* Stavo guardando**lo** ora. | *I was just looking at it now.* |

See also Unit 9 for pronouns used with the imperative form.

4.4 ci

Ci is generally treated in the same way as the object pronouns and is often found with them. It has two main functions: firstly, as a particle meaning *there* or *to there*. It's occasionally replaced by **vi**, but this is far less common in spoken Italian. Secondly, it acts as a pronoun, replacing **a** and a noun.

Mi piace Londra; **ci** abito da sei anni.	*I like London; I've lived there for six years.*
Andando**ci** **di** lunedì, troverete meno gente.	*Going there on a Monday, you will find less people.*
Ti **ci** porto io, se vuoi.	*I'll take you there if you want.*

Ci can be used with a verb which takes **a**, such as **credere, riuscire, pensare**.

| Credi a quello che dice? No, non **ci** credo. | *Do you believe what he says?* *No, I don't believe it.* |

Ci is also used in phrases where the verb **avere** is combined with direct object pronouns **lo, la, li, le. Lo,** la are often abbreviated before **avere** to **l'**. But the plurals **li** and **le** should not be abbreviated.

| Hai il giornale? *Do you have the newspaper?* | No, non **ce** l'ho. *No, I don't have it.* |

It is also used in the idiomatic expression **farcela** (*to manage it, to cope*) ...

Ce la fai a finire quella relazione?	*Can you manage to finish that report?*

... and with the verbs **vedere**, **sentire**, where it has a non-specific meaning.

Non **ci** vedo.	*I can't see anything.*
Ci senti, Chiara?	*Can you hear, Chiara?*

4.5 ne

Ne is a pronoun meaning *of it*, *of them* and used to replace **di** and an object or person.

Quanti figli hai?	*How many children do you have?*
Ne ho tre.	*I have three (of them).*
Quanto pane vuole?	*How much bread do you want?*
Ne prendo un chilo, grazie.	*I'll have a kilo, thanks.*

When there are direct object pronouns, **ne** comes after them.

Me **ne** dai un po'?	*Will you give me a bit (of it)?*

Ne can also be used when no number or quantity is mentioned, meaning *some* or *any*.

Vuoi delle patatine?	*Do you want some crisps?*
No, grazie. **Ne** ho.	*No, thanks. I have some.*
or Sì, grazie. Non **ne** ho.	*Yes, please. I haven't got any.*

Ne can be used meaning *of it* replacing **di** and an object.

Agostino non ti parla mai **della faccenda**?	*Does Agostino ever speak to you about the affair?*
Sì, **ne** parla spesso.	*Yes, he often speaks of it.*

When **ne** is used with a past tense and followed by a number or quantity, the past participle has to agree.

Hai visto dei gabbiani?	*Have you seen any seagulls?*
Sì, **ne** ho visti tre.	*Yes, I have seen three.*

It can also be used when the reference is to **da**.

Sono usciti **dal ristorante**?	*Have they come out of the restaurant?*
Ne escono adesso.	*They're coming out of it just now.*

Ne is used in certain idiomatic expressions.

Me **ne** vado.	*I'm going away.*
Non **ne** posso più.	*I can't take any more.*
Ne va della mia reputazione.	*My reputation is at stake.*

4.6 *Direct object pronouns with a compound tense*

The participle (**mangiato, capito,** etc.) has to agree with a direct object pronoun.

Hai visto i bambini?	*Have you seen the children?*
No, non **li** ho visti.	*No, I haven't seen them.*
Avevi già conosciuto Lidia?	*Had you already met Lidia?*
No, non **l'**avevo mai vist**a** prima.	*No, I had never seen her before.*
Marco avrà già studiato i verbi?	*Will Marco already have studied the verbs?*
Sì, **li** avrà già studiat**i**.	*Yes, he'll have studied them already.*

5 Indefinites

5.1 alcun, ogni, ognuno, ciascuno, tale, altro

For the use of **qualche** and the plural forms of **alcuni, alcune** meaning *some*, see Unit 3.

alcun *(some, any ...)*
The singular forms **alcun, alcuno, alcuna, alcun'** are used only after a negative, with the meaning *any*. They have the same endings as **un, uno**, etc.

Non ho **alcun**'idea.	*I haven't a clue.*
Non c'era **alcuna** ragione.	*There was no reason at all.*
Non ha dato **alcun** motivo.	*She didn't give any reason.*

ogni *(every, each)*
This is always singular, meaning *each*, *every*, and can refer to objects or people.

Ogni cosa è possibile.	*Everything is possible.*
Ogni ospite paga lo stesso.	*Each guest pays the same.*

ognuno *(each one, everyone)*
Like **ogni**, this can only be singular and means *each one*, *everyone*.

Ognuno fa quello che vuole.	*Each does what he wants.*

ciascun, ciascuno *(each, each one)*
This is singular only. As an adjective, it means *each*, and as a pronoun means *each one*. As an adjective, it has the same endings as the indefinite article **un: ciascun, ciascuno, ciascuna, ciascun'**.

Ci sono quattro persone a **ciascun** tavolo.	*There are four people at each table.*

Used on its own as a pronoun, it has just two forms: **ciascuno** and **ciascuna**.

Ciascuno dei bambini ha una camera separata.

Each one of the children has a separate room.

tale, un tale *(such, somebody or other)*
Tale (masculine or feminine) has both singular and plural forms (**tale, tali**).

Used as an adjective, it means *such*.

Ha un **tale** complesso che non riesce neanche a parlare.

She has such a complex that she can't even speak.

Used on its own, it means *somebody* or *other*, *some bloke*, *some guy*.

Ho visto **un tale** che vendeva delle magliette.

I saw some guy selling T-shirts.

altro *(another, other)*
Altro as an adjective means *other*, *another*, and as a pronoun means *anyone/someone else*, *other(s)*, *anything/something else*.

C'è un **altro** modello? *Is there another style?*
L'**altra** mia amica si chiama Maura. *My other friend is called Maura.*
Vuole **altro**? *Do you want anything else?*
Gli **altri** si sono comportati bene. *The others behaved well.*

5.2 qualunque, qualsiasi, chiunque

This group of indefinites includes pronouns and adjectives meaning *-ever*, for example *whatever*, *whichever*, *whoever*.

qualunque, qualsiasi *(any, whatever, any kind of ...)*
The meaning of these two indefinites varies according to their position.

Used *before* the noun, they mean *any* and can only be used with a singular noun.

| Farebbe **qualunque** cosa pur di vederla. | He would do anything just to see her. |
| Pagherebbe **qualsiasi** prezzo pur di avere quella macchina. | He would pay any price just to have that car. |

Used *after* the noun, **qualunque** and **qualsiasi** can be used with a singular or plural noun, meaning *any kind of/any/any whatever/any old*.

| Mettiti un vestito **qualunque**. | Put on any old dress. |
| Vanno bene dei panini **qualsiasi**. | Any sandwiches will do. |

chiunque *(anyone, whoever)*
This has only a singular form and meaning. When meaning *whoever*, as in the second example, it is followed by the subjunctive verb form.

| **Chiunque** può venire. | Anyone can come. |
| **Chiunque** sia, non è molto intelligente. | Whoever he is, he's not very intelligent. |

---

6 Quantity

All the following have a characteristic in common. Used as *adjectives*, they have to agree with the noun they are describing. Used as *nouns* or *adverbs*, their ending does not change.

molto *(much, many, a lot)*

Ci sono **molte** cose da vedere. (adjective)	There are lots of things to see.
Ho mangiato **molto**. (noun)	I've eaten a lot.
Scrive **molto** bene. (adverb)	He writes very well.

troppo *(too much, too many)*

| Ieri c'erano **troppe** persone. | Yesterday, there were too many people. |

Ho mangiato **troppo**.
È **troppo** giovane per andare al pub.

I have eaten too much.
He's too young to go to the pub.

poco (little, few)

Ci sono **poche** cartoline.
Hai dormito **poco**.
Sono un **poco** stanco.

There are only a few postcards.
You haven't slept much.
I am a bit tired.

Poco is often abbreviated to **un po'**.

tutto (all of, everything)

I ragazzi hanno mangiato **tutta** la pizza.
Prendi **tutto**!
Va **tutto** bene per domani sera.

The boys have eaten all the pizza.
Take everything!
It's all fine for tomorrow evening.

tanto (so much, so many; much, many)

Tanti studenti non controllano mai la posta elettronica.
Mi sento male, ho mangiato **tanto**.
È **tanto** gentile con me.

(So) many students never check their e-mail.
I feel ill, I've eaten so much.
She's so kind with me.

parecchio (much, many)

Parecchi italiani passano le vacanze al mare.
Ha girato **parecchio** in Italia.

Lots of Italians spend their holidays at the sea.
She's travelled a lot in Italy.

---

7 Relative pronouns

che (who, what)

La signora **che** lavora nell'ufficio turistico è di Milano.
Il treno **che** parte alle dieci arriva all'una.

The lady who works in the Tourist Office is from Milan.
The train which leaves at ten arrives at one o'clock.

cui *(who/whom, what)*
After a preposition (**con, su, in, per, di, da, a,** etc.), use **cui**.

L'amico **a cui** volevo telefonare è fuori.	*The friend (to whom) I wanted to telephone is out.*
La ragione **per cui** voglio andare a casa è semplice.	*The reason why I want to go home is simple.*

il quale *(who/whom, what)*
Both **che** and **cui** can be replaced by **il quale, la quale, i quali, le quali,** whose form reflects the gender and number of the person or object referred to.

Il canotto **con il quale** giocano i bambini è nostro.	*The rubber dinghy the children are playing with is ours.*

Adding a preposition (**a, di, da, in, su**) produces forms such as **al quale (alla quale, ai quali, alle quali); del quale; dal quale; nel quale; sul quale.**

La moglie del professore **alla quale** abbiamo telefonato è inglese.	*The wife of the teacher we telephoned is English.*

il cui, la cui, i cui, le cui *(whose)*
The form used depends on the gender and number of the object, not on the person owning it.

Il ragazzo **le cui** pinne sono state rubate è inglese.	*The boy whose flippers were stolen is English.*

chi *(he who, those who, etc.)*
Chi is used in proverbs, generalizations and formal notices.

Chi dorme non piglia i pesci.	*The early bird catches the worm! (lit.: He who sleeps doesn't catch the fish.)*

Chi vuole venire in gita ad Assisi deve comprare il biglietto.	*Those who want to come on the excursion to Assisi must buy a ticket.*

In the last example, **chi** can be replaced by (**tutti**) **quelli che,** plural form and meaning.

Tutti quelli che vogliono venire ad Assisi devono comprare il biglietto.

Note these less common, more formal forms:

colui che, colei che, coloro che   *he who, she who, they who*

(tutto) ciò che, quello che *(what, everything which)*
These relatives do *not* refer to a specific thing or person:

Faccio **quello che** mi pare.	*I'll do as I please/what I like.*
Ciò che bisogna fare è parlargli subito.	*What we have to do is speak to him straightaway.*
Tutto quello che impari è utile.	*Everything you learn is useful.*
Prendi **tutto ciò che** vuoi.	*Take everything you want.*

il che (which)
Il che refers back to a *whole* clause or part of sentence.

Mi ha portato dei fiori, **il che** mi ha fatto molto piacere.	*He brought me some flowers, which made me very happy.*

---

8 Prepositions

a
a *to, at, in:*

a scuola	*at school*	a casa	*at home*
a letto	*in bed*	al mare	*at the seaside*

b *Directions and distance*

a destra, a sinistra	*on the right, on the left*
a nord, a sud (etc.)	*North, South (etc.)*
a dieci chilometri	*ten kilometres away*
ad un'ora di strada	*an hour's drive away*

c *Times and seasons*

a Natale, a Pasqua	*at Christmas, at Easter*
A domani!	*See you tomorrow!*
alle cinque, a mezzogiorno	*at five o'clock, at midday*
un pasto al giorno	*one meal a day*

d *Manner in which things are prepared*

pollo allo spiedo	*chicken on the spit*
fatto a mano	*handmade*

e *After certain adjectives or participles*

pronto a	*ready to*
disposto a	*prepared to*

f *After certain prepositions*

accanto a	*besides, next to*
fino a	*as far as, until*
in cima a	*at the top of*
in fondo a	*at the bottom of*
in mezzo a	*in the middle of*
intorno a	*around*
davanti a	*in front of*
in capo a	*at the head/top of*
incontro a	*towards, against*
di fronte a	*opposite*
insieme a	*together with*
quanto a	*as regards*
riguardo a	*on the subject of, as regards*

rispetto a	*in comparison with, regarding*
vicino a	*near*

di

a *Possession, belonging, titles, authorship etc.*

la regina d'Inghilterra	*the Queen of England*
un film di Fellini	*a film by Fellini*

b *Quantity, age, time, etc.*

un litro di vino	*a litre of wine*
un bambino di dieci anni	*a child of age ten*

c *Composition and origin*

un bicchiere di cristallo	*a crystal glass*
una signora di Firenze	*a lady from Florence*

d *Time, seasons*

d'inverno, di primavera	*in winter, in spring*
di mattina, di notte	*in the morning, at night*

e *After certain adjectives and verbs*

Sono stufo del lavoro.	*I'm bored with work.*
riempire di acqua	*to fill with water*

f *Used as an adverb of manner*

di nascosto	*hidden, by stealth*
di corsa	*in a hurry, at a rush*

g *After **qualcosa, niente***

Non c'è niente di speciale.	*There's nothing special.*
Hai fatto qualcosa di bello?	*Have you done anything nice?*

h *With prepositions that require* **di**

a causa di	*because of*
al di là di	*beyond (literally and figuratively)*
fuori di	*outside*
per mezzo di	*by means of*
invece di	*instead of*
prima di	*before*

The prepositions listed below are usually followed by **di** only before pronouns such as **me, te, lui, lei,** etc. Other adverbs and prepositions – those expressing location – are shown in Unit 4.

contro il muro *(against the wall)*	contro di noi *(against us)*
dopo la tempesta *(after the storm)*	dopo di te *(after you)*
fra/tra amici *(between friends)*	fra di noi *(between ourselves)*
senza soldi *(without money)*	senza di te *(without you)*
verso casa *(towards home)*	verso di loro *(towards them)*

da
a *by, from*

È stato riparato dall'idraulico.	*It was repaired by the plumber.*
Il treno in arrivo da Pisa.	*The train arriving from Pisa.*

b *Measurement, quantity, capacity, denomination*

un francobollo da €0,45	*a 45-cent stamp*

c *at the house/shop/restaurant of*

Andiamo da Giovanni.	*We're going to Giovanni's.*
Vado dal medico.	*I'm going to the doctor's.*

d *Physical characteristics*

una signora dai capelli neri	*a woman with black hair*

e *Joining **molto, poco, niente, qualcosa** to the infinitive*

C'è poco da mangiare.   *There's not much to eat.*

f *Indicating manner*

Si è comportato da pazzo.   *He behaved like a madman.*
Sono andati da soli.   *They went by themselves.*

g *Purpose*

una camera da letto   *a bedroom*
un costume da bagno   *a bathing costume*

in
a *Transport*

in bicicletta, in aereo   *by bike, by plane*
in treno, in macchina   *by train, by car*

b *Seasons*

in primavera, in autunno   *in spring, in autumn*

c *Other*

Siamo in quattro.   *There are four of us.*
Se io fossi in te ...   *If I were you, ...*
in orario, in ritardo   *on time, late*
in anticipo   *in advance, early*

d *Dates*

Mio figlio è nato nel 1979.   *My son was born in 1979.*

per
a *for*

I fiori sono per te.   *The flowers are for you.*

b *Duration of time*

Siamo qui per dieci giorni.	*We are here for ten days.*

c *for (destination)*

Sono partiti per la Francia.	*They've left for France.*

d *Place*

Ha buttato la giacca per terra.	*He threw the jacket on the ground.*
Giravano per le strade.	*They were wandering around the streets.*
Scendiamo per le scale.	*Let's go down the stairs.*

e *Means of transport/communication*

Non mandare i soldi per posta.	*Don't send money by post.*
Puoi ringraziarla per telefono.	*You can thank her by phone.*

con
a *with*

Sono andata con Franco.	*I went with Franco.*

b *Manner*

con mia grande sorpresa	*to my great surprise*

c *In expressions or phrases*

E con questo?	*And so what?*

su
a *on or on to*

I bambini sono saltati sul muro.	*The children jumped onto the wall.*

b *out of*

Tre gatti su cinque preferiscono il pesce.

Three out of five cats prefer fish.

c *about, on a subject or topic*

Ha parlato sul problema della droga.

He spoke on the problem of drugs.

d *Expressions or phrases*

sul giornale, sulla rivista
un signore sui cinquanta anni
sul serio
su misura

in the newspaper, magazine
a man of around fifty
seriously
made to measure

fra, tra
a *between* or *among*

La casa è situata tra/fra la ferrovia e la superstrada.

The house is situated between the railway line and the main road.

b *in, within (time)*

Ci vediamo tra un'ora.

See you in one hour.

Combined preposition and article
The prepositions **a, da, in, su, di** combine with **il, la, lo**, etc. to form **al, dal, nel, sul** (Unit 4) and **del** (Unit 10). It is rare for **con** or **per** to do this, but you may see the forms **col** (**con il**) and **coi** (**con i**).

9 Negatives

In Italian, a negative sentence must include **non** as well as a second negative word.

Non siamo **affatto** stanchi.	*We're not tired at all.*
Non siamo stanchi **per niente**.	*We're not tired at all.*
Non viene **nemmeno (neppure)** Luisa.	*Luisa's not coming either.*
Non c'è **nulla** da fare.	*There's nothing to be done.*
Non mi piacciono **né** Mara **né** suo marito.	*I don't like either Mara or her husband.*
Non ci vengo **più**.	*I'm not coming any more/any longer.*

Non comes before the verb, while the other negative comes after.

Preferisce **non** vederlo **più**.	*She prefers not to see him again.*
Non fate **più** queste cose!	*Don't do these things any more!*

In the case of the perfect tense, the negative can also come in between **avere** and the participle (**mangiato**, etc.).

Non ho **ancora** mangiato. or **Non** ho mangiato **ancora**.	*I haven't eaten yet.*
Non è **più** venuto. or **Non** è venuto **più**.	*He didn't come any more.*

The negatives **nulla, niente, nessuno, per niente, alcun, né ... né** come *after* the participle.

Non ho visto **nessuno**.	*I haven't seen anyone.*
Non mi è piaciuto per **niente**.	*I didn't like it at all.*

You can use two or even three negative expressions in one sentence.

Non ci vengo **mai più**.	*I'm not coming here ever again.*

Non mi regala **più niente**.	*He doesn't give me anything any more.*
Non ho **mai** detto **niente a nessuno**.	*I've never told anyone anything.*

The negatives **nessuno, niente** or **nulla, mai, né … né, nemmeno, neppure, neanche** can all be placed at the beginning of the sentence, in which case the **non** is not needed. However – with the exception of **nessuno** – this reversed word order sounds less natural and somewhat dramatic.

Nessuno viene alla festa.	*No one's coming to the party.*
Niente succede in questa città.	*Nothing happens in this town.*
Mai in vita mia ho visto una cosa simile!	*Never in my life have I seen something like this.*

Most of the negatives can be used on their own.

Io non ci vado stasera.	*I'm not going this evening.*
Neanch'io.	*Me neither.*
Sei mai stata in Cina?	*Have you ever been to China?*
Mai!	*Never!*
Pensate di tornare a Nocera?	*Do you think you'll go back to Nocera?*
Mai più!	*Never again!*
Mai visto!	*Never seen anything like it!*

Note the following idiomatic use of negatives:

Credo di **no**.	*I don't think so.*
È arrivato **senza niente**.	*He arrived without anything.*

10 Question words

10.1 Used in direct and indirect questions

Many common question words are covered in the units, for example **dove, quale**. Others are illustrated here.

quando? *(when?)*
Quando can be used in questions.

Quando partite?	*When are you going away?*

It can also be used in indirect or reported questions or statements.

Non mi ha detto **quando** vuole venire.	*He hasn't told me when he wants to come.*

che? *(which, what?)*
Che is usually found with a noun, as in **Che cosa?**

Che cosa vuoi?	*What do you want?*

Using it on its own is considered slightly less elegant.

Che fai?	*What are you doing?*

Che is often used as an adjective, replacing **quale?** (*which?*)

Che macchina hai?	*What car do you have?*

perché? *(why?)*
Perché is used in direct questions ...

Perché ti sei messa quel vestito?	*Why have you put on that dress?*

... and in indirect questions and statements.

Dimmi **perché** sei andata al cinema con Marco.

Tell me why you went to the cinema with Marco.

come? *(how?)*

With **stare** to ask how someone is

Come sta, signora Rossi?   *How are you, signora Rossi?*

With **essere** to ask what someone or something is like

Com'è Marco?   *What is Marco like?*
Marco è alto, bruno.   *Marco is tall, dark.*
Come sono le tagliatelle?   *What is the tagliatelle like?*
Sono salate.   *It's too salty.*

Come is elided before **è** to **Com'è**.

Note the expression **come mai** (meaning *How come?*).

Come mai sei venuto a piedi?   *How come you came on foot?*

10.2 Used in exclamations

Come, che, **quanto** can all be used in exclamations as well:

Quanto sei bello!   *How nice you look!*
Come sei stupido!   *How stupid you are!*
Che antipatico che sei!   *How horrible you are!*

Used as above, **quanto** does not change ending. But when it means *what a lot of*, it must agree with the noun.

Quanti bambini!   *What a lot of children!*
Quanta roba hai comprato!   *What a lot of stuff you've bought!*

11 Conjunctions

Conjunctions join parts of a sentence together; the two simplest examples are **ma** (*but*) and **e** (*and*). (**E** normally becomes **ed** when followed by a vowel, especially **e**.)

Vorrei andare a Parigi **ma** non ho soldi.	*I would like to go to Paris, but I haven't any money.*

11.1 Coordinating conjunctions

Other coordinating conjunctions, which join, or coordinate, parts of a sentence, are:

altrimenti	*otherwise*
anche	*also*
anzi	*rather, on the contrary, in fact*
cioè	*that is, in other words*
infatti	*in fact, indeed*
inoltre	*besides*
insomma	*in short*
invece	*on the other hand*
neanche, neppure, nemmeno	*not even*
o, oppure	*or, or else*
perciò, quindi, pertanto, dunque	*so, therefore*
però, tuttavia	*yet, however, nevertheless*
piuttosto	*rather*

11.2 Subordinating conjunctions

Subordinating conjunctions introduce a dependent, or subordinate, clause. There are two main groups.

a Conjunctions requiring subjunctive

Some conjunctions (for example **perché** meaning *in order to*; **benché**) are followed by the subjunctive. These are illustrated in Unit 19.

b Conjunctions not requiring subjunctive

Examples of conjunctions which do *not* need the subjunctive are:

che, come
Words such as **che** (*that*), **come** (*how, like, as*)

Ha detto **che** era stanco.	*He said he was tired.*
Hai visto **come** era vestita?	*Did you see how she was dressed?*

Words expressing cause
Words such as **perché** (meaning *because*), **poiché, giacché, siccome, dal momento che** (*since*)

Dal momento che abbiamo solo venti minuti, non possiamo fare tutto.	*Since we have only twenty minutes, we can't do everything.*

Perché takes the subjunctive when it means *in order to*.

Words expressing time
Words such as **quando** (*when*), **mentre** (*while*), **dopo che** (*after*), **ogni volta che** (*every time that*), **da quando** (*since*), **(non) appena** (*as soon as*), **finché** (*as long as*)

Resta **finché** vuoi.	*Stay as long as you like.*

When it means *until*, **finché** takes the subjunctive.

Words expressing consequence
Words such as **e così** (*and so*), **al punto che** (*to such an extent that*), **talmente ... che** (*so much so that*)

Ero **talmente** stanca **che** non ci capivo più niente.	*I was so tired that I didn't understand anything.*

---

12 Linking parts of sentences

Take care not to translate English into Italian directly. It doesn't always work. Here are some examples of how Italian and English handle structures in different ways.

12.1 Gerund, infinitive or past infinitive?

For use of the gerund with **stare**, see Unit 6. The English gerund
-*ing* form is sometimes translated by an Italian **gerundio**, sometimes
not. As a general rule, you should use the Italian **gerundio** when
the English gerund has a preposition or a conjunction with it, such
as *as*, *by*, *if*, *when*, mentioned or implied.

Entrando nella stanza, ho visto un disordine totale.	*Coming into the room, I saw a total mess. (As I came into the room, I saw a total mess.)*
Studiando di più, sarai promosso.	*Studying more, you will pass. (If you study more, you will pass.)*

When no preposition or conjunction is mentioned or implied, use
the infinitive form.

Fumare fa male.	*Smoking is bad for you.*

The infinitive is also used after the expressions **prima di, invece di.**

Prima di **uscire**, ha chiuso tutte le finestre.	*Before going out, she closed all the windows.*
Invece di **guardare** la televisione, fai i compiti.	*Instead of watching TV, do your homework.*

With **dopo**, use the past infinitive.

Dopo **aver mangiato**, ha bevuto un digestivo.	*After eating, he drank a digestive liqueur.*
Dopo **essersi alzato** alle cinque, aveva solo voglia di andare a letto.	*Having got up at five, he just wanted to go to bed.*

The gerund also has a past form, formed with the gerund of **avere**
or **essere** and the past participle (**-ato**, etc.).

Avendo studiato poco, sapeva che sarebbe stato bocciato. *Having studied little, he knew he would fail.*

Essendo nato da quelle parti, conosceva bene la zona. *Having been born around there, he knew the area well.*

12.2 Connecting verb and infinitive: introduction

Often a sentence has two connected verbs; the first verb tells us who is carrying out the action (*I, you, he*), while the second is an infinitive (*to go, to do*).

Certain verbs are followed directly by the verb in the infinitive (see Unit 8, **potere**). Other verbs, on the other hand, need to be connected by **di** or **a** or in another way. Below is a list of the most common combinations.

12.3 Verbs linked directly to the infinitive

Auxiliary verbs **dovere, potere, preferire, sapere, volere**

Non **so** nuotare.   *I can't swim.*
Preferisci andare a piedi?   *Do you prefer to go on foot?*

Impersonal verbs and verb phrases
Impersonal verbs **bisogna, basta, conviene**

Basta imparare!   *You only have to learn!*
Non **conviene** risparmiare.   *It's not worth saving.*

Impersonal verb phrases such as è **bello**, è **conveniente**, è **difficile**, è **essenziale**, è **facile**, è **impossibile**, è **necessario**, è **possibile**

È facile imparare l'italiano!   *It's easy to learn Italian!*
Non è **necessario** prenotare.   *It's not necessary to book.*

12.4 *Verbs linked by* **di**

Verbs of ending, finishing
Verbs such as **finire, smettere**, etc.

| **Finisco di** mangiare poi vengo. | *I'll just finish eating then I'll come.* |
| **Smettete di** urlare! | *Stop shouting!* |

Phrases using avere and a noun
These include **aver bisogno, aver fretta, aver tempo, aver intenzione, aver paura, aver vergogna, aver voglia di**

| **Ho bisogno di** cambiare soldi. | *I need to change some money.* |
| **Hai tempo di** parlarmi? | *Do you have time to speak to me?* |

12.5 *Verbs linked by* **a**

Verbs of beginning, starting
Verbs including **cominciare, iniziare, imparare**

| **Comincio a** preparare il pranzo. | *I'll start preparing lunch.* |
| Oggi **impariamo a** fare le lasagne. | *Today, we're learning how to make lasagne.* |

12.6 **Verbs involving more than one person**

When we ask or order someone to do something, we often use a verb which needs one preposition to link it to the person, and another preposition to link it to the infinitive (the action you want that person to carry out). Most commonly, such verbs take a before the person and **di** or **a** before the verb. (See Unit 20.)

| **Chiedo al** cameriere **di** portare il menù. | *I'll ask the waiter to bring the menu.* |
| **Insegno ai** bambini a nuotare. | *I'm teaching the children to swim.* |

At the end of this appendix, there is a list of common verbs showing how they link with the infinitive and/or with a person other than the subject of the verb.

| **suggerire a qualcune di** | *to suggest to someone to* |

12.7 far fare, lasciar fare *(getting something done)*

fare

Fare can be used with an infinitive (for example **entrare, scendere**) to express the idea of getting something done, or making someone do something.

The direct object of **fare** can be an object ...

Faccio riparare la macchina.	*I have/get the car repaired.*

... or a *person.*

Faccio pagare Antonio.	*I get Antonio to pay.*

lasciare

A similar construction is possible with **lasciare** *(to let, allow)*.

Lascio passare la signora.	*I let the lady pass.*

Double object

Look what happens when there are *two* objects (Antonio *and a coffee*) involved.

Faccio pagare il caffè **ad** Antonio.	*I get Antonio to pay for the coffee.*

Now see what happens when we add a person to the first example shown.

Faccio riparare la macchina **al** meccanico.	*I get the car repaired by the mechanic.*

In both cases, the person is now linked to the verb by **a**.

A can be replaced by **da** (*by*).

Faccio pagare il caffè **da** Antonio.   *I get the coffee paid for by Antonio.*
Faccio riparare la macchina **dal**   *I get the car repaired by the*
  meccanico.   *mechanic.*

Pronouns
The person or object can be replaced by a pronoun. The examples above would become:

Lo faccio pagare.   *I get him to pay.*
La faccio riparare.   *I get it repaired.*

Both person and thing can be replaced by pronouns:

Glielo faccio pagare.   *I get him to pay (for) it.*
Gliela faccio riparare.   *I get him to repair it.*

fare *plus infinitive*
Here are some common combinations of **fare** and infinitive.

far avere	*to let someone have something*
far entrare	*to show someone in*
far pagare	*to charge someone (for something)*
far uscire	*to show someone out*
far vedere	*to show someone*
far venire	*to get someone to come, to call someone out*

The **e** is generally missed off the end of **fare** before the infinitive.

---

13 Verbs extra

13.1 Past definite

The past definite tense (*passato remoto*) is more common in written Italian, especially in literary texts. However, it is fairly widely used, even in spoken conversation, in the south of Italy, in situations where northerners would use the perfect tense (*passato prossimo*). It is important for students to be able to recognize it, at least. Here are the forms of the past definite for each verb group.

parlare *to talk, speak*

parlai	parlammo
parlasti	parlaste
parlò	parlarono

vendere *to sell*

vendei/vendetti	vendemmo
vendesti	vendeste
vendé/vendette	venderono/vendettero

dormire *to sleep*

dormii	dormimmo
dormisti	dormiste
dormì	dormirono

There are exceptions to this pattern particularly amongst the **-ere** verbs; the irregular past definite usually follows an alternating pattern of short and long forms, for example:

leggere *to read*

lessi	leggemmo
leggesti	leggeste
lesse	lessero

Common verbs which have an irregular past definite are shown in the verb tables, with the two alternating forms.

13.2 Verbs and verb links

Here is a list of common verbs showing how they link with the infinitive and/or with a person other than the subject of the verb. Where the construction involves another person (**chiedo a qualcuno di fare qualcosa**), this is shown by the abbreviation **qcn. (qualcuno)**.

Verb	Preposition		
abituarsi		a	to get used
accettare		di	to accept
aiutare	qcn	a	to help someone
amare			to love
ammettere		di	to admit
andare		a	to go
aspettare		di	to wait
aspettarsi		di	to expect
augurarsi		di	to hope, wish
bastare			to be enough
bisognare			to be necessary
cercare		di	to try
cessare		di	to cease
chiedere	a qcn	di	to ask someone to
comandare	a qcn	di	to order someone to
cominciare		a	to begin
consigliare	a qcn	di	to advise someone to
continuare		a	to continue
correre		a	to run
costringere	qcn	a	to force someone to
credere		di	to believe, think
decidere		di	to decide
decidersi		a	to decide
desiderare			to desire, want
dimenticare		di	to forget
dire	a qcn	di	to tell someone to
divertirsi		a	to enjoy oneself
domandare	a qcn	di	to ask someone to
dovere			to have to
fare + *inf.*	qcn		to make someone + *inf.*

fare a meno		di	*to do without*
fare meglio		a	*to do better*
fare presto		a	*to hasten to*
fermarsi		a	*to pause, stop*
fingere		di	*to pretend*
finire		di	*to finish*
forzare	qcn	a	*to force someone to*
imparare		a	*to learn*
impedire	a qcn	di	*to prevent someone from*
incoraggiare	qcn	a	*to encourage someone to*
iniziare		a	*to begin to*
insegnare	a qcn	a	*to teach someone to*
invitare	qcn	a	*to invite someone to*
lamentarsi		di	*to complain*
lasciare			*to let, allow*
mandare	qcn	a	*to send someone to*
meravigliarsi		di	*to wonder*
mettersi		a	*to start off*
obbligare	qcn	a	*to oblige someone to*
occorrere			*to be necessary*
offrire		di	*to offer*
ordinare	a qcn	di	*to order someone to*
passare		a	*to stop by*
pensare		a	*to think about*
pensare		di	*to think of, decide to*
permettere	a qcn	di	*to allow someone to*
persuadere	qcn	a	*to persuade someone to*
piacere			*to please*
potere			*to be able*
preferire			*to prefer*
pregare	qcn	di	*to beg someone to*
prepararsi		a	*to get ready*
provare		a	*to try*
ricordarsi		di	*to remember*
rifiutarsi		di	*to refuse*
rimanere		a	*to stay*
rinunciare		a	*to give up*
riprendere		a	*to resume*

riuscire	a		to succeed
sapere			to be able to
sapere	di		to know
sbrigarsi	a		to hurry
sentire			to hear
sentirsela	di		to feel like
servire	a		to be useful for
smettere	di		to stop
sognare	di		to dream
sperare	di		to hope
stancarsi	di		to tire
stare	a		to stay
stupirsi	di		to be amazed
temere	di		to be afraid
tentare	di		to attempt
tornare	a		to return
vedere			to see
venire	a		to come
vergognarsi	di		to be ashamed of
vietare	a qcn	di	to forbid someone to/from
volere			to want

13.3 Common irregular verbs

Only the irregular parts of verbs are given. The full verb pattern for each tense or mood is given in full in the appropriate section of the book. Where alternative forms are possible, these are shown in brackets. *Verbs which sometimes or always take **essere** in the perfect tense are asterisked.

accorgersi *to notice*, realize p.p. **accorto(si)** *
Past definite: mi accorsi, ti accorgesti (etc.)
Similar verbs: scorgere (etc.)

andare *to go p.p.* **andato** *
Present: vado, vai, va, andiamo, andate, vanno
Present subj: vada (etc.) andiamo, andiate, vadano
Imperative: vai (va'), vada, andiamo, andate, vadano
Future: andrò (etc.)
Present conditional: andrei (etc.)

aprire *to open p.p.* **aperto**
Past definite: aprii (apersi), apristi (etc.)
Similar verbs: coprire (to cover), scoprire (to discover) (etc.)

avere *to have p.p.* **avuto**
Present: ho, hai, ha, abbiamo, avete, hanno
Present subj: abbia (etc.) abbiamo, abbiate, abbiano
Imperative: abbi, abbia, abbiamo, abbiate, abbiano
Future: avrò (etc.)
Present conditional: avrei (etc.)
Past definite: ebbi, avesti (etc.)

bere *to drink p.p.* **bevuto**
Most parts of bere are derived from its original form **bevere** and
follow the normal -**ere** pattern.
Past definite: bevvi (bevetti), bevesti (etc.)
Future: berrò (etc.)
Present conditional: berrei (etc.)

cadere *to fall p.p.* **caduto***
Past definite: caddi, cadesti, (etc.)
Future: cadrò *Present conditional:* cadrei (etc.)
Similar verbs: accadere (to happen), scadere (to fall due, expire)

chiedere *to ask p.p.* **chiesto**
Past definite: chiesi, chiedesti (etc.)
Similar verbs: richiedere (to request)
chiudere *to shut, close p.p.* **chiuso**
Past definite: chiusi, chiudesti (etc.)
Similar verbs: rinchiudere *(to shut in)*, schiudere *(to disclose)*

cogliere *to gather, take p.p.* **colto**
Present: colgo, cogli, coglie, cogliamo, cogliete, colgono
Present subj: colga, cogliamo, cogliate, colgano
Imperative: cogli, colga, cogliamo, cogliete, colgano
Past definite: colsi, cogliesti (etc.)
Similar verbs: raccogliere *(to gather, collect),*
        accogliere *(to welcome),* sciogliere *(to dissolve)*

conoscere *to get to know, meet p.p.* **conosciuto**
Past definite: conobbi, conoscesti (etc.)
Similar verbs: riconoscere

correre *to run p.p.* **corso***
Past definite:	corsi, corresti (etc.)
Similar verbs:	occorrere, percorrere, rincorrere, scorrere (etc.)

crescere *to grow p.p.* **cresciuto*** *(sometimes)*
Past definite:	crebbi, crescesti (etc.)
Similar verbs:	accrescere *(to increase)*, rincrescere *(to regret)*

dare *to give p.p.* **dato**
Present:	do, dai, dà, diamo, date, danno
Present subj:	dia, diamo, diate, diano
Imperative:	da' (dai, dà), dia, diamo, date, diano
Past definite:	diedi (detti), desti, diede (dette), demmo, deste, diedero (dettero)
Future:	darò (etc.)
Present conditional:	darei (etc.)
Imperfect:	davo (etc.)
Imperfect subj:	dessi, dessi, desse, dessimo, deste, dessero
Similar verbs:	ridare *(to give back)*

decidere *to give back p.p.* **deciso**
Past definite:	decisi, decidesti (etc.)

difendere *to defend p.p.* **difeso**
Past definite:	difesi, difendesti, (etc.)
Similar verbs:	offendere (to offend)

dire *to say p.p.* **detto**
Present:	dico, dici, dice, diciamo, dite, dicono
Present subj:	dica, diciamo, diciate, dicano
Imperative:	di', dica, diciamo, dite, dicano
Past definite:	dissi, dicesti (etc.)
Imperfect:	dicevo (etc.)
Future:	dirò (etc.)
Present conditional:	direi (etc.)
Similar verbs:	benedire, maledire, contraddire

discutere *to discuss p.p.* **discusso**
Past definite:	discussi, discutesti (etc.)

dividere *to divide p.p.* **diviso**
Past definite:	divisi, dividesti (etc.)

dovere *to have to, to owe* **p.p. dovuto**
Present: devo (debbo), devi, deve, dobbiamo, dovete, devono (debbono)
Present subj: deva (debba), dobbiamo, dobbiate, devano (debbano)
Future: dovrò (etc.)
Present conditional: dovrei (etc.)

essere *to be* **p.p. stato***
Present: sono, sei, è, siamo, siete, sono
Present subj: sia (etc.), siamo, siate, siano
Imperative: sii, sia, siamo, siate, siano
Future: sarò (etc.)
Present conditional: sarei (etc.)
Past definite: fui, fosti, fu, fummo, foste, furono
Imperfect: ero, eri, era, eravamo, eravate, erano
Imperfect subj: fossi, fosti, fosse, fossimo, foste, fossero

fare *to make, to do* **p.p. fatto**
Present: faccio, fai, fa, facciamo, fate, fanno
Present subj: faccia, facciamo, facciate, facciano
Imperative: fa (fai, fa'), faccia, facciamo, fate, facciano
Imperfect: facevo
Imperfect subj: facessi (etc.)
Future: farò (etc.)
Present conditional: farei (etc.)
Past definite: feci, facesti (etc.)

giungere *to reach, to arrive* **p.p. giunto***
Past definite: giunsi, giungesti (etc.)
Similar verbs: aggiungere, raggiungere, soggiungere

leggere *to read* **p.p. letto**
Past definite: lessi, leggesti (etc.)
Similar verbs: reggere, correggere, proteggere

mettere *to put* **p.p. messo**
Past definite: misi, mettesti (etc.)
Similar verbs: ammettere, scommettere, smettere, trasmettere

nascere to *be born* p.p. **nato***
Past definite: nacqui, nascesti (etc.)
Similar verbs: rinascere

nascondere to *hide* p.p. **nascosto**
Past definite: nascosi, nascondesti (etc.)

offrire to *offer* p.p. **offerto**
Past definite: offrii (offersi), offristi (etc.)
Similar verbs: soffrire (to suffer)

perdere to *lose* p.p. **perduto/perso**
Past definite: persi (perdei, perdetti), perdesti (etc.)
persuadere to *persuade, convince* p.p. **persuaso**
Past definite: persuasi, persuadesti (etc.)

piacere to *please* p.p. **piaciuto***
Present: piaccio, piaci, piace, piacciamo, piacete, piacciono
Present subj: piaccia (etc.)
Past definite: piacque, piacesti (etc.)
Similar verbs: compiacere, dispiacere

piangere to *cry, weep* p.p. **pianto**
Past definite: piansi, piangesti (etc.)
Similar verbs: compiangere, rimpiangere

porre to *place, put* p.p. **posto**
The parts of **porre** are derived from its original form **ponere**.
Present: pongo, poni, pone, poniamo, ponete, pongono
Present subj: ponga, poniamo, poniate, pongano
Imperative: poni, ponga, poniamo, ponete, pongano
Past definite: posi, ponesti (etc.)
Future: porrò (etc.)
Present conditional: porrei (etc.)
Imperfect: ponevo
Imperfect subj: ponessi
Similar verbs: disporre, esporre, opporre, proporre, supporre

potere to *be able to* p.p. **potuto**
Present: posso, puoi, può, possiamo, potete, possono

Present subj:	possa, possiamo, possiate, possano
Future:	potrò (etc.)
Present conditional:	potrei (etc.)
Past definite:	potei (potetti), potesti (etc.)

prendere *to take p.p.* **preso**

Past definite:	presi, prendesti (etc.)

ridere *to laugh p.p.* **riso**

Past definite:	risi, ridesti (etc.)

rimanere *to remain, stay p.p.* **rimasto***

Present:	rimango, rimani, rimane, rimaniamo, rimanete, rimangono
Present subj:	rimanga, rimaniamo, rimaniate, rimangano
Imperative:	rimani, rimanga, rimaniamo, rimanete, rimangano
Past definite:	rimasi, rimanesti (etc.)
Future:	rimarrò (etc.)
Present conditional:	rimarrei (etc.)

rispondere *to reply p.p.* **risposto**

Past definite:	risposi, rispondesti (etc.)
Similar verbs:	corrispondere

rompere *to break p.p.* **rotto**

Past definite:	ruppi, rompesti (etc.)
Similar verbs:	corrompere, interrompere

salire *to go up, climb up p.p.* **salito***

Present:	salgo, sali, sale, saliamo, salite, salgono
Present subj:	salga, saliamo, saliate, salgano
Imperative:	sali, salga, saliamo, salite, salgano

sapere *to know, learn a fact p.p.* **saputo**

Present:	so, sai, sa, sappiamo, sapete, sanno
Present subj:	sappia, sappiamo, sappiate, sappiano
Imperative:	sappi, sappia, sappiamo, sapete, sappiano
Future:	saprò (etc.)
Present conditional:	saprei (etc.)
Past definite:	seppi, sapesti (etc.)

scegliere *to choose p.p.* **scelto**

Present:	scelgo, scegli, sceglie, scegliamo, scegliete, scelgono
Present subj:	scelga, scegliamo, scegliate, scelgano
Imperative:	scegli, scelga, scegliamo, scegliete, scelgano
Past definite:	scelsi, scegliesti (etc.)

scendere *to descend, get down p.p.* **sceso***

Past definite:	scesi, scendesti (etc.)
Similar verbs:	ascendere

scrivere *to write p.p.* **scritto**

Past definite:	scrissi, scrivesti (etc.)

sedere *to sit p.p.* **seduto**

Present:	siedo, siedi, siede, sediamo, sedete, siedono
Present subj:	sieda, sediamo, sediate, siedano
Imperative:	siedi, sieda, sediamo, sedete, siedano
Note reflexive form:	

sedersi *to sit (down) p.p.* **seduto(si)***

stare *to be, stay, stand p.p.* **stato***

Present:	sto, stai, sta, stiamo, state, stanno
Present subj:	stia, stiamo, stiate, stiano
Imperative:	sta (stai, sta'), stia, stiamo, state, stiano
Past definite:	stetti, stesti (etc.)
Imperfect:	stavo (etc.)
Imperfect subj:	stessi, stessi, stesse, stessimo, steste, stessero

tenere *to hold p.p.* **tenuto**

Present:	tengo, tieni, tiene, teniamo, tenete, tengono
Present subj:	tenga, teniamo, teniate, tengano
Imperative:	tieni, tenga, teniamo, tenete, tengano
Future:	terrò (etc.)
Present conditional:	terrei (etc.)
Past definite:	tenni, tenesti (etc.)
Similar verbs:	appartenere, contenere, mantenere, ritenere, sostenere, trattenere

togliere *to take away, take off*: see **cogliere**

uscire *to go out* *p.p.* **uscito***
Present:	esco, esci, esce, usciamo, uscite, escono
Present subj:	esca, usciamo, usciate, escano
Imperative:	esci, esca, usciamo, uscite, escano
Similar verbs:	riuscire (to succeed)

vedere *to see* *p.p.* **visto/veduto**
Past definite:	vidi, vedesti (etc.)
Future:	vedrò (etc.)
Present conditional:	vedrei (etc.)

venire *to come* *p.p.* **venuto***
Present:	vengo, vieni, viene, veniamo, venite, vengono
Present subj:	venga, veniamo, veniate, vengano
Imperative:	vieni, venga, veniamo, venite, vengano
Future:	verrò (etc.)
Present conditional:	verrei (etc.)
Past definite:	venni, venisti (etc.)
Similar verbs:	avvenire, convenire, divenire, svenire

vivere *to live* *p.p.* **vissuto*** (optional)
Past definite:	vissi, vivesti (etc.)
Future:	vivrò (etc.)
Present conditional:	vivrei (etc.)

volere *to want to* *p.p.* **voluto**
Present:	voglio, vuoi, vuole, vogliamo, volete, vogliono
Present subj:	voglia, vogliamo, vogliate, vogliano
Future:	vorrò (etc.)
Present conditional:	vorrei (etc.)
Past definite:	volli, volesti (etc.)

Glossary of grammatical terms

active construction all verbs that take an object can either have an active form – *lasciamo la macchina nel garage* (*we leave the car in the garage*) – or a *passive* form – *la macchina viene lasciata nel garage* (*the car is left in the garage*). An active construction is one in which the subject of the sentence is the person carrying out the action, as in the first example. (See also *passive.*)

adjective gives information about a noun. The biggest group of adjectives is that of descriptive adjectives, used to describe objects or people: e.g. size, colour, shape, nationality. Other adjectives can be found under separate categories: see *demonstrative, indefinite, interrogative* and *possessive.*

adverb gives information about a verb, saying how, when or where something is done. Adverbs such as **molto, poco, tanto** can also add further information about an adjective or another adverb.

agreement in Italian, adjectives, articles and sometimes past participles have to agree with the noun or pronoun they refer to in number and gender. This means that their form varies according to whether the noun/pronoun is masculine or feminine, singular or plural.

article Italian has two main types: the definite article **il, lo**, etc. (*the*) which is used to specify the particular person or object and the indefinite article **un, una**, etc. (*a*) which is used to indicate an unspecified person or object. The partitive **dei, delle, degli**, etc. (*some, any*) is also considered to be an article.

auxiliary verbs such as **avere** and **essere** used with the past participle to form compound tenses, both active *ho* **mangiato** (*I have eaten*), **siamo** **entrati** (*we went in*) and passive **è stato ammazzato** (*he was killed*). (See also *modal auxiliary.*)

clause a part of a sentence which contains a subject and a verb. Complex sentences are made up of a series of clauses. The main clause is the part which makes sense on its own and does not depend on any other element in the sentence. A subordinate clause always depends on another clause, and is often introduced by a conjunction such as **che**. Subordinate clauses include time clauses, relative clauses, purpose clauses, result clauses, conditional clauses, clauses of exception.

comparative used to compare one element with another, whether person, object or activity. Specifically, there are comparative adjectives and comparative adverbs.

compound tenses formed by the auxiliary **avere** or **essere**, and the past participle. They include the perfect (*passato prossimo*), pluperfect (*trapassato*), past conditional, future perfect, and, of course, the passive tenses.

conditional not a tense, but a verb mood, with two tenses (present, past). The present conditional can be used on its own, particularly as a polite way of expressing a request, or in conditional sentences, where the statement contained in the main clause is dependent on some condition being met.

conjugation the pattern according to which verb forms change according to the person, tense or mood. It also means the actual groups of verbs ending in **-are**, **-ere**, **-ire** to which regular verbs belong.

conjunction a 'joining' word, usually linking two words, phrases or clauses within a sentence. It can be as simple as e (*and*) or ma (*but*), or more complex. Specific conjunctions include those beginning clauses of condition, result, purpose, exception. Many of these require the use of subjunctive. (See *subordinate clause*.)

countable a noun is countable if it can normally be used in both singular and plural, and take the indefinite article **un**, **una**, etc. An uncountable noun is one which does not normally have a plural, e.g. **latte** (*milk*), or an abstract noun such as **coraggio** (*courage*).

definite article see **article**.

demonstrative a demonstrative adjective or a pronoun is one which demonstrates or indicates the person or object referred to: the most common ones in Italian are **questo** and **quello**.

direct object whether noun or pronoun, it is something or someone directly affected by the action or event. It is always used with a *transitive* verb.

feminine see *gender*.

gender all nouns in Italian have a gender: they are either masculine or feminine, even if they are inanimate objects. Grammatical gender is not always a guide to natural gender: e.g. **giraffa** is female in gender but is used for a male or female giraffe. Gender is important since it determines the form of noun, article and adjective and even past participle.

gerund a verb form ending in **-ando** or **-endo**: **parlando** (*speaking*), **sorridendo** (*smiling*), **finendo** (*finishing*). The gerund can be used with the verb **stare** to express a continuous action or event: **sto mangiando** (*I'm just eating*).

idiomatic an idiomatic expression is one which cannot normally be translated literally, for example **sono morta di sonno** (*I'm dead tired*).

imperative the verb mood used to express orders, commands or instructions.

impersonal (verbs, verb forms) such as **basta** (*it is enough*), **occorre** (*it is necessary*) do not refer to one particular person. They can generally be translated by English it and a third person form. These verbs can be personalised by adding a personal pronoun, usually the indirect object: e.g. **mi basta sapere questo** (*I only need to know this*).

indefinite article see *article*.

indefinite an adjective or pronoun used to refer to a person or thing in a general unspecified way, rather than a definite or specified person or thing. Examples are: **alcuni** (*some*), **certi** (*certain, some*), **qualche** (*some*).

indicative (verb) the verb mood we use most of the time. It has a full range of tenses, e.g. present, perfect, imperfect, future. (See also *subjunctive*.)

indirect object an object, whether noun or pronoun, that is indirectly affected by the action or event. An indirect object can be found in the same sentence as a direct object: **ho mandato delle cartoline** (direct) *ai miei amici* (indirect) (*I sent some postcards to my friends*). It can also be used with an intransitive verb, with a preposition such as **a, da**: e.g. **Marco telefonava al suo amico ogni sera** (*Marco used to phone his friend every evening*).

infinitive the form in which a verb is listed in dictionaries recognised by its endings **-are, -ere, -ire**. It cannot be used on its own but depends on a verb, often a **modal verb: vorrei** *ringraziare* **i collaboratori** (*I would like to thank my collaborators*) or following a **preposition: siamo andati in centro per** *comprare* **i biglietti** (*we took a trip into town to buy the tickets*).

interrogative a word which is used to ask a question or an indirect question. These include **chi** (*who*), **come** (*how*), **cosa** (*what*), **dove** (*where*), **quale** (*which*), **quando** (*when*), **perché** (*why*).

intransitive (verb) a verb which cannot be used with a direct object. Some intransitive verbs can be used with an indirect object, e.g. **telefonare a**. Others are always used without any object, e.g. verbs of movement. Many of these verbs take the auxiliary **essere**, but not all. It is important to remember that sometimes a verb can be used transitively in English e.g. to walk (*to walk the dog*), but its Italian equivalent (**camminare**) cannot be used transitively. Finally, some verbs can be used both transitively and intransitively. (See **transitive verbs**.)

invariable an invariable noun is one that has the same form for both singular and plural: **un** *film*, **dei** *film* or for both masculine and feminine: **un** *artista*, **un'***artista*. An invariable adjective, e.g. **rosa** (*pink*) is one which does not change its form to agree with the noun, whether masculine or feminine, singular or plural.

irregular (noun or verb) one which does not follow one of the standard patterns of forms or endings.

masculine see *gender*.

modal verb (modal auxiliary) a verb which is used with an infinitive, such as **potere** (*to be able to*), **dovere** (*to have to*), **volere** (*to want to*), as in *posso* **lavorare domani** *I can work tomorrow*.

mood the ways in which verbs can express actions or event. The four verb moods are the indicative, subjunctive, conditional and imperative. All of these moods, except the imperative, have a range of different tenses; the imperative only has one.

negative words or phrases that turn a positive statement or question into a negative one. Italian uses mainly double negatives, or pairs of negative elements. Examples of negatives include: **nessun** (*no*), **nessuno** (*nobody*), **niente** (*nothing*), **non ... mai** (*not ever, never*), **non ... ancora** (*not yet*), **non ... più** (*no longer, no more*).

noun indicates a person, place, thing, or event, for example. Nouns are inextricably linked to the articles (**il, un,** etc.) and to any adjectives that accompany them. All nouns have a gender and this determines the form of the adjectives and articles that go with it.

number the distinction between *singular* and *plural*. Verb forms alter according to the number of the subject: **il ragazzo *nuota*** (*the boy swims*), **i ragazzi *nuotano*** (*the boys swim*).

object in grammatical terms, the person or thing affected by the action or event, as opposed to the subject, which is the person or thing responsible for it. (See *direct object*, *indirect object*.)

participle (present, past) verbs normally have a present participle and a past participle. The past participle is used with the verb **avere** or **essere** to form the *passato prossimo* tense. When used with **essere**, it 'agrees' with the subject: siamo andati.

partitive article see *article*.

passive (verb forms) in a passive construction, the subject of the sentence is the person or thing affected by the action or event taking place: **tutti gli studenti sono stati promossi** (*all the students were moved up a class*). (See also *active construction*.)

person the verb subject can be a first person (**io** *I*), second person (**tu** *you*) **third** person (**lui, lei** *he, she*) and so on.

personal pronoun may be a subject pronoun: **io, tu, lui** (*I, you, he*) etc.; direct object pronoun: **mi, ti, lo, la** (*me, you, him, her*) etc.; indirect object pronoun: **mi, ti, gli, le** (*to me, to you, to him, to her*) etc.; disjunctive pronoun, used as a stressed direct object or after preposition (con) **me, te, lui, lei** ((*with*) *me, you, him, her*) etc. (See also *pronoun*.)

plural *see* **number.**

possessive possessive adjectives and/or pronouns denote ownership: *il mio* **orologio** (*my watch*).

preposition a word which gives further information about a person, action or event, referring, for example, to time or place, value or purpose. Examples include **a, con, da, di, in, per, su.**

pronoun a word which stands in for and/or refers to a noun. There are various categories of pronoun: demonstrative, indefinite, interrogative, personal, possessive, reflexive, relative.

question direct questions sometimes begin with a question word: **dove vai stasera?** (*where are you going this evening?*) and sometimes do not: **hai fame?** (*are you hungry?*). Indirect questions are introduced by words such as **chiedere** (*to ask*).

reflexive verb a verb that can be used with a reflexive pronoun, equivalent of English *myself*, *himself*, indicating that the subject and the object are one and the same: **mi lavo** (*I wash*). Sometimes the verb can only be used reflexively, and there is no object mentioned, e.g. **vergognarsi** (*to be ashamed*).

regular a regular noun or verb is one which follows one of the main noun or verb patterns, whose forms and endings can be predicted: e.g., **-are**, **parlare** (*to speak*), **-ere**, **sorridere** (*to smile*), **-ire**, **partire** (*to leave*).

relative a relative pronoun introduces a relative clause, which gives more information about a person or thing mentioned or an event referred to: **ho visto la segretaria *che* lavorava con Di Martino** (*I saw the secretary who worked with Di Martino*).

reported speech also known as indirect speech, a way of relating words spoken or written by someone else. Reported speech is usually introduced by verbs such as **dire** (*to say, to tell*), **scrivere** (*to write*), **annunciare** (*to announce*) and the conjunction **che**.

sentence must have a verb and a subject. It can either be a simple sentence (one subject, one verb): **i bambini dormivano** (*the children were asleep*) or a complex sentence (main clause and one or more subordinate clauses): **mentre i bambini dormivano, i genitori hanno messo in ordine la stanza** (*while the children were asleep, their parents tidied the room*).

singular *see* **number**.

stem *see* **verb stem**.

subject is usually a noun, (subject) pronoun (**io, tu, lei**, etc.) or proper name denoting the person or object performing the action or the event taking place. In the case of a passive construction, the subject is the person or thing affected by the action. With Italian verbs, it is not always essential to have a subject mentioned since it is understood from the verb form:

abbiamo mangiato a **mezzogiorno** (*we ate at midday*).

subjunctive not a tense, but a verb mood, with four tenses (present, perfect, imperfect, pluperfect), used to express doubt or uncertainty. It is almost always used in complex sentences where one clause depends on another. (See *subordinate clause*.) However, it can also be found standing on its own, e.g. when used as an imperative form: **vada via!** (*go away!*).

subordinate clause one that depends on another clause, usually the main clause in a sentence. The subordinate clause may depend on a main verb expressing uncertainty, e.g. **dubitare**, or a conjunction such as **benché**, or a relative pronoun such as **che**. (See also *conjunction*.)

superlative when one or more persons, objects or activities are compared, a superlative form is used to express the one which is superior to all the rest: **la casa di Matilde era *la più grande* del paese** (*Mathilde's house was the biggest in the village*). (See also comparative.)

tense a finite verb form that normally provides a clue as to the time setting (present, past, future) for an action or event: **andremo a New York** (*we will go to New York*).

transitive verb a verb which can always be used transitively, or in other words with a direct object: ***ho fumato* una sigaretta** (*I smoked a cigarette*). Sometimes no object is used: ***ho fumato*** (*I smoked*), but the verb is still a transitive verb since it can take an object. Some verbs can be used both transitively and intransitively: e.g. **aumentare** (*to increase*), **diminuire** (*to decrease*), **cambiare** (*to change*).

verb a word that describes an action, event or state. It always has a subject and can also have an object. Its form varies according to its mood and tense, and the person, gender and number of its subject.

verb stem the 'base', or part of the verb which is left when you remove **-are, -ere, -ire** from the infinitive form. In a regular verb the ending changes but the stem does not normally change. In an irregular verb, the stem may change too.

voice verbs normally have two voices: *active* and *passive*. (See *active* and *passive*.)

Index

Note: The numbers refer to units, not pages; numbers preceded by G refer to the **Grammar appendix**. For details of functions covered, see also the **Contents list**.

Credits

Front cover: Oxford Illustrators Ltd.

Back cover: © Jakub Semeniuk/iStockphoto.com, © Royalty-Free/ Corbis, © agencyby/iStockphoto.com, © Andy Cook/iStockphoto. com, © Christopher Ewing/iStockphoto.com, © zebicho – Fotolia. com, © Geoffrey Holman/iStockphoto.com, © Photodisc/Getty Images, © James C. Pruitt/iStockphoto.com, © Mohamed Saber – Fotolia.com